George Eliot

MIDDLEMARCH

George Eliot

MIDDLEMARCH

[Edited with Introduction, Author's Information, Criticism, Study Questions and Bibliography]

Mansi Sachdeva
B.A. English (Hons), Delhi University;
M.A., M. Phil. (English), IGNOU

ANMOL PUBLICATIONS PVT. LTD.
NEW DELHI - 110 002 (INDIA)

ANMOL PUBLICATIONS PVT. LTD.

H.O.: 4374/4B, Ansari Road, Darya Ganj,
New Delhi-110 002 (India)
Ph.: 23278000, 23261597

B.O.: No. 1015, Ist Main Road, BSK IIIrd Stage
IIIrd Phase, IIIrd Block
Bangalore - 560 085 (India)
Visit us at: www.anmolpublications.com

Middlemarch

First Published, 2009

PRINTED IN INDIA

Printed at Mehra Offset Press, Delhi.

Contents

Preface

On November 22, 1819, the literary genius George Eliot was born. Interestingly, she decided to write novels under a male pseudonym. Her first attempt was Middlemarch, which unfortunately ended in failure. This book was followed by a short novella "Miss Brooke". She integrated this novella into Middlemarch and got published in eight parts. Subtitle of this epic is " A Study of Provincial Life". Thus, it represents lives of common men.

In the history of English literature, Middlemarch is always regarded as an unusual novel. Being a Victorian novel, its several characters are similar to the modern novels. This masterpiece of Eliot has received mixed critical response.

Author

Chaptet 1

Introduction

George Eliot was the male pseudonym of Mary Ann Evans (she would later call herself Marian), born on November 22, 1918 at Arbury Farm in Warwickshire. Her father, Robert Evans, was an overseer at the Arbury Hall estate, a nd Eliot kept house for him after her mother died in 1836. The Mill on the Floss involves many autobiographical details, and it reflects Eliot's close childhood relationships with her father and her older brother Isaac. Eliot was sent to school as a child and at the age of fifteen and underwent a spiritual conversion to Evangelicism, similar to Maggie Tulliver's pious conversion upon reading Thomas a Kempis in Book IV of The Mill on the Floss.

In 1841, Eliot and her father moved closer to the town of Coventry, which was at that time a centre of radical thought. Eliot made friends with a group of Coventry intellectuals, mainly members of the Bray family, and began reading such works as An Enquiry into the Origins of Christianity. Eliot soon gave up her Evangelicism in favor of a non-sectarian spirituality based on a sense of common humanity. She refused to attend church with her father and began work on a translation from German of Life of Jesus, a rationalist reexamination of some Bible sections. Life of Jesus was published in 1846, and on the strength of that accomplishment, Eliot moved to London after her father's death.

In London, Eliot became the assistant editor of John Chapman's Westminster Review and came into close contact with the leading intellectuals of the time, such as Herbert Spencer, John Stuart Mill, and Harriet Martineau. In 1852, Eliot met and became close to George Henry Lewes, a writer and an editor of The Leader. Lewes was living apart from his wife, and Eliot's decision to accompany Lewes to Germany, living as a couple, provoked a degree of scandal in London. In particular, Eliot sacrificed her relationship with her brother Isaac, and she depicted the pain of his disapproval in The Mill on the Floss in Tom's disapproval of Maggie's relationships with Philip and Stephen.

Eliot and Lewes lived together, considering themselves virtually married until his death in 1878. With the encouragement of Lewes, Eliot began writing fiction. Scenes of Clerical Life was published in 1856. Adam Bede (1859), her first full novel, was met with critical acclaim, and the public began to wonder what writer was behind the pseudonym of George Eliot. By the time of the publication of The Mill on the Floss in three volumes in 1860, Marian Evans's authorship had been tentatively guessed by a few London intellectuals and friends. Several well-received novels followed, including Middlemarch, the novel now regarded as her greatest artistic success. Eliot died in 1880.

Eliot's most important contribution to literature was in her treatment of realism. Eschewing the caricature fiction of Charles Dickens, Eliot perfected the genre of psychological realism, paving the way for the later work of the American novelist Henry James. Eliot understood that art should be near to life, valuing observed truths and creating a greater sense of sympathy in the reader by coherently and non-judgementally depicting the psychological motives of characters. Eliot's attention to character is mediated by a strong sense of historical and cultural climate. Thus in The Mill on the Floss, Mr. Tulliver's financial downfall is depicted within the larger context of the increased materialism of the British midlands in the first half of the nineteenth century, but it is also portrayed as the result of minute social and psychological actions and reactions of Mr. Tulliver and the characters that affect him, such as Mrs. Tulliver and Mr. Wakem.

The Mill on the Floss marks a break from the earlier work of Eliot, which was mainly a depiction of provincial life, and it bridged the gap to more wide- ranging later novels, such as Middlemarch, that drew detailed backdrops of the social and economic forces alive in an entire community. The Mill on the Floss is Eliot's only novel to end tragically and the most autobiographical novel.

Middlemarch was first published in 1871 and 1872, as a serial novel in eight parts, which came out every two months. This was Eliot's most comprehensive and sweeping novel to date, and was intended as a study of provincial British life. Eliot worked on several different stories, starting with Lydgate and his trials as a young doctor; then she worked on Dorothea's story, writing the first ten Chapters as they appear in the finished book with only this character and her world in mind. Eliot then decided to build a world around these two characters, and create a more sweeping portrait of an entire town and its various inhabitants; Lydgate and Dorothea acted essentially as the core of the novel, as two somewhat similar figures who were the soul of the novel. Both are alike in their unhappy marriages, their social aspirations, and the way in which they react to societal pressure.

The novel, when it first appeared, was a huge success, both with critics and readers; it made Eliot's name as one of the greatest novelists in Britain, and her fame spread. Her intention with the novel was to analyze recent political, social, and economic threads through a series of personal accounts. The characters and stories told within the novel are meant to show how people are affected by historical change while it happens, and how progress happens in people's lives. Eliot manages to weave in the Catholic emancipation, the death of George IV, the dissolution of Parliament in 1831, the outbreak of cholera in 1832, and the passage of the Reform Bill later that year. Eliot manages to weave these things into the concerns of the characters and the narrative; they are not the focus of the novel, but are balanced with the novel's literary concerns.

One of the most widespread concerns in the novel is change, and how people react to it. All the historical concerns in the novel are involved in this, as are people's reactions under stress, and to progress in their society. Eliot is able to show people acting naturally in close detail, and present criticism on them, while still allowing the readers to form their own opinion of them. Overall, every character in this novel are human; each of them can be liked or disliked according to their personal foibles and flaws. But Eliot's point is that we, like they, are human; we can only judge them as we judge ourselves. She is not totally impartial in the narrative, which would be impossible in making criticisms; but there is still plenty of room for people to make up their own minds, and interpret the characters in their own way.

Eliot's stated goal with writing this novel, along with her others, was to give her readers "a clearer conception and a more active admiration of those vital elements which bind men together and give a higher worthiness to their existence," according to a letter of 1868 that she wrote. The novel, especially the characters of Dorothea and Farebrother, are very much influenced by Eliot's personal belief in the religion of humanity. Her views of marriage are also interjected into the novel; Eliot was not favorable about society's ideas of gender roles and marriage, hence her depictions of Rosamond and Lydgate's marital troubles.

The novel is very much concerned with women's roles, women's lives, and how they should be changed. However, it also exposes Eliot's ambivalence on the subject. Although she had no children and lived with her lover, George Lewes, without being married, at the same time she believed that women should be married, and had obligations to their husbands and children. The novel advocates change in women's roles, and in their spheres of influence; but, at the same time, no woman is happy who isn't married, and in a solid partnership with her husband. This tension in Eliot's personal views forms the struggles that Rosamond, Dorothea, and Celia face, and determines the outcome of their unions according to their character and effectiveness.

If there is one metaphor that serves to sum up the way people and society work in Middlemarch, it is a web. Just as Rosamond and Lydgate spin their own web and get caught in it, every character is bound in a huge web, and if one pulls one way or another, the web shifts, and someone is affected. Things and people are inextricable connected and an event, like Featherstone's funeral, can have a very palpable meaning to someone who has no involvement, like Dorothea. Middlemarch is a very carefully woven work of social commentary and human analysis, with many living, breathing characters who are as real as the historical time period they inhabit.

Chaptet 2

Biography

From Mary Anne Evans to George Eliot

Mary Anne Evans: The Early Years

Mary Anne Evans was born at South Farm, Arbury, on November 22, 1819. The youngest child of Robert Evans and Christiana Pearson Evans, she had four siblings: Robert, Fanny, Chrissy, and Isaac. Mary Anne shared an especially close relationship with her brother Isaac — they were inseparable playmates. However, in 1824, Isaac was sent to school at Foleshill, and Mary Anne was sent to Miss Latham's boarding school. At Miss Lathim's, missing the companionship and comfort of her brother, Mary Anne first turned to books as a source of amusement. Those who knew her found Mary Anne a serious, sensitive, and introspective child. She had straight light-brown hair and a plain face. Mathilde Blind described her as "a queer, three-cornered, awkward girl, who sat in corners and shyly watched her elders".

In 1828, after finishing at Miss Latham's, Mary Anne was sent to Mrs. Wallington's Boarding School at Nuneaton. It was at Mrs. Wallington's that she met the woman who was to be the most influential figure of her early life, Miss Maria Lewis. Maria Lewis, a kind woman with strong evangelical beliefs, was a governess at the school. She took an immediate interest in the shy Mary Anne, and marking the exceptional quality of the child's mind, took it upon herself to foster it. By the time Mary Anne was thirteen, she had learned all that Mrs. Wallington's school had to offer. When she left, however, she maintained a close relationship with Miss Lewis – a relationship they kept up for nearly fourteen years. Upon leaving Miss Wallington's, Mary Anne attended Miss Franklin's school at Coventry. It was here that Mary Anne worked to rid herself of her Midland accent and cultivated the "low, well-modulated, musical voice, which impressed everyone who knew George Eliot in later years". At Miss Franklin's school, Mary Anne became an accomplished pianist, studied French, was admired for her skill at writing, and read widely. She also wrote poetry and fiction.

Drastic changes soon occurred in Mary Anne's life. Her mother had been ill for quite some time. In February of 1839, Mrs. Evans died, and Mary Anne, then 19, left school to take care of her father. Though not the oldest daughter, Mary Anne had always been close to her father, and she tried to fill in for her mother while continuing her education at home (now Griff House). Robert Evans, proud of his daughter, bought Mary Anne any book she wished to have and arranged for her to receive lessons in Italian and German. In 1841, she and her father moved to a new home at Foleshill.

The World of Ideas

Foleshill was a larger town than Griff, and Mary Anne suspected that her father had chosen it in order to enlarge her social circle, and perhaps help her find a husband. However, Mary Anne felt distanced from those around her. Always serious and shy, she "could not help thinking how much easier life would be to her, and how much better she would stand in the estimation of her neighbors, if only she could take things as they did, be satisfied with outside pleasures, and conform to popular beliefs without any reflection or examination". Mary Anne had been entertaining doubts about her religious convictions for some time, but she did not have the courage to relinquish those convictions just yet.

At Foleshill, Mary Anne continued her studies and spent her evenings reading Sir Walter Scott to her father, whose health was failing. On November 2, 1841, Mary Anne was invited to the home of Charles and Cara Bray. Mary Anne found in the Brays the same doubts about Christianity that she had been secretly harboring for quite some time and felt she was among kindred souls. In his autobiography, Bray later wrote, "we became friends at once"; in fact, Charles and Cara Bray were to be Mary Anne's most intimate friends for the next thirteen years.

In 1842, Mary Anne stopped going to church. Her longtime friend Maria Lewis was disappointed and their correspondence dwindled — though no permanent break was made until Christmas of 1846. Mary Anne's father was even more disturbed by his daughter's heresy and refused to speak to her. Eventually, a truce was effected—Mary Anne agreed to go to church with her father and he conceded that she had the right to think what she pleased (as long as she showed signs of outward conformity), but relations between the two remained strained.

Mary Anne continued her friendship with the Brays. They were open-minded intellectuals, and they brought the shy Mary Anne out of her shell. After five years in their company, she could not be called shy at all. Charles Bray had connections to some of the most important thinkers of the time, and Eliot's acquaintance with him served to bring her closer to "the world of ideas." Mary Anne met many interesting and important people at the Bray's home, including Ralph Waldo Emerson, who was quite taken with her and commented, "that young lady has a calm and serious soul".

At Rosehill (the Bray's home), Mary Anne also met some of the people who were to become her closest friends: Sara Hennell, Charles Hennell, and Elizabeth (or Rufa) Brabant (later Mrs. Charles Hennell). In 1844, Mary Anne began work on an English translation of David Friedrich Strauss' Das Leben Jesu, one of the most influential works of religious thought read in England at the time. This translation took her two years to complete, and while her name did not appear on the publication, it did later bring her some little fame in London when people discovered that it was her work. Meanwhile, Mary Anne's father's health continued to fail, and Mary Anne was his caring nurse. He died in June of 1849. Mr. Evans seemed to soften towards Mary Anne a bit in his final years, but left her little in his will. Mary Anne was twenty-nine.

Alone

Though emotionally and physically exhausted from nursing her father, Mary Anne agreed to take a Continental tour with the Brays just five days after the funeral. In July, rather than returning home with them, Mary Anne announced her intention to stay in Geneva alone. She returned to England in 1850, and resolved to move to London. She first spent seven months at Rosehill with the Brays, where she came into contact with John Chapman, a London publisher and bookseller. Having read her translation of Strauss, he asked her to write an article for the Westminster Review. Mary Anne finished this article in November. It was an impressive piece. She delivered the article herself to Chapman in London and took up lodgings in Chapman's London home at 142 Strand, where Chapman lived with his wife, Susanna, and his mistress, Elisabeth Tilley.

Chapman was a tall, handsome, magnetic man and a notorious philanderer. Soon after Mary Anne moved into the Strand, he took a great interest in her and they began to spend an inordinate amount of time together, often at strange hours. Both his wife and his mistress were jealous. When Susanna caught her husband holding Mary Anne's hand, things blew up. Susanna and Elisabeth joined forces against Mary Anne and demanded of Chapman that she move out immediately. Mary Anne agreed to return to Coventry.

In 1851, Chapman purchased the Westminster Review. He needed an editor, and he wanted someone who would be willing to let him take all the credit and work behind the scenes anonymously. Mary Anne was his first choice. However, he needed her in London, and knew it would prove difficult to persuade Susanna and Elisabeth to agree. Eventually, he did get the ladies to agree, and Mary Anne moved back into 142 Strand. Things were different this time — Mary Anne saw the true nature of Chapman, and made a vow to keep her relationship with him strictly professional. This was a vow she kept. Mary Anne edited the Westminster Review for two years and ten issues. Under her direction, it again became the important intellectual journal it had once been under former editor John Stuart Mill. Mary Anne's social circle continued to grow. London had become a centre of enlightened radicalism and there were many parties at the Strand where she met some of the most important thinkers of the time. Though she was physically unattractive, most people who met Mary Anne were quite taken with her. They were charmed by her expressive face and eyes, her gentleness, her beautiful, low voice, and her great intellect.

George Henry Lewes

Mary Anne was growing tired of editing the Review and of living in the Chapman home. She became depressed and her health was failing. She suffered from awful headaches. Mary Anne was now nearly thirty-three and feeling lonely. She met George Henry Lewes in October of 1851. Lewes was an unattractive man, but loved by most who came near him because of his outgoing personality and wit. Lewes had married Agnes Jervis in 1841. About eight years into the marriage, Agnes began an affair with Lewes's close friend Thornton Hunt. Both Lewes and Agnes were believers in "free love" and felt that feelings were stronger than legal bonds. So when Agnes gave birth to Hunt's son, Lewes claimed the illegitimate child as his own. In the coming years, she would bear Hunt four more children. George claimed all of them, but he ceased to view Agnes as his wife.

When Mary Anne met Lewes, his marriage had long been over in every sense but the legal one. Lewes came to visit Mary Anne at the Strand often, often enough that by April of 1853, their intimacy had grown far beyond what either of them could have expected. In September of 1853, Mary Anne moved out of 142 Strand and found her own lodgings. This move gave her the opportunity to spend more time with Lewes, and by November they had grown extremely close. In July of 1854, her translation of Feuerbach's Essence of Christianity was published, with her name appearing on the title page. This was the first and last time "Marian Evans" appeared on a work of hers.

In June of 1854, Mary Anne went to Rosehill for the last time. She knew that her friends Sara Hennell and Cara Bray would not approve of what she had made up her mind to do. Mary Anne had decided to live openly with George Lewes as his lover and spiritual wife. The decision was not an easy one. Mary Anne knew that this bold move would bring public censure and that if George ever left her, she would be alone and outcast. She wrote the following to John Chapman on the subject, "I do not wish to take the ground of ignoring what is unconventional in my position. I have counted the cost of the step I have taken and am prepared to bear, without irritation or bitterness, renunciation of all my friends. I am not mistaken in the person to whom I have attached myself".

"Married" Life

In July of 1854, George and Mary Anne departed for the Continent. They spent eight months in Germany, first at Weimar and then in Berlin, so that George could work on his biography of Goethe. Mary Anne wrote to friends that she was quite happy. Upon their return, Mary Anne took lodgings in Dover, and George went to London to settle his affairs. Mary Anne did not see George for five weeks. She had stipulated that George must separate permanently from his wife, Agnes. She knew, of course, that a divorce was impossible, but she wanted to be assured that there was no possibility of reconciliation before she would move to London with George. Agnes confirmed that a reunion was not possible. With this assurance, Mary Anne moved to London in April. She and George took rooms as Mr. and Mrs. Lewes, and their "marriage" was officially begun.

Chapman soon asked Mary Anne to take over the "Belle Letters" section of the Westminster Review at a fixed salary of fifty pounds a year. Mary Anne happily agreed to this extra income. She wrote countless book reviews which gave her ample cause to think about what exactly made good fiction. The couple received few visitors at first, but both Rufa and

Bessie Parks broke the taboo and risked their reputations by paying calls at the Leweses.

George Eliot is Born

In June of 1856, Mary Anne and George moved to Tenby on the coast of South Whales. When Barbara Leigh Smith visited them in July, she remarked that the couple was very happy. At Tenby, Mary Anne began to think more and more about her childhood dream of writing fiction. She felt that she could competently write the descriptive passages of a novel, but feared that she lacked the talent to render dramatic and dialogue passages effectively. When she shared these thoughts with George, he encouraged her to try her hand at fiction writing. In August, the Leweses moved back to London, and on September 23rd of 1856, Mary Anne began to write "The Sad Fortunes of the Reverend Amos Barton," which would later become a part of Scenes of Clerical Life. Despite his avowed confidence in her, George still had some doubts about Mary Anne's ability to write fiction. Those doubts were removed when he read her Amos Barton story.

Her fears were unfounded — she could write good dialogue and she could create drama to stir the emotions. Lewes sent her story to his publisher, John Blackwood, claiming it was the work of a (male) friend who wanted to remain anonymous. The story was published on New Year's Day, 1857, less than two months after Mary Anne's thirty-seventh birthday. Mary Anne then adopted George Eliot as her nom de plume. She later told John Cross that she chose the name because "George was Mr. Lewes's Christian name, and Eliot was a good mouth-filling, easily pronounced word".

In May of 1857, Mary Anne finally decided to tell her family of her marriage to George. At first, she kept the details to herself, but when pressed, she revealed that the marriage was not a legal one. Urged by Isaac, Mary Anne's sisters wrote letters renouncing Mary Anne. She was now an outcast in the eyes of her family.

After the publication of Scenes of Clerical Life, there was much talk about the supposed identity of George Eliot, but

Mary Anne kept her secret (she didn't even tell Blackwood until February of 1858). In October of 1857 she began work on Adam Bede. The Leweses spent the middle of that year in Munich, Vienna, and Dresden. Mary Anne continued to work on Adam Bede while they were abroad, and finished it in September of 1858, shortly after their return to England. When Adam Bede made it into print, the critics praised the book highly. It was a sensational success. Even Queen Victoria loved it. And the public still had no idea who George Eliot was!

Mary Anne's private life afforded her much joy. She and George were very happy together. He was constantly looking to protect her from her friends and critics alike. In 1859, they purchased their first home: Holly Lodge at Southfields. By this time the secret of George Eliot's identity wasn't very secret. Herbert Spencer and John Chapman had informed many of the members of the literary circle in London that George Eliot was none other than the unprepossessing Mary Anne Lewes.

When the truth about George Eliot's identity was firmly established, Blackwood balked at publishing Mary Anne's new novel, The Mill on the Floss. He feared that the controversy surrounding Mary Anne's life with Lewes would keep it from selling. Eventually Blackwood did publish the novel with George Eliot appearing on the title page, and when the book came out, it was a success despite all the worry about the controversial nature of Mary Anne's relationship with Lewes.

Finding their country home too far from town, the Leweses moved back to London in late 1860. Mary Anne became depressed in her new surroundings. Not even George could revive her spirits. Mary Anne attributed much of her depression to the social ridicule she felt. Since she had become famous, her private life with George Lewes had become public business. While the public adored her novels, they often criticized her personally for her defiance of the marriage convention. She resented the fact that she was seen as a violator of the marriage vow while George's unfaithful wife, Agnes, appeared a long-suffering victim. In such a social climate, the Leweses received few visitors (they could count the number of their female visitors on one hand). Rufa Hennell, the first woman to call on the Leweses, also became the first to invite them to dinner. However, the greater part of their social circle remained male, even as it widened with Eliot's increasing fame.

In April of 1861, after the publication of Silas Marner, Mary Anne left for Italy to begin research for her next novel, Romola, to be set in fifteenth century Florence. Mary Anne researched furiously — she often fell into depression because of self-doubt and the overwhelming nature of the task before her. In May of 1862, she accepted an offer from George Smith to publish the novel serially in the Cornhill Magazine. Serial publication proved problematic for Mary Anne, who was very sensitive about her work and easily disturbed by the reviews that came out on earlier parts of her work while she was working on the later ones. Lewes eventually began to suppress almost all negative commentary from his wife. He knew that such negativism would stall her writing, as she was still given to bouts of depression, so he offered her only the good. This policy of Lewes has often been blamed for the "abstruseness" of Eliot's later novels, but without it, she very likely would not have written at all—she certainly was no longer in need of money, having earned nearly 16,000.

As Eliot's fame increased and her renown grew, her social circle continued to widen. The more popular Eliot's novels grew, the more accepting London society became of her relationship with Lewes. Mary Anne's family continued their silence, but it is apparent that they, too, read her novels and found them worthy of the sister they remembered. Her siblings probably would have been surprised to know how conservative Mary Anne had become by this time, in spite of her unconventional love of Lewes.

Mary Anne began serious work on Middlemarch in 1869, though she'd been thinking about this "English novel" for years. Progress was slow, but it was published by Blackwood in parts from 1871-2. The novel was a success with the public. If George Eliot was famous before, she was doubly famous after the publication of Middlemarch. She was also very rich. Once socially ostracized, now the couple could not get away from a constant stream of visitors. Their dream was to move out into the country so that they could spend time alone with one another as in the old days. They searched for the perfect house for four years without ever finding a permanent residence. By 1876, the public seemed to have forgotten the unofficial marriage status of its beloved author, George Eliot. There were even rumors that her marriage had been made official by the death of Agnes Lewes, but they were false. Agnes was alive and well in Kensington.

In 1874, Mary Anne began work on what would be her final novel, Daniel Deronda. Mary Anne's old fears about the worth of what she was doing returned. She hoped desperately that she was not just "adding to the heap of books". As usual, Lewes did his best to comfort her. Illness followed depression. Mary Anne began to suffer from kidney stones in February of 1874—the pain would plague her until her death. Daniel Deronda came out in 1876. Mary Anne's health continued to falter, and her fame continued to grow. She was now regarded as "the greatest living English novelist". Her fans were wild about her; she received scores of letters from all over the world.

Alone Again

Eventually, the Leweses managed to stem the tide of visitors to their London home and only saw the few people that they wished to see. One person who was always invited on Sundays was John Cross, their business manager of sorts, whom they referred to as their "dear nephew." In November of 1876, John Cross found a lovely house for George and Mary Anne, and they finally had the country home of which they had been dreaming. They enjoyed their new home immensely, finding their frequent walks in the countryside "so much better than Society!".

In mid-1878, Lewes began to suffer from horrible cramps every night. Though he did not know it at the time, it was a sign of serious illness. The cramps continued to plague him and the attacks were coming more and more often, but he maintained his high spirits, concealing the seriousness of his illness. By November, he could no longer conceal his agony and Mary Anne wrote, "I have a deep sense of change within, and of a permanently closer companionship with death". Mary Anne was right, by the end of the month, her lifelong partner and support was dead. He passed away at their home in London on November 30, 1878. Mary Anne did not leave her room for a week, and did not go to the funeral. She could bear to see no one. Cross pressed her to accept him as a visitor, fearing that too long of a solitude might prove fatal to Mary Anne. She refused, writing on February 7, 1879, "each day seems a new beginning—a new acquaintance with grief". She finally saw him on February 23.

Mary Anne began the task of completing Lewes's unfinished Problems of Life and Mind and decided to establish a trust in his name, the George Henry Lewes Studentship in Physiology. She saw Cross often as he was still helping her to manage her finances. In March, she began to see other friends as well. She and Cross grew closer — they began to read Dante together. In August of 1879, Cross hinted for the first time that he wished to be more than a friend. That November, Mary Anne turned 60 and faced the one-year anniversary of Lewes's death. She still mourned him.

Mary Anne finally accepted Cross's proposal of marriage (which had been extended three times) on April 9, 1880. Cross had just turned 40. The ceremony was in May of that year. In November, Mary Anne turned 61. On the evening of December 19, Mary Anne became suddenly ill. She was diagnosed as having laryngitis, and the doctor saw no cause for worry. A few days later her kidney problem began to bother her again, and she was in much pain. With little warning, she passed away at ten o'clock, the night of December 22, 1880. Her new husband was left alone after only seven months of marriage. Mary Anne was buried in Highgate Cemetery, London, next to her spiritual husband George Lewes.

Chaptet 3

Chronology of George Eliot

George Eliot: A Brief Chronology

George Eliot (Mary Ann Evans) was born on November 22, 1819, in Chilvers Coton, Warwickshire, near Nuneaton, Warwickshire. Eliot is famous for works like "Middlemarch" (1871-72), "The Mill on the Floss" (1860), and "Silas Marner" (1861). Read more about the life and times of George Eliot.

1819 George Eliot was born on November 22 at South Farm, Arbury, Warwichshire. She was the youngest of three children of Robert Evan's second marriage (to Christina Pearson). Eliot was baptized Mary Ann Evans at Chilvers Coton on November 29.

1820 The family moved to Griff House, where her father was an agent for the Arbury estate of Francis Newdigate.

1825-27 She attended Miss Lathom's School, Attleborough, with her sister Christina.

1828-32 She attended Mrs. Wallington's School, at Nuneaton, where she met Miss Lewis, the principal governess and a strong evangelical.

1832-35 She attended Miss Franklin's School, at Coventry, which was operated by the daughters of a Baptist minister.

1835 She left school at Christmas.

1836 Her mother died on February 3. She took charge of her father's household. She learned Italian and German from a Coventry teacher, and began to read Greek and Latin with the headmaster of Coventry Grammar School.

1838 She started a chart of ecclesiastical history.

1840 Her first publication, a religous poem, appeared in the "Christian Observer" in January.

1841 Her brother Isaac married, and took over the house at Griff. In March, Robert Evans and his daughter moved to a house in Foleshill Road, Coventry. Her faith was challenged.

1842 She refuseed to attend church with her father from January to May, but finally agreeed to accompany him. She translated parts of Spinoza for Charles Bray.

1843 She visited Dr. Brabant of Devizes in November with his daughter, who had undertaken a translation of David Friedrich Strauss's work of historical criticism, "Das Leben Jesu" (1835).

1844 She took over the translation of Strauss. She began to study Hebrew.

1846 "The Life of Jesus" was published in 3 volumes in June after much labour and many complaints of being "Strauss-sick."

1849 She translated Spinoza's "Tractatus" as a calming occupation during her father's last illness. Her father, Robert Evans died on May 31. She journeyed abroad in June with the Brays, and stayed in Geneva by herself for eight months.

1850 She returned to Coventry and lived with the Brays for seven months.

1851 She went to London to assist John Chapman in editing the "Westminster Review," and contributed a review of Mackay's "The Progress of the Intellect" to the January number. In March, she was driven away from 142 Strand by the jeolousy of Chapman's wife and mistress. In September, she returned to edit the journal. She met Herbert Spencer.

1852 She met Bessie Parkes and Barbara Leigh-Smith (later Madame Barbara Bodichon). On January 1, the first issue of "Westminster Review" was published under her editorship. She began a friendship with Lewes. She translated Feuerbach's "Das Wesen des Christentums" ("The Essence of Christianity"). Her friendship with Herbert Spencer caused rumors of an engagement.

1853 She moved from Chapman's to her own lodgings George Eliot is a famous English novelist. Read more about her life and works—in this brief chronology!

1854 Her translation of Ludwig Feuerbach's "The Essence of Christianity" was published in July. She went with George Henry Lewes to Germany on July 20. She stopped in Weimar, and then spent the winter in Berlin. She began translating Spinoza's "Ethics" in November. Lewes could not obtain a divorce because he had condoned his wife's adultery.

1855 George Eliot and Lewes returned to England in March, where Lewe's "Life of Goethe" was published. They settled in Richmond.

1856 She finished translating Spinoza's "Ethics" on February 19. She began writing "The Sad Fortunes of Reverend Amos Barton," on September 23.

1857 "Scenes of Clerical Life" was published in "Maga" ("Blackwoods Magazine") under pseudonym George Eliot. She began to write "Adam Bede" on October 22.

1858 "Scenes of Clerical Life" was published in two volumes by Blackwood in January.

1859 "Adam Bede" was published by Blackwood in three volumes, on February 1—to critical acclaim (16,000 copies were sold in the first year). They settled at Holly Lodge, Wandsworth, where she formed a friendship with Mr. and Mrs. Richard Congreve. Her sister, Chrissey, died on March 15. She began writing "The Mill on the Floss."

1860 She began an Italian journey with Lewes in March. "The Mill on the Floss" was published by

Blackwood in three volumes in April. She started work on a historical novel—based on the life of Savonarola.

1861 "Silas Marner" was published by Blackwood in April. They returned to Florence and began to collect material for "Romola" (which she had previously abandoned). She began writing the novel in October.

1862 "Romola" appeared—in 14 monthly installments—in "Cornhill Magazine," beginning in July.

1863 "Romola" was published in three volumes by Smith, Elder, and Co. She and Lewes bought the Priory at 21 North Bank, Regent's Park.

1864 She set off for Italy with Lewes and F. W. Burton. She began to study Spanish.

1865 George Eliot took a January holiday in Paris. She begn to write "Felix Holt, the Radical," and went to Brittany in November.

1866 "Felix Holt" was published by Blackwood in June. She went to Holland, Belgium, Germany, and Spain.

1867 She went to Germany with Lewes.

1868 "The Spanish Gypsy" was published by Blackwood, on May 25. She went to Germany and Switzerland with Lewes.

1869 She travels went to Italy with Lewes. In April, she met John Walter Cross in Rome. She began to write "Middlemarch" in August. Lewe's second son, Thornton, returned from Natal in May with spinal tuberculosis, and died October 19. She wrote poems, which would later be titled "The Legend of Jubal and Other Poems."

1870 She stopped work on "Middlemarch" and she began to write "Miss Brooke."

1871 George Eliot integrated "Miss Brook" into the first section of "Middlemarch." Book I of "Middlemarch" was published in December.

1872	She was ill a great deal. She traveled to Germany with Lewes in September and October. Book VIII of "Middlemarch" was published in December. The complete novel was also published in four volumes.
1873	She took a holiday in France and Germany from June through August. Thornton Hunt died in June. In November, she was "simmering toward another book.'
1874	She made her first "Sketches toward Daniel Deronda" in January. "The Legend of Jubal and Other Poems" was published. She went to France and Belgium with Lewes in October.
1875	Herbert Lewes (Bertie) died in Natal.
1876	"Daniel Deronda" was published on the same plan as "Middlemarch" in February (the last part appeared in September). She went to France and Switzerland with Lewes. In December, they bought The Heights at Witley in Surrey as a summer residence.
1878	Lewes became very ill in June. Lewes worsened in October and November, and then died on November 30. She refused to see anyone for several weeks. She occupied herself with completing and preparing his major philosophical work, "Problems of Life and Mind," for the press.
1879	She agreeed to see Cross in February. She helped Cross to learn Italian. "Impressions of Theophrastus Such" was published in June. John Blackwood died in October.
1880	In April, she agreed to marry Cross. She married John Walter Cross in May. She took a trip to the Continent. She moved to 4 Cheyne Walk on December 3. She died on December 22 and was buried in Highgate Cemetary.

Chaptet 4

Major Works

Chronological List by Date of Publication of George Eliot's Novels, Short Stories and Poems

1857	Scenes of Clerical Life.
1859	Adam Bede.
1859	The Lifted Veil.
1860	The Mill on the Floss.
1861	Silas Marner: the Weaver of Raveloe.
1862-3	Romola.
1864	Brother Jacob.
1866	Felix Holt, The Radical.
1868	The Spanish Gypsy.
1871-2	Middlemarch.
1876	Daniel Deronda.
1869	Agatha. (Later included in The Legend of Jubal and Other Poems. 1874.)
1869	Brother and Sister.
1869	How Lisa Loved the King.
1870	The Legend of Jubal.
1871	Armgart.
1874	Arion.
1874	A Minor Prophet.
1874	Stradivarius.
1878	A College Breakfast Party. (Reprinted in The Legend of Jubal and Other Poems. 2nd edition. 1879.)
1879	The Death of Moses.
1879	Impressions of Theophrastus Such.
1919	Early Essays. (Dating from the period of about 1846. Three essays only included in the Dictionary.)

Chaptet 5

Plot Synopsis

A Brief Summary

Dorothea and Celia are two Middlemarch sister of marriageable age. Dorothea chooses Casaubon, a dried-up old scholar, for her husband, much to everyone's dismay. Celia, more sensible, chooses Sir James Chettam, a local nobleman who wanted to marry Dorothea, before she turned him down. Celia and Mr. Brooke, Dorothea's uncle, try to counsel her against marrying Casaubon, though she will not listen. Dorothea likes him because he is educated, and she wants to learn, though the marriage is a total mistake.

Dorothea and Casaubon get married; Casaubon hopes for someone to comfort and serve him, and Dorothea wants to be of use in his work. They go on honeymoon in Rome, and there they meet Will Ladislaw, Casaubon's young cousin, whom Casaubon dislikes. Dorothea and Will become friends immediately; they love to talk to each other, and seem to have a real connection, which Casaubon is very jealous of. The honeymoon turns out to be a disaster; Dorothea feels alone and unwanted, as her husband devotes his full time to his studies, and none to her.

Fred Vincy is an irresponsible young man who is used to people providing all the money he needs. He was unable to finish college because he had no aptitude for it, and He has a gambling debt against him, which he cannot pay because he has no job. He has Caleb Garth, an honest family man, co-sign for the debt. Fred receives money from his uncle Featherstone with which to pay the debt. However, he wastes this money, and the Garths, who have little money, end up having to pay it. Fred is very sad, since he believes that this will jeopardize his hopes for Mary, their oldest daughter.

A young doctor named Lydgate moves to the town; he has new methods in medicine, which make some of the older, more established doctors his enemies. Rosamond, the Vincys' vain daughter, takes to him immediately, because he has good connections, and is new to Middlemarch. He likes her, but doesn't plan to marry; she believes he is all hers, and will propose very shortly. Lydgate takes the controversial step of charging patients for his service. Some people don't like this new way of doing things, but Lydgate is also able to cure some difficult cases, so his renown is mixed.

Lydgate is drawn toward Bulstrode, who is very influential though not too well-liked in the town. Lydgate is also compelled to vote with Bulstrode on certain issues, like who to serve as hospital chaplain; he does this to please Bulstrode, though he does not please his conscience.

Featherstone, an old cranky man who is a relative of the Garths and the Vincys, is dying; his relatives all come to visit, hoping that he will put them in his will, since he has tons of money and property. Fred has special hopes that he will get money, being as close to the old man as most people can be. Featherstone's relatives turn up in droves when he is sick, all hoping to be put into his will and get some money. He ignores all of them, and has Mary Garth, who is his housekeeper, either entertain them, or have them go away. He dies, and leaves everything to his illegitimate son, Mr. Rigg, leaving Fred very disappointed.

Dorothea's marriage continues to be a very unpleasant thing; the dynamic of their marriage does not change, though Casaubon grown more irritable. He expects her to devote all her time to making him feel better, soothing his insecurities, etc.; however, he doesn't tell her what he wants her to do, leaving her completely confused about everything. He doesn't expect that Dorothea should be a human being, with her own opinions and ideas; Dorothea becomes less and less content in the marriage.

Will Ladislaw moves to Middlemarch, much to Casaubon's displeasure. Mr. Brooke, Dorothea's uncle, has bought a newspaper, The Pioneer, and hires Will to work on it. Will and Mr. Brooke are politically progressive, which means that they are not well-liked in the neighborhood. Mr. Brooke decides to try and run for office; but he is mocked a great deal and gives up. Will is very politically adept, though, and should go into politics himself someday.

Lydgate, though he has no intent of marrying so soon, proposes to Rosamond; she accepts, and they are to be married. The couple are warned that they are not suited to each other; Rosamond has no sense of money, and likes things that are too expensive. However, the two are married, as Rosamond soon begins spending more than Lydgate actually has saved.

Casaubon is in a bad condition; Lydgate says that it is a heart ailment, and can kill him suddenly. Casaubon asks Dorothea to promise to follow his wishes after he dies; she does not promise immediately. But, before she can give him her answer, he is dead, and she is widowed.

There is a clause in Casaubon's will about Dorothea not marrying Will, or else she forfeits her property. This clause is a shock, and does not speak well of Will's character. Dorothea goes to visit her sister and Sir James, and their new baby, Arthur. However, she soon finds out about the clause, and is deeply troubled by it.

Fred is told to get a job by his father; instead, all that he can do is go back and finish school, which makes Mary a little happier. The Garths come upon a great deal of good fortune; Caleb Garth gets some new properties to manage, which means that the family has some money at last. Farebrother and his family also start doing well; Dorothea gives them her large parish, and the extra income will allow Farebrother to marry, and will ensure that they have enough money to live a little better. Meanwhile, Lydgate is deeply in debt; he cannot pay back his loans, and his business is failing quickly. Rosamond applies to her father and his uncle for loans, but nothing seems to work. He is in a nervous, desperate state, and the marriage is not looking too good either. Rosamond begins to hate him because he tries to deny her all the nice, expensive things that she likes. She treasures her precious things more than she does her husband, who is too stressed to pay attention to her. She begins keeping company with Will Ladislaw, and fancies that he loves her. He does not, but it keeps Rosamond content for some time.

Will finds out about the clause in Casaubon's will, and becomes determined to leave. He sees Dorothea one last time, and they have a very heated confrontation. He leaves and goes to London, to find another job; she stays and tries not to think of him too often.

Fred does not want to go into the clergy, and he has Farebrother speak to Mary for him. Mary says that she is determined to marry Fred if he will make good on his promise to get a job, but says he should not be a preacher. Fred decides, quite by accident, to become an assistant to Mary's father. His parents are not very pleased by this, but this is all he wants to do, or has any aptitude for.

Bulstrode buys Stone Court from Mr. Rigg, who decides to leave town and go back to the coast. Bulstrode meets Mr. Raffles, a man from his past, very much by accident; Mr. Raffles was in a questionable business of selling stolen goods, and will blackmail Bulstrode if he doesn't get money. Raffles also married Rigg's mother; but Rigg wouldn't give him any money, and told him to leave immediately.

Rigg comes again and again to haunt Bulstrode; Bulstrode pays him to leave, but Raffles comes back, and he is very ill. Raffles tells Mr. Garth about Bulstrode's past; but Mr. Garth is too scrupulous to spread this knowledge around, so Bulstrode thinks that he is safe. Raffles dies at Bulstrode's house, under Lydgate's care; this doesn't look good, but Raffles died of natural causes relating to alcoholism. Bulstrode offers Lydgate a large loan to keep him from going bankrupt; Lydgate takes it, though it looks really bad, like a bribe. Bulstrode also found out that he had married Will Ladislaw's grandmother, and had deprived Will of his rightful inheritance. He tries to repent by offering Will a good deal of money, but Will refuses, which is good.

Will comes back, but Dorothea catches him with Rosamond, in what looks like a bad situation. Dorothea is disappointed, and angry with Will; Will is in turn angry with Rosamond for making things look like he loved her, when he didn't at all. Will debates whether to go and see her or not; Sir James wants him out of the neighborhood again, thinking that he is no good, and he needs to protect his sister-in-law.

Raffles told his story to a few more people than just Caleb Garth; the story gets around to Middlemarch, and things start looking very bad for Bulstrode. Lydgate is also connected with this, as the loan is thought of as some kind of bribe for being quiet about the circumstances regarding Raffles' death. Dorothea, however, believes that Lydgate is innocent. She, Farebrother, and a few others convince him to stay; in time, public opinion is not so much against him, though his practice continues to diminish.

Bulstrode, however, has to leave Middlemarch because the scandal is so bad. His wife is very sorry, because she had no idea that his past was so dirty; she is a very good person, and makes up her mind to stay with him no matter what. He leaves in disgrace, though Lydgate, who is innocent, stays behind.

Fred is doing well in his work for Mr. Garth; Mrs. Bulstrode leaves him the management of Stone Court, and he gets to live there as he takes care of the property. He and Mary become engaged, though Farebrother also wishes to marry her. But their engagement will be long, while Fred continues to prove himself through work, and saves money for marriage.

Dorothea bails out Lydgate with money to pay Bulstrode back. Finally, Will comes to see her; though she cannot marry him or else lose her property, she decides she doesn't want to lose him. Dorothea gives up all of Casaubon's money and property to marry Will; Celia and Sir James are shocked, though she has made the right decision. Sir James continues to think badly of the marriage; but Will and Dorothea go to London, Will is elected to Parliament, and they are very happy.

Chaptet 6

Historical Background

Victorianism - Find the Victorian Period

The Victorian Era generally coveres a period of time when Queen Victoria was on the throne, from 1837 to 1901. The Industrial Revolution was taking place. Writers from this period include: Charles Dickens, Sir Arthur Conan Doyle, Anne Brontë, Charlotte Brontë, Emily Brontë, Oscar Wilde, and others.

Victorian Period - A Time of Change

(1837 -1901)

"All art is at once surface and symbol. Those who go beneath the surface do so at their own peril. Those who read the symbol do so at their own peril."—by Oscar Wilde, Preface, "The Picture of Dorian Gray"

The Victorian Period revolves around the political career of Queen Victoria. She was crowned in 1837 and died in 1901 (which put a definite end to her political career). A great deal of change took place during this period—brought about because of the Industrial Revolution; so it's not surprising that the literature of the period is often concerned with social reform. As Thomas Carlyle (1795-1881) wrote, "The time for levity, insincerity, and idle babble and play-acting, in all kinds, is gone by; it is a serious, grave time."

Of course, in the literature from this period, we see a duality, or double standard, between the concerns for the individual (the exploitation and corruption both at home and abroad) and national success—in what is often referred to as the Victorian Compromise. In reference to Tennyson, Browning and Arnold, E. D. H. Johnson argues: "Their writings... locate the centers of authority not in the existing social order but within the resources of individual being."

Against the backdrop of technological, political, and socioeconomic change, the Victorian Period was bound to be a volatile time, even without the added complications of the religious and institutional challenges brought by Charles Darwin and other thinkers, writers, and doers.

Victorian Period: Early & Late

The Period is often divided into two parts: the early Victorian Period (ending around 1870) and the late Victorian Period. Writers associated with the early period are: Alfred, Lord Tennyson (1809-1892), Robert Browning (1812-1889), Elizabeth Barrett Browning (1806-1861), Emily Bronte (1818-1848), Matthew Arnold (1822-1888), Dante Gabriel Rossetti (1828-1882), Christina Rossetti (1830-1894), George Eliot (1819-1880), Anthony Trollope (1815-1882) and Charles Dickens (1812-1870).

Writers associated with the late Victorian Period include: George Meredith (1828-1909), Gerard Manley Hopkins (1844-1889), Oscar Wilde (1856-1900), Thomas Hardy (1840-1928), Rudyard Kipling (1865-1936), A.E. Housman (1859-1936), and Robert Louis Stevenson (1850-1894).

While Tennyson and Browning represented pillars in Victorian poetry, Dickens and Eliot contributed to the development of the English novel. Perhaps the most quintessentially Victorian poetic works of the period is: Tennyson's "In Memorium" (1850), which mourns the loss of his friend. Henry James describes Eliot's "Middlemarch" (1872) as "organized, moulded, balanced composition, gratifying the reader with the sense of design and construction."

It was a time of change, a time of great upheaval, but also a time of GREAT literature!

Victorian Age

The last completed period of English literature, almost

coincident in extent with the reign of the queen whose name it bears (Victoria, queen 1837-1901), stands nearly beside The Elizabethan period in the significance and interest of its work. The Elizabethan literature to be sure, in its imaginative and spiritual enthusiasm, is the expression of a period more profoundly great than the Victorian; but the Victorian literature speaks for an age which witnessed incomparably greater changes than any that had gone before in all the conditions of life—material comforts, scientific knowledge, and, absolutely speaking, in intellectual and spiritual enlightenment. Moreover, to twentieth century students the Victorian literature makes a specially strong appeal because it is in part the literature of our own time and its ideas and point of view are in large measure ours. We must begin by glancing briefly at some of the general determining changes and conditions to which reference has just been made, and we may naturally begin with the merely material ones.

Before the accession of Queen Victoria the 'industrial revolution,' the vast development of manufacturing made possible in the latter part of the eighteenth century by the introduction of coal and the steam engine, had rendered England the richest nation in the world, and the movement continued with steadily accelerating momentum throughout the period. Hand in hand with it went the increase of population from less than thirteen millions in England in 1825 to nearly three times as many at the end of the period. The introduction of the steam railway and the steamship, at the beginning of the period, in place of the lumbering stagecoach and the sailing vessel, broke up the old stagnant and stationary habits of life and increased the amount of travel at least a thousand times.

The discovery of the electric telegraph in 1844 brought almost every important part of Europe, and eventually of the world, nearer to every town dweller than the nearest county had been in the eighteenth century; and the development of the modern newspaper out of the few feeble sheets of 1825 (dailies and weeklies in London, only weeklies elsewhere), carried full accounts of the doings of the whole world, in place of long-delayed fragmentary rumors, to every door within a few hours. No less striking was the progress in public health and the increase in human happiness due to the enormous advance in the sciences of medicine, surgery, and hygiene. Indeed these sciences in their modern form virtually began with the discovery of the facts of bacteriology about 1860, and the use of antiseptics fifteen years later, and not much earlier began the effective opposition to the frightful epidemics which had formerly been supposed to be dependent only on the will of Providence.

Political and social progress, though less astonishing, was substantial. In 1830 England, nominally a monarchy, was in reality a plutocracy of about a hundred thousand men—landed nobles, gentry, and wealthy merchants—whose privileges dated back to fifteenth century conditions. The first Reform Bill, of 1832, forced on Parliament by popular pressure, extended the right of voting to men of the 'middle class,' and the subsequent bills of 1867 and 1885 made it universal for men. Meanwhile the House of Commons slowly asserted itself against the hereditary House of Lords, and thus England became perhaps the most truly democratic of the great nations of the world. At the beginning of the period the social condition of the great body of the population was extremely bad.

Laborers in factories and mines and on farms were largely in a state of virtual though not nominal slavery, living, many of them, in unspeakable moral and physical conditions. Little by little improvement came, partly by the passage of laws, partly by the growth of trades-unions. The substitution in the middle of the century of free-trade for protection through the passage of the 'Corn-Laws' afforded much relief by lowering the price of food. Socialism, taking shape as a definite movement in the middle of the century, became one to be reckoned with before its close, though the majority of the more well-to-do classes failed to understand even then the growing necessity for far-reaching economic and social changes. Humanitarian consciousness, however, gained greatly during the period. The middle and upper classes awoke to some extent to their duty to the poor, and sympathetic benevolent effort, both organized and informal, increased very largely in amount and intelligence. Popular education, too, which in 1830 had no connection with the State and was in every respect very incomplete, was developed and finally made compulsory as regards the rudiments.

Still more permanently significant, perhaps, was the transformation of the former conceptions of the nature and meaning of the world and life, through the discoveries of science. Geology and astronomy now gradually compelled all thinking people to realise the unthinkable duration of the cosmic processes and the comparative littleness of our earth in the vast extent of the universe. Absolutely revolutionary for almost all lines if thought was the gradual adoption by almost all thinkers of the theory of Evolution, which, partly formulated by Lamarck early in the century, received definite statement in 1859 in Charles Darwin's 'Origin of Species.' The great modification in the externals of religious belief thus brought about was confirmed also by the growth of the science of historical criticism.

This movement of religious change was met in its early stages by the very interesting reactionary 'Oxford' or 'Tractarian' Movement, which asserted the supreme authority of the Church and its traditional doctrines. The most important figure in this movement, who connects it definitely with literature, was John Henry Newman (1801-90), author of the hymn 'Lead, Kindly Light,' a man of winning personality and great literary skill. For fifteen years, as vicar of the Oxford University Church, Newman was a great spiritual force in the English communion, but the series of 'Tracts for the Times' to which he largely contributed, ending in 1841 in the famous Tract 90, tell the story of his gradual progress toward Rome.

Thereafter as an avowed Roman Catholic and head of a monastic establishment Newman showed himself a formidable controversialist, especially in a literary encounter with the clergyman-novelist Charles Kingsley which led to Newman's famous 'Apologia pro Vita Sua' (Apology for My Life), one of the secondary literary masterpieces of the century. His services to the Catholic Church were recognized in 1879 by his appointment as a Cardinal. More than one of the influences thus hastily surveyed combine in creating the moral, social, and intellectual strenuousness which is one of the main marks of the literature of the period. More conspicuously than ever before the majority of the great writers, not least the poets and novelists, were impelled not merely by the emotional or dramatic creative impulse but by the sense of a message for their age which should broaden the vision and elevate the ideals of the masses of their fellows. The literature of the period, therefore, lacks the disinterested and joyous spontaneity of, for example, the Elizabethan period, and its mood is far more complex than that of the partly socially-minded pseudo-classicists.

While all the new influences were manifesting themselves in Victorian literature they did not, of course, supersede the great general inherited tendencies. This literature is in the main romantic. On the social side this should be evident; the Victorian social humanitarianism is merely the developed form of the eighteenth century romantic democratic impulse. On the esthetic side the romantic traits are also present, though not so aggressively as in the previous period; with romantic vigour the Victorian literature often combines exquisite classical finish; indeed, it is so eclectic and composite that all the definite older terms take on new and less sharply contrasting meanings when applied to it.

So long a period naturally falls into sub-divisions; during its middle part in particular, progress and triumphant romanticism, not yet largely attacked by scientific skepticism, had created a prevailing atmosphere of somewhat passive sentiment and optimism both in society and in literature which has given to the adjective 'mid-Victorian' a very definite denotation. The adjective and its period are commonly spoken of with contempt in our own day by those persons who pride themselves on their complete sophistication and superiority to all intellectual and emotional weakness.

But during the 'mid-Victorian' years, there was also a comparative healthiness in the lives of the well-to-do classes and in literature which had never before been equalled and which may finally prove no less praiseworthy than the rather self-conscious freedom and unrestraint of the early twentieth century.

The most important literature of the whole period falls under the three heads of essays, poetry, and prose fiction, which we may best consider in that order.

Chaptet 7

List of Characters

Character List

Dorothea Brooke

Oldest of two daughters, and raised by her bachelor uncle, Mr. Brooke. Dorothea is an excessively religious, pious girl‹to the extent that she withdraws from the activities she likes most, and convinces herself to marry a man, Mr. Casaubon, who cannot satisfy her emotionally or mentally. Dorothea, although she is fairly well-educated, is naïve about the outside world; when her marriage disappoints her, she is forced to learn that she cannot make a life through other people, and that she must fulfill her purpose in life through her own effort.

Celia Brooke

Dorothea's younger sister, the more calm and ordinary of the two. Although she makes no challenges to convention, Celia is sensible, and very perceptive when it comes to people and the Middlemarch world around her. She marries the kind and sensitive Sir James Chettam, a much better match, and made for better reasons, than her sister's union.

Mr. Brooke

Dorothea and Celia's guardian and uncle, brother to their deceased father. He is a strong-willed man, with definite, though outdated, ideas about what women should and should not do. Mr. Brooke means well, however, and has few qualms about flying in the face of Middlemarch conventions and politics, if need be.

Edward Casaubon

Dorothea's middle-aged husband, a crusty old scholar with an inability to feel emotion or love. He slaves away on a project called "The Key to All Mythologies," a work that is supposed to integrate his life's learning. However, Casaubon really has no intention of writing or finishing it, and has lost his ability to live and his will to achieve in the musty pages of books. He is also a man prone to jealousy and insecurity, which places a great burden on his young wife, Dorothea.

Sir James Chettam

Begins pursuing Dorothea at the beginning of the novel, but gives her up for her sister Celia when Dorothea becomes engaged to Casaubon. Chettam is an affable, kind man, who listens ardently to Dorothea's plans for improving the life of rural folk, and then takes great measures to make her plans a reality.

Unlike many of the men in this novel, he does not subscribe to ideas that women should be weak, ornamental, and limited in their activities to household affairs; this makes his union with Celia a happy one, and cements his friendship with Dorothea.

Mr. Cadwallader

Preacher of Sir James' parish, and a trusted friend and advisor to him as well. He is kind, though has strong opinions in certain issues. He is often at Freshitt, Sir James' estate, for casual occasions and conversations.

Mrs. Cadwallader

Wife of Mr. Cadwallader, also rather kind-hearted, though with a tendency to be a bit of a busy-body. She knows all about neighborhood affairs, showing perhaps a little too much interest in other people's business.

Will Ladislaw

Young cousin of Mr. Casaubon, whom Casaubon has little regard for. He is kind though proud, and very intelligent. But, he is of lower social and economic standing than Casaubon because both his mother and grandmother married beneath themselves, and were disowned as a result. He is Dorothea's true love, and both of them bring out the best in each other.

Dr. Tertius Lydgate

Young man of about 30, of good family and social connections. He is the newest doctor in Middlemarch, and gains a lot of criticism from the old guard for his new methods and outsider status. He is proud to a fault, bright, and thinks that he has the capacity to be a great innovator in medicine. He falls in love with Rosamond and marries her, though his finances are less than ideal.

Rosamond Vincy

Very vain, empty-headed young woman, though her social graces and manner are perfect. She loves Lydgate because he is an outsider with impressive connections, and flatters her often. She needs constant attention from male suitors, even after marriage, and only the finest things around her. She treasures expensive possessions and furniture even more than her husband Lydgate, which causes great discord.

Mr. Vincy

Rosamond and Fred's father, mayor of Middlemarch. His family is one of the foremost in local society, and he is a merchant of good standing, dealing in cloth. Their family is not all rich, but got money from business. Mr. Vincy is very economical and works hard, though the rest of his family does not.

Mrs. Vincy

Wife to Mr. Vincy, and originator of many of her daughter Rosamond's flaws. She is also rather empty-headed, materialistic, and impractical; she gets Rosamond used to a very high standard of living, beyond even her husband's needs. She is not a bad woman, though she is recognized as being flawed, and not as steady as her husband.

Fred Vincy

The Vincys' only son; he starts out as a spendthrift and a very irresponsible young man, though by the end of the novel, he is doing decidedly better. He is in love with Mary Garth, though she is below him in social standing. However, Mary is much more sensible than he is, and gets him to work hard and prosper.

Mary Garth

Oldest child of the Garths, she works for Mr. Featherstone at Stone Court until his death. She is an intelligent girl who knows a good bit of literature, and she also has good experience with human nature. Mary is very affable, practical, and independent. She also helps Fred to improve himself immeasurably.

Caleb Garth

Mary's father, a hard-working man who manages estates and does improvements and construction projects on properties. He is far from rich, and very generous in spirit; overall a good man, who is always honest, and treats people well. He has a number of children, Mary being the most prominent. Fred becomes his apprentice when he cleans up his act.

Mrs. Garth

Wife of Caleb, just as honest and upstanding. She gives lessons to her own children and to village children as well, making extra money from this. She prizes responsibility, education, and honesty, and makes sure all of her children have these traits. She is a harder judge than her husband, but they are still a good match.

Mr. Featherstone

Owner of Stone Court, and very wealthy; related to both the Vincys and the Garths through his two childless marriages. He is a stern, unkind old man who uses his wealth as a threat to other people. He leaves his estate to his illegitimate son Mr. Rigg, which disappoints the Vincy family a great deal.

Mr. Rigg

Illegitimate son of Featherstone; he is disliked by people in Middlemarch for his common origins, and for being an outsider. He handles business and accountancy matters, and sells Stone Court to Mr. Bulstrode. He is stern and not very social, but not as mean as his father.

Mr. Bulstrode

Another prominent figure in Middlemarch, who runs a bank, a hospital, and other institutions. He has a good deal of money, and is prosperous; but his tendency to sermonize and keep an absurdly pious façade in public means that he is very unpopular with many people.

Mrs. Bulstrode

Mr. Vincy's sister; she is a very good woman, honest, upstanding, and faithful. She is also very good at evaluating other people, and their affairs. She gives excellent advice to Rosamond about marrying, and to the Vincys as well. Though her husband got his start in London, she is a true Middlemarcher, with a long family history there.

Mrs. Waule

Mr. Featherstone's sister, whom Mr. Featherstone does not like. She only comes to see him when he is dying, with the expectation that he will give her money in his will. A rater unpleasant woman, and not good company either.

Farebrother

A very honest and good man, though he is also human and would be the first to say so. He is in the clergy, and makes very little money; he supports his sister, mother, and aunt with this money, which is a bit of a strain. He is a good friend to Ladislaw, Lydgate, and others; he is also in love with Mary Garth, and she regards him highly.

Mr. Tyke

Another clergyman in the area, though his preaching is more sanctimonious, and favored by Bulstrode. He gets the position as the chaplain at the hospital instead of Farebrother for political reasons, although Farebrother is favored personally and as a preacher by most of the neighborhood.

Naumann

Will's painter friend in Rome, who appreciates Dorothea's beauty.

Trumbull

Town auctioneer, and business advisor to Featherstone. He seems to know Featherstone better than almost anyone, and is the only person other than Rigg who receives anything from his will.

Mr. Raffles

Rigg's stepfather, a good-for-nothing. Also a former business partner of Bulstrode's. He helped Bulstrode in some very disreputable trades, and comes back years later to blackmail him. He effectively blackens Bulstrode's name, then dies of alcoholism while under his care.

Christy Garth

The Garths' oldest son; he is a real academic excelling in languages and other subjects. He is responsible, upright, and everything that the Garths treasure in a person's character.

Captain Lydgate

Lydgate's flighty, wealthy, and airheaded cousin. Lydgate doesn't care for him at all, though Rosamond adores him because he pays her a lot of attention.

Godwin Lydgate

Lydgate's very wealthy uncle, who turns down Rosamond's request for a loan. He seems rather haughty, and not generous at all.

Miss Noble

Farebrother's aunt, who has never married. She is kindly, and Will is a very good friend to her.

Ned Plymdale

Vain suitor of Rosamond's, though she rejects him. He goes on to do well financially, and get married to someone else.

Mrs. Plymdale

Ned's mother, very proud and boastful about her son's success. Bitter that Rosamond rejects him.

Chaptet 8

Symbol, Image, Motif in George Eliot's Middlemarch

Responsibility

This is a major theme of Fred's story, and he must becomes responsible for his finances and his choices. Will does too, to a certain extent. Both men must learn how to rely on themselves, not infringe upon others, and how to become independent in many ways.

Stubbornness

A big issue of character. Rosamond is extremely stubborn, meaning that if things aren't done her way, she will go behind other people's backs to do things the way she thinks they should be done. Societal stubbornness is responsible for Lydgate's failure with his medical practice; people want what they want, for whatever reasons, which means that they are blind to things that might be best for them.

Prejudice

A theme that Lydgate and Will Ladislaw cannot seem to beat. People in Middlemarch dislike anyone who is not from Middlemarch, or anyone whose reputation seems questionable. Will and Lydgate are both good people, but it is initial prejudice, sometimes based on invalid or circumstantial reasons, that means that they are never liked or accepted in Middlemarch.

Conformity

An issue that is related to societal expectation, but is somewhat different. People are supposed to conform to certain social ideals and norms‹Dorothea is supposed to be a proper wife and then a proper widow, and follow society's set guidelines about how to fill each position. Will fits no position that society tries to group him into, so he is disliked; he refuses to be conventional or proper, or to fit into that society and its ideas of how someone like Will should act.

Love

Love keeps people together, or the lack or it lets them drift apart. Those who are truly in love‹like Will and Dorothea, Mary and Fred‹are bound together by it, and are very alike in temperament and outlook. Those who lack it‹like Lydgate and Rosamond, Casaubon and Dorothea‹are ill-suited to each other in marriage, and are very disappointed by their unions.

Unity of Middlemarch

The decisions made by every person in Middlemarch seem to have a direct effect on at least one other person. Mary's decision to marry Fred means that Farebrother is without a wife. Dorothea's decision to choose Casaubon leads Sir James to choose Celia. Bulstrode's dirty dealings with regard to Raffles mean disgrace to both Lydgate and Will Ladislaw. Everyone in Middlemarch is intimately connected, and it seems that no one can move around without disturbing someone else.

Societal Expectations

Closely linked to society's hierarchy, are ideas about how everyone should act in certain situations. Lydgate proposes to Rosamond because society expects that he should do it. Dorothea is pushed to live with someone else or marry again after she is widowed, because society expects that it is right. People don't necessarily follow these expectations, nor should they; but they do exist, and play a part in people's lives.

Vanity

Especially relevant to Rosamond and her suitors. Rosamond is exceptionally vain about her charm and her appearances, so much so that it is a shock to her when her friend Ladislaw says he doesn't love her. Her unsuccessful suitors are all equally vain, and blame Lydgate, rather than Rosamond's lack of interest, when she won't return their favor.

Self-discovery

There are certain truths which every character learns about himself in the course of trials; Lydgate and Rosamond find out more about their characters through their money troubles, though they do not always adjust accordingly. Dorothea makes the most dramatic journey of self-discovery, and changes a great deal within the course of the novel.

Reality vs. Expectations

Many characters' preconceived ideas, especially of marriage, are proven tragically wrong in the course of the book. Casaubon and Dorothea both have unrealistic ideas about marriage, and are disappointed. Lydgate and Rosamond have the same idea, and are let down. Life often defies what one expects, or could predict of it; and the people who are happiest are the ones who have few expectations, or are most flexible.

Conscience vs. self-interest

This is a question that comes to play in Lydgate's life in particular. Does one do what one thinks is right, or what gives one the most benefit? Lydgate often goes for self-interest, though it gets him into trouble.

Gender roles and expectations

Especially relevant to Dorothea. Middlemarch society has very defined ideas of what people of each gender should do within the society, and people, especially women, who deviate from this norm, are looked down upon. Dorothea is tolerated because she is of good family and does not disrupt the society she is in. However, she faces a great deal of pressure to change herself, conform to others' ideas, and submit herself to male leadership at all times.

Progress

Much is changing in the world of Middlemarch; English society is evolving in social, economic, technologic areas. Socially, ideas of gender and class are in flux, as women are proving more and more competent, and the Industrial Revolution is causing a greater amount of social mobility. The economy of England is changing, from an aristocratic, inheritance- based system of holding wealth and land, to one based on commerce, business, and manufacturing. Technology is also changing, in medical science, and in areas like transportation, and these are changes that are beginning to sweep through Middlemarch.

Pride

This is something which both helps and hinders many people in the book, and is most applicable to Dorothea, Will Ladislaw, and Lydgate. With Lydgate, pride is a tumbling block, something that keeps him from putting his affairs in order, and sometimes doing what is necessary in his marriage and practice.

Dorothea and Will's pride is more involved in who they are personally‹neither of them likes to be regarded poorly, will defend themselves and their decisions if needed, and follow their own course with regards to everything.

Money

Money is the root of many evils, but much good, in the novel. Lydgate gets desperate for want of it, Fred despairs when he has little, Dorothea becomes generous when she has too much, and the Garths save carefully since their money is limited. Money has a profound effect on character within the novel, and though many people are judged by how much money they have, many of the best people in the novel, like Will Ladislaw and Mr. Farebrother, have very little.

Strength of rumor

Rumor can do a great deal of damage in Middlemarch, having even more weight than fact in some cases. Both Bulstrode and Lydgate are blackened by rumors passed around society, and Will is blackened as well, though he is falsely accused.

Politics

Everything is political in Middlemarch, with most people strongly backing the conservative party. Personal alliances and aversions are based on matters of politics and political identification. But even political matters, like all things, get personal; people decide who or who not to support by how they like them, even more so sometimes than any dependence on issues.

Family obligation

People within the novel have varying ideas of family obligation in the novel, though it is a strong force in Middlemarch society. Mr. Featherstone's relations believe they are entitled to money; Mrs. Bulstrode believes that she must help and advise her family in order to show support. Sir James shows his regard for his family by being very protective and a constant advisor as well. Casaubon dispenses of his obligation through money, and Bulstrode attempts also to do the same.

Social position

Social position means a great deal in Middlemarch; it means how much respect a person gets, how people treat them, how they are regarded, etc. People of high status are generally treated more delicately than people with little money, like Lydgate and Will Ladislaw. Birth and connections are also important in determining a person's place, and also what benefits they will receive from society.

Dorothea, the Dodo Bird in Middlemarch

Dorothea and her sister Celia probably learned about the

dodo bird, which became extinct in the seventeenth century, in their early education. Celia probably thought her sister's name had an amusing phonic resemblance to the extinct bird. "Dodo," she thought, "can be my term of endearment for Dorothea." One can only speculate about the origin of Dorothea's nickname in the novel Middlemarch because George Eliot does not provide its history. Fortunately, the history of the dodo bird is well documented, as is Dorothea's fictional life, and comparison of the two produces many intriguing parallels that provide insight into the caged and flightless lives of Victorian women.

The dodo bird lived undisturbed on the island of Mauritius in the Indian Ocean for so long that it lost its need and ability to fly. Most Victorians with money or "unquestionably 'good'" connections are isolated from the limitations and social ills outside their little microcosms, thus islands unto themselves metaphorically speaking. Islanded by her family's respectability and wealth, Dorothea is "educated... on plans at once narrow and promiscuous, first in an English family and afterwards in a Swiss family at Lausanne". After completing her education, she lives in "a quiet country-house, and attend[s] a village church hardly larger than a parlour" at Tipton Grange — Dorothea's physical microcosmic island: "Her mind was theoretic, and yearned by its nature after some lofty conception of the world which might frankly include the parish of Tipton and her own rule of conduct there". Since Dorothea's uncle, Mr. Brooke "dread[s] so much the sort of superior woman likely to be available" to be a "guide and companion to his nieces," Dorothea "preside[s] over... [his] household, and did not at all dislike her new authority, with the homage that belonged to it."

Like most middle-class Victorian women, Dorothea's "homage" was restricted to the domestic sphere. She had no power to effect the changes on her uncle's property which she saw fitting. One such change is the improvement of the "pig-sty cottages" in which her uncle's tenants reside: "'Worth doing! yes, indeed,' said Dorothea... 'I think we deserve to be beaten out of our beautiful houses with a scourge of small cords — all of us who let tenants live in such sties as we see round us. Life in cottages might be happier than ours, if they were real houses fit for human beings from whom we expect duties and affections.'" Mr. Brooke apathetically files the poverty of his tenants under political economy while Dorothea looks on helplessly, wishing to spread her unused wings and lift some of the tenants' burdens: "In Mr. Brooke the hereditary strain of Puritan energy [i]s clearly in abeyance; but in his niece Dorothea it glow[s] alike through faults and virtues, turning sometimes into impatience of her uncle's talk or his way of 'letting things be' on his estate". Imprisoned by the cage of her youth, Dorothea settles for drawing architectural plans of new cottages in preparation for the auspicious time "when she would be of age and have some command of money for generous schemes."

Mr. Brooke's unconscious prejudice towards Dorothea's sex and age represents the social limitations that keep most Victorian women forever "thinking of [their] wings and never flying". When she delivers a compassionate and humane response to Sir James Chettam's entreaty, her uncle clips her lofty sentiments with a brusque chauvinistic bullet: "'Young ladies don't understand political economy'" (The disjointed points he makes to discredit his niece only prove to support her opinion: "'The fact is, human reason may carry you a little too far — over the hedge, in fact.... I have always been in favour [sic] of a little theory: we must have Thought; else we shall be landed back in the dark ages." Dorothea's eloquent insightfulness did not originate from any "theory" or "reason" based on textbooks.

Her rectitude and social conscience produce the antithesis of political economy's core principle: "'It is not a sin to make yourself poor in performing experiments for the good of all.'" Mr. Brooke again slights Dorothea when he rejects her proposal to help sort his papers, telling her "young ladies are too flighty" to "meddle with... documents"). The adjective used to describe young women is pregnant with hypocrisy and irony. If anyone is given to flightiness, it is Mr. Brooke, a man of "acquiescent temper, miscellaneous opinions, and uncertain vote". He "was held... to have contracted a too rambling habit of mind" with "conclusions [that] were as difficult to predict as the weather." The flightiness he hypocritically accuses his niece of possessing is ironic in respect to Dorothea's nickname (Dodos were flightless birds). As the narrator's psychological analysis of Mr. Brooke's motivation reveals, his remark was totally unconscious, even involuntary: "[T]he remark lay in his mind as lightly as the broken wing of an insect among all the other fragments there, and a chance current had sent it alighting to her". His instinctive response represents that though most women have wings to fly, Victorian society unconsciously places them in sexist cages from the cradle to the grave.

When the Portuguese sailors first arrived on the island of Mauritius, the dodo birds, having no natural predators, had no fear of them or their animals. The sailors hunted the island's avian inhabitants for food and sport, while the dogs and pigs made short work of the birds' eggs. Just as the dodo birds were oblivious to the predatory motives of the new visitors on their island, Dorothea, in her tranquil microcosm without a middle-aged woman to guide her, is oblivious to Sir James's intention to stuff and hang her on his mantelpiece as a trophy wife:

She was open, ardent, and not in the least self-admiring; indeed, it was pretty to see how her imagination adorned her sister Celia with attractions altogether superior to her own, and if any gentleman appeared to come to the Grange from some other motive than that of seeing Mr. Brooke, she concluded he must be in love with Celia: Sir James Chettam for example, whom she constantly considered from Celia's point of view, inwardly debating whether it would be good for Celia to accept him. That he should be regarded as a suitor to herself would have seemed to her a ridiculous irrelevance.

In Sir James's hunt for a wife to "whom he could say 'What shall we do?' about this or that, who could help her husband with reasons and would also have the property qualifications for doing so", Dorothea falls into his sights: "She was thoroughly charming to him, but of course he theorised [sic] a little about his attachment." He picks Dorothea as if she were live game or a "young woman... tied up to be chosen, like poultry at market" and proceeds to track and set traps for his prey — the Brooke sister he feels is "in all respects superior". One such trap Sir James uses is illusory predominance: "In short, he felt himself to be in love in the right place, and was ready to endure a great deal of predominance, which, after all, a man could put down when he liked. Sir James had no idea that he should ever like to put down the predominance of this handsome girl, in whose cleverness he delighted". He coaxes Dorothea out of her nest, closer to the cage of domesticity, by giving her the monetary means to effect "generous schemes" denied by her youth and uncle:

"Do you know, Lovegood was telling me yesterday that you had the best notion in the world of a plan for cottages — quite wonderful for a young lady, he thought. You had a real genus, to use his expression. He said you wanted Mr. Brooke to build a new set of cottages, but he seemed to think it hardly probable that your uncle would consent. Do you know, that is one of the things I wish to do — I mean, on my own estate. I should be so glad to carry out that plan of yours, if you would let me see it.... But after all, it is worth doing." [

Both the predator and the prey are unaware of the other's intentions. Only Dorothea's sister Celia can see that both parties use "preconceptions either confident or distrustful" to misinterpret each other's actions and manners: "Celia was present while the plans were being examined, and observed Sir James's illusion. He thinks that Dodo cares about him, and she only cares about her plans. Yet I am not certain that she would refuse him if she thought he would let her manage everything and carry out all her notions. And how very uncomfortable Sir James would be! I cannot bear notions"). After his trophy eludes him, Sir James proves himself better than most Victorian men: "Although Sir James was a sportsman, he had some other feelings towards women than grouse and foxes, and did not regard his future wife in the light of prey, valuable chiefly for the excitements of the chase".

Mistaking their lack of fear for a lack of intelligence, the Portuguese sailors called the avian inhabitants on the newly discovered island of Mauritius "dodo," Portuguese for "doudou," which means "simpleton." When Edward Casaubon first discovers Dorothea, he mistakenly believes that her unworldliness and initial appreciation of a man who "take[s] pains to talk to her, not with absurd compliments, but with an appeal to her understanding" will make her an excellent helpmate... [and] enable him to dispense with a hired secretary, an aid Mr. Casaubon had never yet employed and had a suspicious dread of. (Mr. Casaubon was nervously conscious that he was expected to manifest a powerful mind.) Providence, in its kindness, had supplied him with... [a] wife, a modest young lady, with the purely appreciative, unambitious abilities of her sex... sure to think her husband's mind powerful.

More than a "helpmate," Casaubon wishes Dorothea to be a "housemaid" to "rub" his "pier-glass or extensive surface of polished steel... [that is] minutely and multitudinously scratched in all directions." When directly applied to Edward's life and works, the pier-glass parable illuminates the catacombs of his psychological makeup. His "abundant pen-scratches" are the "minutely and multitudinous" scratches on a pier-glass — the many volumes of his notations that "go everywhere impartially" — which he initially believes Dorothea will "observe... with the uncritical awe of an elegant-minded canary bird." His notations are on "amplitude of paper[s]," which is the equivalent of an actual pier-glass. The "egoism" of Casaubon "produces the flattering illusion of concentric arrangement" of "all the mythical systems or erratic mythical fragments in the world":

He told her how he had undertaken to show (what indeed had been attempted before, but not with that thoroughness, justice of comparison, and effectiveness of arrangement at which Mr. Casaubon aimed) that all the mythical systems or erratic mythical fragments of the world were corruptions of a tradition originally revealed. Having once mastered the true position and taken a firm footing there, the vast field of mythical constructions became intelligible, nay, luminous with the reflected light of speedy correspondences. But to gather in this great harvest of truth was no light or speedy work. His notes already made a formidable range of volumes, but the crowning task would be to condense these voluminous still-accumulating results and bring them... to a fit little shelf.

The years of toil produce nothing but more pen-scratches and paper and wear his candle to a mere stub. With the winds of death threatening to extinguish his low, flickering flame, Edward needs Dorothea to carry his torch:

But it was clear enough to her that he would expect her to devote herself to sifting those mixed heaps of material, which were to be doubtful illustration of principles still more doubtful.... And now she pictured to herself the days, months, and years which she must spend in sorting what might be called shattered mummies, and fragments of tradition which was itself a mosaic wrought from crushed ruins — sorting them as food for a theory which was already withered in the birth like an elfin child.... She could understand well enough now why her husband had come to cling to her, as possible the only hope left that his labours would ever take a shape in which they could be given to the world.

Had her husband not betrayed her trust with the codicil of his will, Dorothea would have remained a prisoner in her marital tomb: "[S]he simply felt that she was going to say 'Yes' to her own doom: she was too weak, too full of dread at the thought of inflicting a keen-edged blow on her husband, to do anything but submit completely". Already "paying hidden visits" to her "best soul in prison", Dorothea's altruistic passions would have shared the same fate as the extinct dodo birds had her soul not been pardoned by her husband's treachery. The parallels between the lives of the dodo birds and Dorothea reveal how life for Victorian women took place in a series of aviaries built by a male-chauvinistic society, which keep them flightless and oppressed. George Eliot shows Dorothea's various cages, which take the form of the frustratingly confining world of her girlhood and the suffocating "virtual tomb" of her marriage, as the movelist tries to save the souls, passions, and talents of women from extinction.

The Women in Window

Social and moral concerns are reflected in the presentation of landscape throughout George Eliot's fiction. Felix Holt, for example, opens with a dioramic view of the midlands countryside circa 1832 as it passes before a hypothetical passenger on the outside box of a stagecoach. The reader is offered a rich description of such natural beauties as meadows, watercourses, ponds, lanes, willows, elders, yews, hedgerows, wildflowers, ricks, and cattle.

But the landscape, as Arnold Kettle has pointed out, is sociological as well as pictorial (p. 100); For an opposing view, see Conrad, Victorian Treasure-House, pp. 39-40. It offers what Eliot, in the "Impressions of Theophrastus Such," calls "a piece of our social history in pictorial writing" (2:40). The narrator of Felix Holt not only places a shepherd in the scene but pauses to characterize his mental horizons. She contrasts an impoverished, benighted cluster of laborers' cottages ("their little dingy windows telling, like thick-filmed eyes, of nothing but the darkness within") to a more prosperous, better-schooled village. Many of the visual details take on an emblematic moral significance, as they do so often in Ruskin's great set-piece descriptions.

Both Adam Bede and Middlemarch are deeply influenced by Ruskin's critique of the picturesque. The landscape of Adam Bede consistently reflects a Ruskinian awareness of the dark underside of an apparently Edenic setting. Loamshire at first seems the classic paysage riant, ideally fertile and perfectly suited to man's needs. But a close scrutiny of the opening prospect reveals some ominous tints. In the following passage the nameless Gilpinesque traveller begins and ends in the picturesque, but symbolic elements intervene.

On the side of the Green that led towards the church, the broken line of thatched cottages was continued nearly to the church [145/146] yard gate; but on the opposite, northwestern side, there was nothing to obstruct the view of gently-swelling meadow, and wooded valley, and dark masses of distant hill. That rich undulating district of Loamshire to which Hayslope belonged, lies close to a grim outskirt of Stonyshire, overlooked by its barren hills as a pretty blooming sister may sometimes be linked in the arm of a rugged, tall, swarthy brother; and in two or three hours' ride the traveller might exchange a bleak treeless region, intersected by lines of cold grey stone, for one where his road wound under the shelter of woods, or up swelling hills, muffled with hedgerows and long meadow-grass and thick corn; and where at c very turn he came upon some fine old country-seat nestled in the valley or crowning the slope, some homestead with its long length of barn and its cluster of golden ricks, some grey steeple looking out from a pretty confusion of trees and thatch and dark-red tiles.

The distant glimpse of Stonyshire introduces a touch of mountain gloom into the agreeable vista (Creeger). Bleakness and barrenness, according to Gilpin, are distinctly nonpicturesque; here they function as emblematic reminders of an alternate and far less pleasant state of nature.

The traveller proceeds to analyze the landscape in the approved Claudian terms of foreground, middle distance, and background. The prospect accommodates this conventional zoning, first by falling away from the viewer, who occupies a middle elevation, and then by rising in the distance to its maximum elevation in the form of large hills. But the description emphasizes that the zoning is nature's rather than man's; and the foreground, with its "level sunlight lying like transparent gold among the gently curving stems of the feathered grass and the tall red sorrel, and the white umbels of the hemlocks lining the bushy hedgerows," is far more Pre-Raphaelite than Claudian (2:23).

Moreover, a strong consciousness of time invests the consideration of space. Although the moment is 18 June 1799, the description evokes the grand perennial cycle of nature, so that the reader seems to glimpse the same landscape under different seasonal]aspects. The passage of time brings renewal to nature, but has a different meaning for mortal man. The "keen and hungry winds of the north" and the "sound of the scythe being whetted [which] makes us cast more lingering looks at the flower-sprinkled tresses of the meadow" remind man of his finite term, as they often do in traditional pastoral literature. The description suggests that man will be swallowed up from view, much as the "tall mansion" and its landscaped park are swallowed up from view by the woods and meadows

In his picture of Dinah Morris Preaching on Hayslope Green (1861), E. H. Corbould neatly solves the problem posed by George Eliot's detailed and richly significant landscape description. He simply turns Dinah around, so that her backdrop is not the panoramic vista, as in the novel, but Hayslope village and a piece of the intervening green, an altogether more manageable subject.

The truly Ruskinian landscape always contains intimations of mortality as well as of immortality. The bay into which Romola's boat drifts is spectacularly beautiful and peaceful but contains a plague-stricken village. As Norma Jean Davis points out, "both Ruskin and Romola discover, in their exploration of Italian landscape, that behind the apparent picturesque beauty and green luxuriance are elements of death and decay".

In Adam Bede Eliot twice introduces overt memento mori into apparently idyllic landscapes. Early in the novel Adam and Seth carry a coffin through a scene of "Eden-like peace and loveliness," creating, as the narrator says, "a strangely-mingled picture" (4:73). A moment later they come upon their drowned father's body. This effect of moral chiaroscuro is repeated in the setting through which the pregnant Hetty sets off in search of Arthur.

The early February landscape is astir with signs of spring and hope, but the narrator thinks of the wayside crucifix one might encounter in a Continental countryside on such a day: an image of a great agony — the agony of the Cross. It has stood perhaps by the clustering apple — blossoms, or in the broad sunshine by the cornfield, or at a turning by the wood where a clear brook was gurgling below; and surely, if there came a traveller to this world who knew nothing of the story of man's life upon it, this image of agony would seem to him strangely out of place in the midst of this joyous nature.

He would not know that hidden behind the apple-blossoms, or among the golden com, or under the shrouding boughs of the wood, there might be a human heart beating heavily with anguish; perhaps a young [147/148] blooming girl, not knowing where to turn for refuge from swift-advancing shame; understanding no more of this life of ours than a foolish lost lamb wandering farther and farther in the nightfall on the lonely heath; yet tasting the bitterest of life's bitterness. [35:112]

This appeal for sympathy is a virtual reprise of the third and fourth paragraphs of Ruskin's "Mountain Gloom." There, too, a naive traveller comes upon "a cross of rough-hewn pine, iron-bound to its parapet" amidst an inspiring landscape. This cross is an emblem of the misery of the peasants who inhabit the landscape and who die contemplating images of the suffering Christ. Eliot's comparison of the incomprehending Hetty to a biblical lost lamb may have been prompted by Ruskin's comparison of the insensible Swiss peasants to the wild mountain goats which take no "passion of joy in all that fair work of God" surrounding them (6.387-89). The cross in the landscape is a reminder of unseen moral forces in nature. The moral intrudes upon the picturesque again in the climactic recognition scene of Adam Bede. Adam, passing through the Fir-tree Grove, stops to contemplate a beech-tree as Gilpin himself might have done in his Remarks on Forest Scenery. The sensitive carpenter registers aesthetic detail as well as potential board-feet:

Adam delighted in a fine tree of all things; as the fisherman's sight is keenest on the sea, so Adam's perceptions were more at home with trees than with other objects. He kept them in his memory, as a painter does, with all the flecks and knots in their bark, all the curves and angles of their boughs; and had often calculated the height and contents of a trunk to a nicety, as he stood looking at it. No wonder that, notwithstanding his desire to get on, he could not help pausing to look at a curious large beech which he had seen standing before him at a turning in the road, and convince himself that it was not two trees wedded together, but only one. For the rest of his life he remembered that moment when he was calmly examining the beech, as a man remembers his last glimpse of the home where his youth was passed, before the road turned, and he saw it no more. The beech stood at the last turning before the Grove ended in an [148/149]archway of boughs that let in the eastern light; and as Adam stepped away from the tree to continue his walk, his eyes fell on two figures about twenty yards before him. [27:10]

This is the moment of Adam's psychic fall from innocence to experience. His innocent perception of the picturesque variegation of tree-trunks and boughs gives way to a shattering recognition of Eve with her seducer. The recognition is still pictorial, since the "archway of boughs" makes a perfect frame; but the picture now admits the existence of treachery and evil in the idyllic scene. This episode may have been the model for the great recognition scene in Henry James's The Ambassadors, in which Lambert Strether, like Adam, sees two trusted friends in a compromised position amidst a landscape which only moments before had been a pleasant picture.

The Fir-tree Grove in Adam Bede is a delusory paradise for all who enter it. It is the regular trysting-place of Hetty and Arthur, and the scene of the seduction that has such tragic consequences. Michael Squires has rightly related the setting to the tradition of the locus amoenus in pastoral poetry, the erotic and magical pagan paradise which changes those who enter it (Squires, pp. 60-67; the Red Deeps in The Mill on the Floss is a vestigial locus amoenus. Compare Ware Commons in chapter 12 of John Fowles's The French Lieutenant's Woman). But George Eliot treats the topos with a Protestant distrust that recalls Spenser's handling of the Bower of Blisse in The Faerie Queene. In pictorial terms, the grove is a Claudian mythological landscape, peopled with figures from Ovid. This ideal landscape is the symptomatic product of a mind that avoids reality to indulge in fantasies of self-gratification.

She thought nothing of the evening light that lay gently in the grassy alleys between the fern, and made the beauty of their living green more visible than it had been in the overpowering flood of noon: she thought of nothing that was present. She only saw something that was possible: Mr. Arthur Donnithorne coming to meet her again along the Fir-tree

Grove. That was the foreground of Hetty's picture; behind it lay a bright hazy something — days that were not to be as the other days of her life had been. It was as if she had been wooed by a river-god, who might any time take her to his wondrous halls below a watery heaven. 113:201-02]

In other words, Hetty prefers a Heroic Landscape with Poseidon and Tyro to a more realistic picture along the lines of, say, Millais's Waiting (1854). Claude's presumed avoidance of the nature immediately surrounding him makes him the chief villain in the historical drama of landscape painting presented by Ruskin in Modern Painters. By the same token, Claudian landscape is something of a villain in Adam Bede.

The aesthetic and the moral remain compatible in Adam Bede. Ruskin's critique of the surface-picturesque opens the way to a true landscape which intimates the possibility of salvation through moral struggle. The same is true in Middlemarch, but in the later novel the vision of true landscape is much more problematic. George Eliot explores more deeply than ever before the disturbing possibility that the aesthetic and the moral are incompatible, that art itself has no worthy human use. As Barbara Hardy has said: "The art/ life antithesis is a very important subject in Middlemarch.... Many characters are defined and even tested by their response to art, and art itself is defined and even tested by its relevance and meaning for human beings of different kinds".

These issues are crystallized in Chapter 39, which narrates Mr. Brooke's visit to the farm of his tenant, Dagley. Here the lower picturesque is precisely what Ruskin called it: an eminently heartless ideal.

It is true that an observer, under that softening influence of the fine arts which makes other people's hardships picturesque, might have been delighted with this homestead called Freeman's End: the old house had dormer-windows in the dark-red roof, two of the chimneys were choked with ivy, the large porch was blocked up with bundles of sticks, and half the windows were closed with grey worm-eaten shutters about which the jasmine boughs grew in wild luxuriance; the mouldering garden wall with hollyhocks peeping over it was a perfect study of highly mingled subdued colour, and there was an aged goat (kept doubtless on interesting superstitious grounds) lying against the open back-kitchen door. The mossy thatch of the cow-shed, the broken grey barn-doors, the pauper labourers in ragged [150/151]breeches who had nearly finished unloading a wagon of corn into the barn ready for early thrashing [sic]; the scanty dairy of cows being tethered for milking and leaving one half of the shed in brown emptiness; the very pigs and white ducks seemed to wander about the uneven neglected yard as if in low spirits from feeding on a too meagre quality of rinsings, — all these objects under the quiet light of a sky marbled with high clouds would have made a sort of picture which we have all paused over as a "charming bit," touching other sensibilities than those which are stirred by the depression of the agricultural interest, with the sad lack of farming capital, as seen constantly in the newspapers of that time. But these troublesome associations were just now strongly present to Mr. Brooke, and spoiled the scene for him. [39: 182-83]

At Freeman's End, picturesque unevenness betokens neglect and brown emptiness signifies want. As Eliot says in Daniel Deronda, again echoing Ruskin: "What horrors of damp huts, where human beings languish, may not become picturesque through aerial distance!" for. The narrator of Middlemarch will not indulge the nostalgia for "dear, old, brown, crumbling, picturesque inefficiency" which gives pleasure to the narrator of "Amos Barton" (1:4). Even Mr. Brooke's connoisseurship gives way to a true perception of his tenant's misery.

The aestheticist view of life is questioned throughout Middlemarch. We have seen that Will Ladislaw accuses Naumann of looking at the world "entirely from the studio point of view". By the same token Dorothea's conscience is troubled by aesthetic apprehension as such. She is unable to bring the "severe classical nudities and smirking Renaissance-Correggiosities" in her uncle's art collection at Tipton Grange into "any sort of relevance with her life". Her trip to Rome helps her better to understand what Will calls the "old language" of classical and Renaissance art, but it does not bridge the gap between that art and her own sense of purpose. As Richard S. Lyons has pointed out in "The Method of Middlemarch (p. 43), Dorothea renews her attack upon Mr. Brooke's collection after her return from Rome: "I used to come from the village with that dirt and coarse ugliness [like a pain within me, and the simpering pictures in the drawing room seemed to me like a wicked attempt to find delight in what is false, while we don't mind how hard the truth is for the neighbours outside our walls". As the novel progresses, Ladislaw becomes less the aesthete, but Dorothea does not become more the connoiseuse.

Dorothea can find relevance in simple portraiture, which she values more for iconic than for aesthetic reasons. The miniature of Ladislaw's grandmother sustains her through some bad times because it reminds her of Will himself and of his great regard for her. Dorothea is also sustained by a hard-won vision of the English landscape, a vision that is partly pictorial but not sentimentally picturesque. She tends from the first to envision her own destiny as somehow involved with the midlands countryside. Even in the sculpture gallery of the Vatican Museum her first thoughts are of the English landscape: "She did not really see the streak of sunlight on the floor more than she saw the statues: she was inwardly seeing the light of years to come in her own home and over the English fields and elms and hedge-bordered highroads; and feeling that the way in which they might be filled with joyful devotedness was not so clear to her as it had been". Dorothea values nature and duty more highly than art, and her priorities reflect certain moments in George Eliot's own museum-going.

The landscape that matters most to Dorothea upon her return from Rome lies immediately outside the west window of her boudoir at Lowick. The window gives onto an avenue of lime-trees leading to an entrance-gate, beyond which may be seen a bit of road and a large expanse of open, flat field. Dorothea views this prospect under several different diurnal, seasonal, and emotional aspects, so that it affords a series of landscape images in which objective and subjective elements strive to achieve a stable balance. E. D. H. Johnson has pointed out in "The Truer Message" that the sequence of views from Dorothea's boudoir window provides an index to her growth toward self-knowledge.

The most important views occur in chapters 28, 54, and 8 0;and they form a progression from despair through indifference to affirmation which corresponds roughly with the progression outlined by Carlyle in Sartor Resartus from the Everlasting Nay through the [152/153]Centre of Indifference to the Everlasting Yea. In Chapter 28 Dorothea is at an ebb, having suffered the disappointment of virtually all her marital hopes. The landscape outside her boudoir reflects her mood of cold constriction and drab imprisonment: she saw the long avenue of limes lifting their trunks from a white earth, and spreading white branches against the dun and motionless sky. The distant flat shrank in uniform whiteness and low hanging uniformity of cloud.... Her blooming full-pulsed youth stood there in a moral imprisonment which made itself one with the chill, colourless, narrowed landscape.

Dorothea's subjectivity dominates this landscape of despair. The description borders on the pathetic fallacy, a concept which George Eliot noted with interest in "Arts and Belles Lettres," her review of the third volume of Modern Painters. The novelist here displays what John Stuart Mill called "the power of creating scenery, in keeping with some state of human feeling; so fitted to it as to be the embodied symbol of it, and to summon up the state of feeling itself, with a force not to be surpassed by anything but reality". Mill was speaking of Tennyson's earliest poems, especially of "Mariana"; and indeed it is of "Mariana" and Millais's splendid painting of Tennyson's heroine (1851) that one is reminded most strongly by chapter 28 of Middlemarch Dorothea's duty is no clearer to her in Chapter 54, but as a widow she suffers less acutely than she did as a wife. She has recuperated from the worst of her bereavement, and her condition is now comfortable but neutral and aimless. Again the landscape reflects her spiritual state:

She had not yet applied herself to her work, but was seated with her hands folded on her lap, looking out along the avenue of limes to the distant fields. Every leaf was at rest in the sunshine, the familiar scene was changeless, and seemed to represent the prospect of her life, full of motiveless ease — motiveless, if her own energy could not seek out reasons for ardent action.

The prospect is no longer jaundiced by Dorothea's despair, but it is still dominated by her subjectivity. There is no fruitful interchange between objective and subjective, between nature and the perceiving mind.

The possibility of a more balanced relationship with the landscape is adumbrated in chapter 37 and realized in chapter 80. "She had been so used to struggle for and to find resolve in looking along the avenue towards the arch of western light," we are told in the earlier instance, "that the vision itself had gained a communicating power". Once the vision itself communicates, it can offer the joy and moral strength that work through time and memory to make up Wordsworthian maturity. Dorothea attains such maturity in Chapter 80, after suffering through a night of dark despair brought on by Will Ladislaw's apparent rejection of her love. Her psychic resurrection is assisted by her recognition of an independent life in the landscape outside her boudoir window.

She opened her curtains, and looked out towards the bit of road that lay in view, with fields beyond outside the entrance-gates. On the road there was a man with a bundle on his back and a woman carrying her baby; in the field she could see figures moving — perhaps the shepherd with his dog. Far off in the bending sky was the pearly light; and she felt the largeness of the world and the manifold wakings of men to labour and endurance. She was a part of that involuntary, palpitating life, and could neither look out on it from her luxurious shelter as a mere spectator, nor hide her eyes in selfish complaining.

The landscape is no longer problematic; its objective reality affords Dorothea an alternative to self-pity, and makes possible a creative interaction between her mind and the world outside it. Though faith is gone, the world remains; and work still has meaning, as it does for Carlyle's Teufelsdrockh in the phase of the Everlasting Yea. The perception of otherness is not sickening, as in Sartre's La Nausée, but healing. The recuperation of Rex Gascoigne in Daniel Deronda begins with a similar act of attention to a landscape peopled by working figures immediately outside his own window (8:122-23).

The vista in chapter 80 of Middlemarch holds its Wordsworthian and Carlylean elements within a highly pictorialized structure. The window provides a frame, and the prospect is divided into foreground, middle distance, and background. The lighting is specified and the figures in the scene are precisely located. Critics have sought analogues for the description in the paintings of Rubens and Millet, but the details given by Eliot are so minimal and generic as to defy identification with the work of any particular artist. They are at any rate not conventionally picturesque; they manifest no roughness, irregularity, vivid chiaroscuro, or ruin. Eliot is evoking not the surface-picturesque but the noble picturesque, which consists, according to Ruskin, in the unconscious expression of human suffering "nobly endured by unpretending strength of heart... the world's hard work being gone through all the while, and no pity asked for, nor contempt feared").

The best pictorial analogue for the window-scenes in Middlemarch is not to be found in landscape painting at all but in a popular motif of nineteenth-century Romantic genre painting: the figure looking out a window who presents his or her back to a viewer located inside the room. The motif is operative in European painting from the seventeenth century well into the twentieth; its classic nineteenth-century embodiment is in the work of Caspar David Friedrich, especially the Frau am Fenster of about 1822.66 Millais's Mariana belongs to this tradition, as does Moritz von Schwind's Morgenstunde, a picture George Eliot might have seen at Munich in 1858. The real subject of such paintings, at least in the nineteenth century, is usually the spiritual interaction between the spectator and the prospect. Romantic

Fensterbilder are an appropriate analogue to the window-scenes in Middlemarch because Dorothea's presence in those scenes is always visualized as carefully as the landscape itself, and because the quality of her apprehension is the true centre of the audience's interest.

In natural description, then, no less than in characterization and domestic scenes, George Eliot was deeply influenced by pictorial conventions. Her vision of nature was shaped by eighteenth-century traditions of the picturesque and topographical, and by nineteenth-century modes of landscape sensibility which came to her through Wordsworth, Ruskin, and the Pre-Raphaelites She was well aware that the beholder's share of perception may be conditioned by the experience of art. She lends this awareness to Daniel Deronda as he contemplates a Gothic capital at the Abbey:

'I wonder whether one oftener learns to love real objects through their representations, or the representations through the real objects,' he said, after pointing out a lovely capital made by the curled leaves of greens, showing their reticulated underside with the firm gradual swell of its central rib. 'When I was a little fellow these capitals taught me to observe, and delight in, the structure of leaves.'

These remarks are in the spirit of Ruskin, as Henry Auster has pointed out, but they must also reflect many of George Eliot's own encounters with the natural world (p. 97). She knew that art can help one see and feel, and indeed she valued art chiefly because it can.

But what happened to Eliot's descriptive art when it became, in turn, subject to someone else's imagination — when, in short, an illustrator set about to render it into visual forms? Inevitably the pictures were modified from what the author had conceived. The next chapter will examine Frederic Leighton's illustrations of Romola, both for the light they throw upon the text and for the questions they raise concerning literary illustration in general.

Chaptet 9

Summary and Analysis of Middlemarch

Chapter 1: Summary:

The novel begins in the upper-class Brooke household in Tipton, inhabited by Mr. Brooke and his two nieces, Dorothea and Celia. Dorothea and her sister Celia are well-connected, sensible girls from a good family; they believe in economy of dress and are rather mainstream in their beliefs and behaviour. Dorothea is drawn to sacrifice and grand, intellectual things, while Celia has fewer aspirations in the world of academics and religion. Their uncle, Mr. Brooke, is careful with his money, and rather Puritan in his disposition, which Dorothea is also.

Two suitors, Sir Chettam and Mr. Casaubon, make visits to the house; Sir Chettam likes Dorothea, but Dorothea believes he is more inclined toward her sister. Celia has more sense than her sister, but Dorothea is very steadfast in her Puritan ways.

Analysis

Middlemarch is supposed to be a microcosm for semi-rural England in the early 19th century; the novel takes place in the years around 1830. The novel is more focused on upper- and middle-class people than on anyone of lower financial and social status; most of these people are not at all representative of the average Briton of the period in terms of income, lifestyle, etc. However, appropriate gender roles are represented and commented upon in the novel, and even in the first chapter; Celia is more representative of the proper woman in this time period, with Dorothea embodying many less desirable qualities.

Dorothea, Celia, and Mr. Brooke do not represent the average family either; with Mr. Brooke being so averse to women, it is a mystery how Dorothea and Celia were brought up, and by whom. Though it was not uncharacteristic in this period for women to die in childbirth and leave children behind, Dorothea and Celia are in a very interesting situation. Orphaned children with competent relations would likely be left to a married female relative, or to another mother-like figure. Mr. Brooke must have hired governesses and other women to raise the girls, because he certainly could not have handled them himself, nor would it seem socially proper.

Through the comparison of Celia and Dorothea in this chapter, Eliot conveys what were and were not considered suitable qualities for women during this time period. Dorothea is a woman with strong opinions, who is more interested in the world of faith and intellect than in reality; these qualities are considered strange and undesirable, according to Eliot, and are impediments toward her getting married. Socially, in Eliot's world and in the world of this novel, a silent, self-sacrificing, weak-willed woman was still ideal, though Eliot's high regard of Dorothea and her eccentricities is a criticism of this ideal model.

Celia is clearly more suited to the time period in which she lives, able to be herself and have her own opinions without appearing out of place. But, then the question arises‹should Dorothea become more suited to her society, or should society have to learn to accept different kinds of women? This is one theme in the novel that is very pertinent to Dorothea's life. It is true that Dorothea has a lot to learn, since she lives more in her mind than in the world she inhabits; but though she is mistaken in some of her appraisals of life, doesn't necessarily mean that she needs correction in everything.

At the same time, Dorothea herself has rather outmoded views on marriage, as is made clear by Eliot's tone. The statement that Dorothea wants to marry "great men whose odd habits it would have been glorious piety to endure," exposes Dorothea's outmoded views on marriage, and her particularly interesting personality. Husbands aren't supposed to be some kind of religious trial, and one shouldn't marry in order to seek martyrdom for putting up with their eccentricities; Eliot makes it clear that Dorothea is indeed mistaken, and has much to learn, though her rebuke is soft and conveys no dislike of Dorothea as a character.

Chapter 2: Summary:

Sir James and Casaubon are over for supper, with Sir James trying to appeal to Dorothea, while Dorothea begins to admire Casaubon. Dorothea hopes that Sir James will try to appeal to her sister Celia, rather than to herself, and Dorothea continues her perverse fascination with Casaubon.

Analysis:

Casaubon is the very creature that Dorothea should avoid turning into; he lives completely in his mind, with very little knowledge of the world in which he lives, so it is ironic that Dorothea favors him since these are the very qualities that endanger her good sense. And it is also ironic that Dorothea is so quick to slight the man who listens to her plans for the public good, and seeks to cater to the things she loves to do. That Dorothea tries her best to run from the things that would do her the most good shows a kind of perverseness inherent in her nature, that may do her a bit of harm.

Mr. Brooke holds very unkind views of females, and has no reservations about expressing his somewhat socially acceptable, though incorrect views, before his two nieces. Mr. Brooke represents an older way of thought, that is dying out, but still present; he is of past generations, who firmly believed women to be flighty and irresponsible, and hardly able to do work of merit. Mr. Brooke is very vocal on the theme of gender expectations, and airs many views typically held in his day. In contrast with Mr. Brooke is Sir James, who believes that Dorothea has valuable things to say, and has no compunctions about recognizing the merits of Dorothea's plans. Another irony is that Dorothea bristles when Mr. Brooke belittles her capabilities, while she herself believes that she can be no more than an assistant to another man's work. Dorothea, too, adopts older, incorrect views about women, views that will do her no good if she really means to make a difference in the world, which she desperately wants to do.

There is a great contradiction in Dorothea; on one hand, she totally underestimates her intellect and her ability to be her own guide, and on the other hand, she trusts herself with making workable plans to benefit a great number of people. That Dorothea doesn't trust herself intellectually, yet values her ability to create solutions, is a character issue that needs to be resolved in the course of the book.

Sir James represents progress in society's ideas about women; he is of the opposite opinion of Mr. Brooke, giving some regard to women's ideas and good sense. Though Sir James has not totally given up on established ideas of men's dominance, he is far more permissive of a woman's individuality, as shown by his acceptance Dorothea as a potential wife. Sir James, in this respect, embodies the theme of progress that is seen throughout the novel, in social, technological, and ideological areas.

Chapter 3: Summary:

Dorothea continues to admire Casaubon, especially admiring his vast studies and knowledge. She understands that Casaubon has some regard for her, and feels honored, despite Casaubon's complete inability to show emotion. She is blind to the fact that he wants to marry her to fulfill his needs, and is taking advantage of her naiveté in this decision. Casaubon actually tries to show consideration for her in the things he chooses to speak to her about, and in the way he regards her. Still, Dorothea's refusal to see Casaubon as anything other than a beacon of knowledge and good, and Sir James as an annoyance who is useful for carrying out her plans, shows how her stubbornness blinds her in judging people's characters, and in making important decisions as well.

Analysis:

Dorothea's allusion to the "affable archangel" of Paradise Lost, in explaining her feelings about Casaubon, shows a divide between what Dorothea believes to be true, and what is actually so. Dorothea takes Casaubon's pedantic and patronizing qualities to be generosity with his learning; she views everything he says and does through the lens of her good favor, disregarding anything that would give her an unappealing impression of the man. Dorothea certainly means well, but her misappraisal of Causabon's character reinforces the necessity of careful consideration, of thinking about things from all angles, rather than just from an optimistic one. Dorothea is blind to the truth about Casaubon because she chooses to be, and this trait is more foolish than good-natured.

That Dorothea wrests herself away from the things she loves most‹riding horses, planning public improvements illuminates a certain perversion inherent in her nature. It is not a contradiction that she will be happy living with, and its existence, and the way that this flaw keeps her from being happy, foreshadows a necessary self-examination on Dorothea's part. She will need to decide whether to continue with her habits of self-denial and sacrifice, at the detriment of her happiness and greatest desires.

Eliot may not be in favor of Dorothea and Sir James marrying, but she does interject a bit of her own social commentary, stating that Sir James might be well-served by following Dorothea's plans, as other men would benefit from the ideas of strong women. This highlights a particular paradox in Victorian era society; although men are acknowledged as head of their households and leaders outside the home, it is "feminine direction" which creates men from children, and often guides their spouses. Women are not acknowledged as leaders, and they do lead; and Eliot professes a belief that more female leadership would do even more good.

Chapter 4: Summary:

Sir James has acted on Dorothea's plan, and made new, more pleasant cottages for his poor tenants; Dorothea is still determined not to think highly of him, though Celia is rather fond of Sir James. Dorothea admits to her sister that she does not like Sir James, although he plainly likes her; Celia cannot believe that Dorothea could so easily dismiss a man who loves her. When Dorothea gets back, her uncle tells her that he went to visit Casaubon, and Casaubon inquired about marrying Dorothea. Mr. Brooke is against it, because of Casaubon's tendency to mope about and live in books; but, when Dorothea says that she would accept Casaubon over Sir Chettam, Mr. Brooke speaks diplomatically, while laying out before her the realities of marriage. Though Dorothea listens, she does not seem to absorb all the important things he says. Mr. Brooke has brought back a letter of proposal to Dorothea, and she is determined to accept.

Analysis:

Celia, who has remained in the background up until this point, is finally revealed as a very sensible, perceptive girl; she makes the most accurate appraisal of Dorothea's character so far, telling her sister that "you always see what nobody else sees yet you never see what is quite plain" (36). Also, Dorothea prefers to blame people around her when their words or actions make her see, on some unconscious level, that she is wrong; Celia knows about Dorothea's faults, though Dorothea refuses to realise them herself. The theme of hiding in knowledge is introduced, as Dorothea, almost instinctively, turns to books and the library after she realizes that she is acting unfairly toward Sir James. Knowledge is indeed a noble pursuit, but plunging into it to save one's self from confronting reality is definitely unhealthy, and is a habit that Dorothea will need overcome.

Here, Dorothea is confronted with the issue of expectations vs. reality for the first time. Her uncle cautions her on what to expect and what not to expect for marriage; although she says she has some idea of what to expect if she marries Casaubon, in reality she has no idea what it will be like. Dorothea presumes to know more than any sheltered girl of 18 ever could know; but at least she takes Mr. Brooke's advice with some weight. Still, the emphasis on Mr. Brooke's warnings, and Dorothea's attention to those warnings, foreshadow that there is some truth in what Mr. Brooke says. Dorothea indeed will have to face the difference between what she expects from marriage, and what she is going to get.

Chapter 5: Summary:

Dorothea reads Casaubon's letter, and is touched by it; she immediately writes out an acceptance, taking the letter to mean that he feels the same about her as she does about him. Celia has no idea what has happened until Casaubon joins them all for dinner, and she, at least, knows that her sister has made a serious mistake, and perhaps can be swayed from it. Dorothea, however, is convinced that she has made the right choice; Casaubon expresses happiness at their engagement, and Dorothea completely overlooks his lack of passion.

Analysis:

Casaubon's letter is a perfect expose of his stoic, remote character; he refers to his material "need" in wanting her as a wife, and mentions her "fitness to supply that need" But, what Dorothea fails to notice is that he states his feelings as being "sincere devotion," far short of the infatuation/ love with which she regards him. Dorothea sees the letter as a confirmation of Casaubon and her won mutual feelings; what she does not see in the letter is its stark confession that he needs her help and companionship, without the troubles of passion and an equal union. Dorothea loves Casaubon for his learning and his mind; but her vitality and her passion, the two things that energize and support her, will receive no nourishment from Casaubon's cold, emotionless self. She mistakes his practical proposal for a confession of "loving [her]," another instance where her naivete and her blindness to the truth deceive her. Dorothea's shows of passion overwhelm Casaubon, and also betray his feelings that Dorothea owes him something in this union; not once does he ask himself whether he is good enough for her, and this foreshadows a rocky start to their marriage.

Eliot says as much concerning the union-to-be; Eliot draws special attention to Casaubon's frigid rhetoric, which, although it is sincere in its intent, again conveys how emotionless Casaubon really is. Dorothea's inability to see what is before her plainly is a theme that becomes important with this union.

As Eliot notes, "Dorothea's faith supplied all that Mr. Casaubon's words seemed to leave unsaid"; Dorothea, for better or for worse, is a "believer," and nothing that Casaubon says or does can truly be unpalatable to her in this blind state.

Eliot makes Dorothea's flaws and oversights very clear, but does not chastise her for them; Eliot seems to hope that Dorothea will find her own way, letting the characters flow through the work, rather than bending them artificially to the author's own desires. Eliot has much in common with Austen, as regards the tone, purpose, treatment of characters, and criticisms of society in their novels; Eliot, like Austen, is able to display human follies and shortcomings, show where their respective societies fall short, and are able to criticize without being disparaging, keeping a rather objective tone throughout their works.

Chapter 6: Summary:

Mrs. Cadwallader is finally introduced, a shrewd, somewhat manipulative, and meddling woman whom Mr. Brooke has little affection for. Mrs. Casaubon and Mr. Brooke talk politics for a little while, which Mr. Brooke does not want to do; finally, Celia tells Mrs. Cadwallader that Dorothea is going to marry Casaubon, which displeases Mrs. Cadwallader, a great advocate for Sir James, greatly. Sir James finds out, and is greatly displeased; but Mrs. Cadwallader tells him that Celia admires him greatly, and won't give him as much trouble. Mrs. Cadwallader is the archetype of the country woman, with her narrow interests, her meddling ways, and her great concern in anything involving people she knows. Sir James is able to conquer his disappointment, and realizes that courting Celia is what he should begin to do.

Analysis:

At last, something of Middlemarch life and politics

becomes clear. In such a rural area, everyone seems to know everyone, and also knows everyone else's business as well. It is the kind of place where people show a great amount of concern for one another, although gossip takes precedence over privacy. Politically, Middlemarch is a narrow-minded place; since liberals are the minority, they are looked down upon, and there seem to be great rivalries between people of different parties. Mrs. Cadwallader is a symbol of how this country life works, with everything out in the open, and the outside world not daring to interfere; she believes in the privileges of good birth and class, and takes great interest in the marriages and relationships of those she knows, even going so far as trying to play matchmaker between Sir James and Dorothea.

However, even she is not to be underestimated; she can sense Dorothea's reasons for marrying Casaubon, and knows how the marriages will go even before it begins. Appearances can be deceiving, even in Middlemarch; sometimes a woman who seems as clueless as Mrs. Cadwallader has the benefit of perceptiveness on her side, and the good judgment to understand people and their hidden motivations.

Pride is another theme running through the course of the book; it is what keeps Dorothea from realizing and admitting she is wrong, stops Casaubon from asking himself whether his upcoming marriage will benefit Dorothea, and smothers Sir James' disappointment in a new surge of hope for his marriage prospects. As Eliot says, pride can be a good thing; in a sensible, even-tempered person like Sir James, pride does not deceive him, and can be a rather beneficial thing. But pride also works in harmful ways, and has certainly doomed Dorothea and Casaubon's marriage even before it has begun.

Chapter 7: Summary:

Casaubon has exhausted his meager reserves of passion already, and looks forward to married life, which he expects will be more pleasant and fulfilled. Not once does he stop and consider his duties for Dorothea, showing himself to be an unsuitable partner who will be hard-pressed to make her happy. Dorothea is eager to begin learning, out of her own desire to be able to understand and know things. Mr. Brooke cautions Casaubon that Dorothea, as a woman, might not be capable of such learning; Dorothea resents such talk, and tries to ignore it.

Analysis:

Dorothea begins to show an inkling of her real desires, beginning with her desire to know Latin and Greek not because it would help her husband, but because it will help her become a more well-learned person. Dorothea and Casaubon are foils in the way they treat their relationship; Dorothea believes it is her duty mostly to give, and is swayed by her emotion and passion. Casaubon feels little passion, and expects to receive without giving; he believes he is owed every comfort in his endless pursuit of knowledge, and thinks of Dorothea as an instrument, rather than as a person. He enjoys her being ignorant, though she does not; he wants dominance in the relationship, and she expects the relationship to be something resembling an exchange, with knowledge and enlightenment as the pay for her pains. Dorothea and Casaubon have nothing in common except their regard for learning; because of this, their marriage will certainly be very trying for both of them, and probably will not be a pleasant experience for either.

Mr. Brooke again shows himself to be a symbol of the old ways of thinking about gender roles and society. His speech about women not being suited to real learning, and needing to be limited to the arts and other light pursuits was widely believed during this time period; although he seems to trust his nieces' good judgment, he still airs his ultra-traditional beliefs about women and their capabilities at every turn. Dorothea is infected by these ideas, with her beliefs about self-sacrifice of women and her possible inability to learn like men do; but, deep down she does not believe in them, as she first demonstrates with her distaste for her uncle's assertion that women should be involved in light, artistic pursuits.

Chapter 8: Summary:

Sir James, in spite of Dorothea's engagement, begins to

like visiting the Grange, her home, once again; he is stung by her rejection, and cannot understand her attraction to Casaubon at all. He goes to speak to Mr. Cadwallader, a great friend, to clear his mind about this issue. Sir James cannot help his great pride, but at least he is very civil to Dorothea, and does not let his distaste for her marriage interfere with his plans to make the cottages she proposed.

Analysis:

Sir James compares Dorothea, after her unexplainable rejection, to Desdemona; the allusion is not quite fitting, since Casaubon has none of the passion for his future wife that Othello showed for his. However, it is likely that this comparison will prove more apt than it appears; for, with the inequality of the match, it is certain that Dorothea will be greatly wronged at one point or another by her cold, loveless mate, as Desdemona was by hers.

Sir James does prove to be a good fellow, despite his pride; like many people who know about Dorothea and Casaubon's match, he is greatly concerned, and hopes to bring the girl to her senses. And this desire on his part is due more to his regard for her well-being than his pain at being jilted; Sir James proves himself to be a decent and kind-hearted man, and a good friend to Dorothea's who is certainly worthy of respect and good regard.

Chapter 9: Summary:

Dorothea gets her new home, Lowick, ready for her impending residence there. The house is rather big, but not particularly cheery; in fact, it rather resembles Casaubon in its looks. Dorothea, however, finds it agreeable, as she finds Casaubon also; but, chances are, she will soon find that she is mistaken, as the newness and novelty of this entire situation wears off. Celia herself dislikes anything that Dorothea accepts, and as such, dislikes Lowick and Casaubon equally.

Casaubon introduces the party to Will Ladislaw, his cousin; he dislikes Dorothea immediately, because of the way she speaks poorly of herself before others, and because she is marrying his sour, humorless cousin. Will is young, rather handsome, and an artist as well; he seems much better suited to Dorothea, though a better match than Casaubon is certainly not hard to find. Ladislaw is without occupation, so Casaubon is, reluctantly, providing for him; but Casaubon and his cousin seem not to get along at all.

Analysis:

Obvious parallels between Casaubon and his house become clear, and the parallels are bad omens for Dorothea's marriage. The house is stern, melancholy-looking, and rather plain and uninviting, qualities which Casaubon also possesses; any chance of the house, or Casaubon, becoming more cheery and friendly depend upon Dorothea, though the challenge is great and will probably be too difficult to achieve.

The dour look of the house, combined with unanimous displeasure in the area about the marriage, and Casaubon's ungenerous, cold demeanor mean doom for the marriage, even before it starts; too many events, judgments, and signs have foreshadowed a bad end for the marriage, and taken together, they cannot be denied. Dorothea seems to be overcompensating for her youth and "ignorance" by insisting on being the obedient, weak-willed wife, though these qualities are not in her nature. In comparison, Celia does seem a bit trivial in some of her judgments and dislikes, but Celia and Dorothea are girls not even out of their teens; at least Celia acts like the girl she is, while her sister belies her own nature with her attempts to be as agreeable as possible to Casaubon.

Ladislaw certainly seems like an interesting character; he immediately senses the falseness of Dorothea's profession of ignorance, and figures that she and his cousin must be ill-suited, or else she is a very disagreeable person. Ladislaw is young, and seems rash, like Dorothea can be; he is also a person of strong opinions, with a great deal of pride. Indeed, Dorothea and Ladislaw seem to have more in common even at this brief meeting than she and Casaubon ever could; he does become more important later in the work, and some kind of conflict between Ladislaw and Casaubon is foreshadowed by their mutual dislike, and Casaubon's distaste for providing for Ladislaw, and for his non-academic temperament.

Chapter 10: Summary:

Ladislaw leaves suddenly for Europe; he has a view of life and work completely opposed to Casaubon's, and is much more impulsive and full of passion than his dull cousin. Casaubon, to his credit, does try to be more joyful about his marriage, and to understand his young bride better; but, he is fundamentally unsuited to this relationship, and cannot make himself more amenable to it. They decide to go to Rome on their honeymoon, a decision partially motivated by Casaubon's single-minded pursuit of information, to the detriment of his fragile relationship with Dorothea.

Casaubon and Dorothea attend a local dinner party, where many of the prominent citizens of the town are discussing their displeasure at Casaubon and Dorothea's marriage, and the arrival of the new doctor, Lydgate. Many of the townspeople prove completely pedestrian in their opinions, liking decorative, weak-willed women, and disapproving of any experimentation, especially relating to medicine. These are people who like routine and tradition, and will be hard-pressed to accept any progress or any outsiders in their community.

Analysis:

Eliot again proves herself an objective narrator, bringing to light Casaubon's good traits and explanations for his less desirable ones; Casaubon is definitely not as bad as he seems to be, and does deserve some sympathy for his shortcomings. Casaubon is a very lonely man, whose hopes of feeling happier and less lonely upon marrying are dashed; his high expectations of finally giving up bachelorhood prove false, and Casaubon does struggle to try and draw more emotion out of himself.

Dorothea, to her credit, is also misled‹by society's requirement that women derive their fulfillment from men, and do not seek to achieve on their own. Dorothea believes that she will gain the knowledge and the purpose she needs from Casaubon because he is a man of learning, and if he cannot give her this, no one can; Dorothea is too young to see that society is often wrong, and that she has to gain her purpose and drive from within. Metaphorically, she wants the lamp of knowledge, but thinks she needs to seek the lamp's oil elsewhere, as Eliot puts it; Dorothea does not see the fault in this metaphor, that she can only get this oil from herself.

The townspeople, as seen at the dinner party, are definitely a mixed bag; they do have an overly harsh opinion of Casaubon, but on the other hand, are perfectly correct in their appraisal of the marriage's prospects. They are unfriendly to the coming of progress, which could be a very negative characteristic; and their tendency to be wary of outsiders is also unfair. The people of Middlemarch, like the many characters in the book, have both positive and negative qualities; they are human, and hence they are flawed, but as Eliot points out, we should not be quick to condemn them for things they cannot control.

Chapter 11: Summary:

Lydgate, the new doctor, is already enamoured of Rosamond Vincy, the mayor's daughter. She is attractive and affable, but he is not economically set for marriage yet. Lydgate believes that women should be quiet, obedient, and beautiful; he is not looking for a partner, but rather an adornment, for a wife. Rosamond seems determined to escape from the tangled web of Middlemarch marriages, in which case Lydgate seems suited to her. Rosamond's brother, Fred Vincy, is an aimless young man who failed to get his degree at college, and seems to do very little besides hang about the house and bother his sister.

Analysis:

Lydgate embodies many of the misconceptions that men have about women, and believes that the qualities that would be considered shortcomings in men are well-suited for women. Like Mr. Brooke, he believes women should not be knowledgeable, opinionated, or make decisions; he wants a woman who is pleasant, shallow, pretty, and vain. Rosamond Vincy is exactly this, a woman who delights in fripperies, and embodies all of the useless qualities that society of the time prized in women. Rosamond Vincy represents the "ideal" Victorian woman, with all her foibles and failings, and Eliot uses her to criticize this ideal, and show how little service it does to women and men alike.

Rosamond is also the embodiment of the social-climbing snob as well; she cannot bear to think that her mother was the daughter of a simple innkeeper, or that her father's family is merely middle-class. Rosamond has no idea of the value of money, nor does she have any conception of how little such things as class matter in the scheme of things. Lydgate, too, is one of this kind; he too would like to deny his origins, and pretend that he is better or higher class than he actually is.

Summary and Analysis of Chapters 12-22

Chapter 12: Summary:

Fred and Rosamond travel to Stone Court, the house of their wealthy uncle, Mr. Featherstone. Mrs. Waule, Mr. Featherstone's sister, is there; and though she is also well off, she tries to get even more money from her brother. Mary Garth is Mr. Featherstone's servant, and Fred admires her very much. Mrs. Waule's visit is to lobby for more money in Mr. Featherstone's will, and she tries to discredit Fred, of whom Mr. Featherstone is very fond, by alluding to rumors about Fred's gambling debts.

Mr. Featherstone bothers Fred on this subject, and Fred insists he has done nothing of the sort; Mr. Featherstone continues to shame and embarrass Fred, and finally insist that he get proof in writing from Bulstrode, who started this rumor, that it is indeed false.

Mary Garth is plain and amiable, and very honest and kind. Rosamond continues to be supremely interested in Lydgate, whom Mary has met and does not think terribly highly of. Lydgate and Rosamond finally meet, and it seems like their romance has already been destined to occur.

Analysis

Despite Rosamond's snobbish disposition, she has no compunctions about socializing with Mary Garth, a servant; although Rosamond has certain ideas about social class, at least she does not hold these ideas of hers against long-standing friends. Rosamond is pleasant enough to her friends, and to her uncle, though she does show hostility to people who do not strike her fancy, like Mrs.Waule.

The weight of rumor is a theme that is very relevant to Middlemarch life; rumors are circulated like currency, and a person's reputation certainly depends on what people say or think about them.

Rumors are also given a lot of credibility in this provincial life; it is a rumor that causes Featherstone to threaten to take away Fred's inheritance, and this rumor is given some credit because it originated with Bulstrode, one of the most well-known citizens of the town. Rumors are often vicious, and just as often untrue, and represent the more pernicious and flawed aspects of human nature; still, they are important in determining the reputation and caliber of the many people of Middlemarch, and rumors are also an integral part of social life there as well.

Rosamond and Lydgate's romance, though nonexistent at this point, seems to be foreshadowed by Rosamond's own stubborn conceptions about falling in love with a stranger, and him falling in love with her almost immediately. Rosamond decides to like Lydgate, since he is young, good looking, has good prospects, and is of good family; emotional connection doesn't seem to enter into the equation, and they are as shallow as a couple as they are about the opposite sex.

Chapter 13: Summary:

Mr. Vincy goes to see Mr. Bulstrode at the bank on his son Fred's behalf; Lydgate is already there with Bulstrode, talking about the construction of a new hospital in town. Bulstrode likes Lydgate, and expects that he will make reforms and improve medical care in the town, but both are aware of the professional jealousy that will arise from Lydgate's new position, if he is indeed elected as head of the hospital. Bulstrode, for some reason, wants a man named Mr. Tyke to be chaplain of the new hospital, in place of another man named Mr. Farebrother.

Mr. Vincy enters, and broaches the subject of Fred and his need for Bulstrode's reassurances; Mr. Bulstrode does not want to be involved. Bulstrode criticizes Fred's upbringing and personal qualities, making the matter more personal than it needs to be. This matter is complicated by the fact that Bulstrode and Vincy are brothers-in-law, and Vincy believes it is Bulstrode's family obligation to comply, though Bulstrode does not.

Analysis:

Lydgate's case in this chapter shows how small-mindedness, jealousy, and petty squabbles between people can impede progress completely; in Middlemarch, this is an important issue, and one that will thwart Lydgate, as an outsider. Middlemarch is exceedingly political, as becomes apparent in the scene with Mr. Bulstrode; friends will be made and lost through political alliances, and it seems that Lydgate's hopes depend on his siding with Bulstrode in a matter that does not concern him at all.

Bulstrode is an arrogant, self-important man who would use his power to tell people where they are right and wrong. Much like other characters, who are embodiments and representation of certain forces in society, Bulstrode is symbolic of Middlemarch politics and power, and how both of these can lead to pettiness and an inflated ego. That he and Mr. Vincy are married to sisters complicates things; family members have some kind of obligation to one another, but on the other hand, people must do what they feel compelled to do. Middlemarch is a place of tangled family alliances, old grudges, and strong headed personalities; no decision is simply clear-cut, and many people are trying to fulfill their own interests, rather than trying to help other people.

The importance of family is a theme that reappears within the novel; what do people really owe to their family, and are there stronger ties between people than the blood ties of kinship? Friendship can certainly be a powerful bond; Sir James' friendships with Dorothea and Celia are strong enough not to be broken by Dorothea's marriage. However, there are many different views within the novel of how family ties obligate people to behave; the Vincys believe that Featherstone owes an inheritance to Fred, as his nephew, Mr. Vincy believes that Bulstrode, as a relative, should help Fred, and Casaubon believes that he is obligated to support his cousin Ladislaw for some time. But when personal interests, like greed, mingle with these ideas of family obligations, things become very tricky, and intentions are not always honorable.

Chapter 14: Summary:

Bulstrode writes out a letter to the effect that Fred has not borrowed money on his inheritance from Featherstone, because his wife Harriet, Fred's aunt, wishes him to do so. In fact, Fred is in debt, and is given some money by Featherstone on the spot, though it is not enough to unburden him. Fred is grateful, but not as grateful as he could be; Featherstone takes pleasure in the fact that the young man depends on him for funds, and uses this to threaten Fred as well. Fred tries to talk to Mary Garth, whom he has feelings for, about his living and his feelings for her as well. Mary is realistic about his prospects, and knows that he cannot marry until he finds a living and a stable income.

Analysis:

The importance of money is a theme that is intermingled with Fred Vincy's story; indeed, money is an important thing, and how a person uses money shows a great deal about his character. Featherstone is as much of a financial miser as he is an emotional one; his joys in the power to hold back money from people is perverse, and he is miserly in his friendliness as he is with his funds. Fred is full of hope that fate will get him out of any scrapes he gets into; he spends money with this belief in mind, his naïve optimism getting him into trouble, and into debt.

Socially, money also determines a person's place; Lydgate is socially disadvantaged because he is poor, and Sir James is highly regarded not only because he is friendly, but because he is wealthy too.

Although family connections are important in determining a person's place and how much respect they receive, middle-class people who are able to make money for themselves, like the Vincys, are able to lift themselves into a higher class through their gains in wealth. That isn't to say that the British class system, which is determined by birth, is dead at the time of this novel; but the class system is becoming more solvent because of the money being made by ordinary people, and allows those people to climb up the social ladder.

There is great irony in the fact that the only young couple who are truly suited and know each other well, Fred and Mary Garth, cannot get married for financial reasons. Unlike Casaubon and Dorothea, and Lydgate and Rosamond, these two are close friends, and regard each other with the greatest love and respect. As a couple, they contrast greatly with all the other young couples in the book; they seem to be the most compatible emotionally and practically, yet it comes down to a decision of finances about whether they should be joined.

Mary Garth, for her plain and humble appearance, is a clever girl with a good deal of knowledge. That she is able to make allusions to Shakespeare and Victorian literature so easily demonstrates her good grasp of literature, and that she is fairly well read‹certainly more well-read than Fred, and he has even gone to college.

Mary is not a flirt, but she is good at understatement; though she loves Fred, she avoids getting his hopes up by replying to his questions of whether she loves him by merely stating, playfully, "my experience is rather mixed" (138). Mary is a very realistic girl, however; she disregards Fred's romantic, hopeful, and somewhat unrealistic tone when speaking to her of marriage, and she maintains a considerate, even-tempered, but informed tone when replying to him. Where Fred is flighty, Mary is dependable; he is too idle to deserve her, but together, they could do well for each other.

Chapter 15: Summary:

Eliot begins the chapter with a bit of narration about the scope of the book, and then begins to delve into Lydgate's background. Lydgate was very intelligent as a young man, and fell in love with anatomy at a young age. He is a hard worker, driven to succeed in his field and make innovations, and to help people get better rather than make money, which seems to be the focus of many doctors of the time.

Analysis:

Here, Eliot takes a bit of a break from the novel, in order to insert some commentary, which is not an uncommon occurrence in the English novel. Previously, the novel had simply flowed over the events and characters involved; Eliot, as a narrator, becomes a kind of transparent presence, allowing the reader a direct window into the proceedings, without placing herself in the way. Eliot's purpose in suddenly interjecting in the proceedings is to convey the overall purpose of the novel; the purpose is to delve into the lives, motivations, personalities, and circumstances of people in a rural English community, and show the workings of human nature in the characters she chooses to create.

Middlemarch is not necessarily meant to provide a wide-ranging view of Victorian society, or to serve as a commentary on English society of the time; although the novel may have elements of social criticism included in it, this is meant as a focused study and not a sociological of epic proportions. This explains why Eliot chooses to have the narrator relate the events, with little commentary relating the people and happenings of Middlemarch to the outside world of the time.

Lydgate, as the sole outsider of Middlemarch, is an interesting case; the way that people regard him and treat him is not due to who he is, but what they believe him to be and how they feel about strangers. Lydgate stands in stark contrast with people like Fred Vincy, who feel no particular call or motivation; Lydgate, along with Dorothea, is one of few whose passion is improving the lives of the people of Middlemarch, with little concern for politics or anything that would hinder his greater purpose. Lydgate's intentions and his drive are honorable, like Dorothea's are; but it will not be so simple for him to fulfill his purposes in the tangled world of Middlemarch politics and connections.

A bit about Lydgate's personality is laid bare, and it indicates that Lydgate is susceptible to making mistakes in love. This major weakness in his nature foreshadows that he will not be able to choose wisely when it is time to marry; he can be rash when it is least convenient, especially when it comes to affairs of the heart. His overstated resolve, to "take a strictly scientific view of a woman," is certainly not supported by the way that he views Rosamond, nor by the criteria by which he judges her; Lydgate is weak when it comes to women, and his weakness is not expected by the people of Middlemarch.

The way in which Middlemarch society works concerning strangers is laid bare; if a person is considered worthy, people rush to accept him and make him one of the community. This theory of assimilation, however, is neither carefully considered nor does it take into account some people's resistance to change. It also leaves out a crucial examination of the person in consideration, which could mean the person that is accepted is not the same person who lives among them.

Chapter 16: Summary:

Mr. Bulstrode's power becomes plain; as a banker, he has some control over those he lends money to, and he defends people in return for certain expected favors. There is a debate going on whether Bulstrode's choice of Mr. Tyke for the chaplain's position at the hospital is indeed correct; Lydgate, Mr. Vincy, Mr. Chichely, and Dr. Sprague debate this question, with Mr. Vincy firmly supporting Farebrother. Lydgate is soon able to sneak away and talk with Rosamond, whom he finds very refined and beautiful. He meets Farebrother, whom he also finds agreeable. Lydgate is in no hurry to marry, since he has no money yet; but he will certainly keep Rosamond in mind in the meantime. Rosamond, however, is sure that Lydgate is in love with her; and, with little else to think about, she sets her mind on marrying Lydgate.

Analysis:

Mr. Bulstrode is a very shrewd politician; he makes sure he carries a great deal of influence not only through his financial role in the town, but through the favors he chooses to do for people and the obligations he chooses to create. Politics is a theme that has great importance in a Middlemarcher's life, and, if one is as politically adept as Mr. Bulstrode, a great deal of power and influence can result. Bulstrode insists that he is gaining power "for the glory of God"; but the truth is that he does it out of selfish ambition, and certainly is not as clean-living as he seems. Bulstrode's great ambition and his wily ways foreshadow a fall from grace, if he dares to do anything corrupt; just as people fear and are grateful to him, many people dislike the power that Bulstrode wields, and seek to bring him low.

Politics and people blend in an interesting way; and the regards in which politics influences people's decisions and behaviour toward one another is an issue that Lydgate, at least, will have to deal with. Soon, Lydgate will find himself torn between deciding on Mr. Tyke, in order to curry more favor with Bulstrode, or Farebrother, in which case Mr. Vincy would be most pleased.

Lydgate also finds that "it was dangerous to insist on knowledge as a qualification for any salaried office" in Middlemarch, as certain positions are usually held by people who are not quite suited to them; this is a great irony, and one that Lydgate does not want to face. Some Middlemarch traditions are impractical and nonsensical, but yet people still cling to them; this is another example of the theme of progress vs. tradition, and in this case, tradition seems to be the more stubborn.

Lydgate soon finds himself becoming fond of Rosamond, but it is her beauty and her good manners, rather than her personality, which attracts him. He rhapsodizes about her fair looks, which he describes as being "as if the petals of some gigantic flower had just opened and disclosed her"; he devotes this elaborate simile to her attractiveness, yet can say nothing of her personality except that she is "clever". He attributes "ready, self-possessed grace" not to her, but to her hair; the personification may do honor to her beauty, but he is missing the essence of Rosamond's personality entirely. Lydgate certainly does not realise that she is nothing, as Eliot's simile declares, "like a kitten" that is innocent and sincere; she has been trained and taught, and these graces and looks with which he falls in love have little to do with her real self.

The differences between the worlds of men and women are made clear by the juxtaposition of Rosamond and Lydgate. Lydgate, like most men, has a profession, plenty to do outside the home, and many professional goals; he is a very busy man, which means that marrying and starting a household come second for him. However, Rosamond, as a proper young woman, has no other interests besides marrying and living in her own home; she has the temporary diversions of music, socializing, and other light tasks, but nothing to consume her time and thought other than dreams and thoughts about marriage. The worlds of Lydgate and Rosamond contrast greatly, and there will probably be a conflict between Rosamond's eagerness and Lydgate's wish to wait for marriage.

Chapter 17: Summary:

Lydgate goes to see Farebrother at home, and observes his domestic situation. Farebrother's mother engages Lydgate in a debate about changes in religion, which Farebrother and Lydgate seem to espouse. Farebrother is a man of science, like Lydgate; they get along well, which makes Lydgate question Bulstrode's championing of Mr. Tyke even more. However, Farebrother is knowledgeable about Middlemarch politics, and knows that Lydgate must vote with Bulstrode if he wants to get ahead; Lydgate listens to this advice, but wants to vote with his conscience instead.

Analysis:

There are quite a few parallels in the lives and personalities of Lydgate and Farebrother. Both are men of scientific minds, with a great amount of interest in natural things and natural processes. Neither is in a great financial situation, meaning that marriage is not in the cards; and both are somewhat worldly and progressive-minded, clinging to changes that are being made in their own professions. Farebrother and Lydgate are also of the same opinion of many of the people of Middlemarch; they know that they must humour many people and speak very carefully to all those people who they really regard as idiots.

Farebrother is also able to inform Lydgate about a great deal regarding Middlemarch politics, of which Lydgate still has much to learn. Lydgate alludes to Voltaire when explaining his reservations about Bulstrode; but it does not matter what Lydgate's feelings about the man are, it all comes down to whose support he wants. Farebrother describes Bulstrode and his set more correctly; he posits the metaphor that "mankind [is] a doomed carcase which is to nourish them for heaven," and knows that Bulstrode and his ilk can be as unpleasant as they are ignorant. Farebrother shows great generosity and honesty in advising Lydgate to vote with Bulstrode; Farebrother is a truly intelligent and perceptive man, with a good understanding of the way Middlemarch politics work, and of how to keep from getting burned by them.

Chapter 18: Summary:

Lydgate is compelled to vote for Farebrother, at the expense of any help from Bulstrode; he debates this with himself, and the outcomes of either decision. Lydgate wants to secure Farebrother the much needed money, but also wants to keep in Bulstrode's good graces, and knows that Tyke might be better suited to the position. The voting meeting begins, with Lydgate still waffling; people have their various reasons for voting for Farebrother or for Lydgate, and they all vary widely. Lydgate finally decides upon Mr. Tyke.

Analysis:

Lydgate finally realizes the importance of money, a theme within the book that touches on many characters, especially Fred Vincy and Farebrother. Lydgate does not feel that his lack of funds is all that important, especially since he is in no hurry to marry; but, he sees that with a man like Farebrother, who makes a very slender living and has relatives to support, money is a thing of great consequence. Money has determined how Farebrother has lived and his inability to marry; money has also dictated Fred's inability to marry, and has kept him from being truly respectable. Money can limit the way a person lives, and how much respect they are accorded; money can mean happiness or unhappiness, which Lydgate finally realizes.

The influence of one's conscience becomes an issue with which Lydgate, and many of the other men voting, are preoccupied with; when trying to make a decision, should you support the man whom you know to be a better human being, or should you support the man that will get you farther? It is a battle between conscience and self-interest, another important theme, and with Lydgate, self-interest wins; this is something that every person voting had to decide upon, with various results from each of them. Conscience does not necessarily outweigh self-interest; one must debate the merits of each choice, and go with the one that seems most important and beneficial.

In choosing Tyke, Lydgate contradicts the very essence of his nature. He must resign his pride, and vote according to the wishes of a man whom he does not like; he also must override his feelings, and rationalize himself out of making the more palatable choice. Lydgate is a man who is swayed by friendship, yet he cannot let that make his decision in this case; Lydgate, ironically, forswears the instincts that are most natural to him, and somewhat regrets the decision.

Chapter 19: Summary:

Dorothea is at last in Rome on her honeymoon, and Will Ladislaw is there too, spotting her but not daring to approach. Will's friend, Naumann, is there too, is taken with her beauty and wants to paint her picture; Will is still under the influence of his negative first impression of her, and does not want to see her at the risk of finding her as unpleasant as he suspects.

Analysis:

At the beginning of this chapter is one of the first indications of the time period in which this book is taking place. Although Eliot wrote this book in the 1870's, the setting is at the close of the reign of George IV, and the beginning of the era of Queen Victoria. The romantic movement had not yet hit its peak, and times were more innocent of the world at large, according to Eliot.

Eliot's book reflects upon the past, and the stories contained within it may illuminate the progress and the changes in attitude that have happened since. Likely, Eliot chose this time period because of the many forces which were beginning to clash; industrialism vs. the bucolic, the class system vs. new money, tradition vs. progress, superstition vs. science, all of which are issues contained within the novel.

Wisdom says that appearances are usually deceiving, but in the case of Dorothea, the way she appears to others conveys exactly what she is. Will's friend Naumann pegs her as a "Christian Antigone," the interesting allusion conveying perfectly her "sensuous force controlled by spiritual passion" (190). Will is moved by her in spite of himself, actually admitting to admiring her voice; he seems to like her though his protestations would convey other feelings.

Chapter 20: Summary:

Dorothea is in shock by the combination of lately having become a wife, being in a place so foreign to her as Rome, and being completely alone, with the absence of her husband due to his study. Dorothea appeals to her husband to let her help, so that he may get his work finished and published; in her desperation for some emotional response, she sobs, which immediately makes Casaubon even more remote. Casaubon wants her support and affection, which she is giving him, but not in the way he wishes. They have a fundamental communication block, which upsets both of them, especially since it is their honeymoon. Casaubon continues his studies, and nothing is resolved.

Analysis:

Dorothea is just beginning to realise how her marriage cannot live up to her expectations. Casaubon is the same as he ever was, but pays little attention to her, and she cannot talk to him for fear of upsetting him. Dorothea already finds herself lacking emotional support and a like mind, and as she continues to grow out of her naivete and learn more about her marriage, these requirements will probably become more plain to her.

Casaubon's lack of emotion or passion finally dawns on Dorothea, though she has not yet realized that the deficiencies she feels in the marriage are due to her being unsuited to her husband, rather than from any deficiency on her part. As Eliot states, "Dorothea's ideas and resolves seemed like melting ice floating and lost in the warm flood"; Eliot's simile emphasizes how lost and hopeless Dorothea feels, and how her plans and aspirations are left unfulfilled by this union. To Casaubon, Dorothea becomes little more than "a personification of that shallow world which surrounds the ill-appreciated or desponding author"; this view is ironic and unfortunate in light of Dorothea's extensive efforts to support, encourage, and aid her husband.

On this honeymoon, Casaubon and Dorothea's completely contrasting natures first come into conflict. Every time Casaubon tries to express himself with his cold, academic tone, Dorothea is exacerbated to some display of affection or emotion, which Casaubon is desperate to avoid. Dorothea thinks of achieving, of Casaubon writing and publishing his great work, with her help; Casaubon is not so goal-oriented, and is threatened by her insistence that he do something that he is ill-qualified to finish. Casaubon and Dorothea could not contrast more than they already do; and their inability to communicate and understand each other means that there will be more conflicts to come.

Chapter 21: Summary:

Just as Dorothea is beginning to despair again, Will

Ladislaw comes to visit her. Will is surprised to find that she is nice, friendly, and far better than his dried-up old cousin could ever deserve; Will's bad first impression is proven completely wrong. They discuss art, which Dorothea can't understand; Will admits that he has not found his calling in art, and Dorothea is bewildered by his ability to be at leisure all the time. Will also realizes that Dorothea holds Casaubon in unnaturally high regard; he resents this, and wants to get her to realise how she is mistaken. Casaubon returns home, and is not pleased by his cousin's presence. Nevertheless, he invites Will back, and Dorothea senses that she has found a valuable friend.

Analysis:

Will finally learns that Dorothea does not fake ignorance in order to insult; he mistook her remark as having a tone of sarcasm, when in fact she meant what she said with all sincerity. Will returns to his metaphor of the "Aeolian harp" to describe her, in her wonder and beauty; still, he cannot help but be bewildered about someone of such beauty and emotion marrying such a passionless man. Just as Dorothea and Casaubon are completely different kinds of beings, Casaubon and Will contrast in almost every possible way. Where Will is impulsive and emotional, Casaubon is ordered and reserved; Will lives life, and Casaubon seems content to learn about it.

Will and Dorothea actually seem very much alike in temperament, emotional disposition, and in their honesty. That Dorothea finds him the only person she has ever met who seems "likely to understand everything" is very significant; this impression upon such a brief meeting foreshadows that Dorothea and Will shall become close, and that she will take the chance to open her heart to him and express her feelings, which will deepen the relationship. The brief conversation with Will also brings her to an important realization, that she cannot expect emotional fulfillment or understanding from Casaubon. She begins to know that he also has an emotional void and is not the pillar of strength she thought he was; she starts to realise her husband's humanity, but also that her marriage is fundamentally unsatisfying to her.

Chapter 22: Summary:

Will impresses Dorothea with the way he is able to listen to Casaubon and make him feel at ease; Will is also able to engage Dorothea in the conversation, and draw some statements out of her that make Casaubon proud of his well-spoken wife. Will gets Casaubon to agree to bring Dorothea to the studio; once there, Naumann gets Casaubon to sit as a model for Thomas Aquinas, which allows Naumann to also paint Dorothea without Casaubon feeling slighted. Will goes to visit Dorothea later, when Casaubon is not at home; they speak, and Will tells her plainly that she will not be happy with Casaubon, and that her piety is completely unnatural.

Analysis:

The relationship between Will and Dorothea begins to change at a rapid pace; within a space of days, Will has become a "worshipper" of Dorothea, his "soul's sovereign"). The metaphor relates how intensely Will loves Dorothea, and how highly he regards her; in turn, Dorothea begins to appreciate Will, and finally learns to understand a bit of art from his passionate mind and eager explanations.

How ironic that she married her husband so that he could teach her, yet the only man she has learned from is the last one she expected to meet. Dorothea is beginning to find emotional fulfillment and intellectual stimulation in places other than her marriage; if this, and her attachment to Will, continues, her marriage to Casaubon will then be without purpose.

In Will's most impressive bit of conversation with Dorothea so far, he is able to diagnose the nature of her piety, and tell her exactly how she will be affected if she continues to follow her ideas so religiously. Dorothea counters with absolute frankness about her nature and habits, saying things aloud and before company that she has scarcely been able to admit to herself previously.

Dorothea has started on her journey of self-discovery, and from this point on, self-discovery will continue to be one of the most vital themes in her story. Will's passion becomes plain when he adopts a very passionate tone, and riddles his speech with hyperbole. He is saddened by Dorothea's apparent lack of youth, overstating this sentiment by saying that she acts as if she "had a vision of Hades in [her] childhood" (. He also states, with passion-fueled hyperbole, that she has been unfairly haunted by "Minotaurs" in some of the things she has been led to believe. Will's hyperbole and overstatement reflect his great concern for Dorothea, and the thought which he has devoted to her person.

Dorothea responds to Will's emotion with equal zest; she is relieved and energized to find someone who understands her so well, and does take the opportunity to open her mind and her heart to him. This is the first time in the novel that Dorothea speaks with real frankness, and dredges up many of the emotions that have been haunting her during these first few days of her marriage.

Will is able to bring her out of her shyness and her unnatural brooding, and makes a very big impression on her as well. Will's influence and his aid in helping her understand her situation and her plight has given Dorothea fuel for her attempts to find usefulness and happiness. She already has some idea that she will find neither of these with Casaubon, and if she takes Will's advice to heart, she can stop blaming herself and start to see the error she made in her marriage and become a less naïve person.

Summary and Analysis of Chapters 23-33

Chapter 23:

Summary:

Fred still has a debt to pay, and the money he got from Featherstone will not cover the balance; even worse, his dear Mary's brother, Caleb, co-signed on Fred's debt and will be held responsible if he defaults. Fred decides to make money to pay his debt by speculating on horses; unfortunately, he buys a horse that lames itself in a stable accident, and has even less money with which to pay his debt. Fred is a fool to risk all that he has on such an uncertain plan; but the boy is slow to learn, and cannot help himself.

Analysis

The Vincy household certainly did their children no favors in giving them no idea of the value of money; Rosamond has expensive tastes that mean she requires a wealthy husband, and Fred has already gotten himself into trouble because he expects others to pay off his own debts. Those who have little money, like Farebrother and Lydgate, are more responsible and essentially less materialistic; money is a necessary evil, but for those who have no income and rely on other people to provide for their foolishness, it is a great liability as well.

There is a sobering irony at work in Fred's life, almost like fate is trying to get him to be responsible. Of course, as we find out at the beginning of the next chapter, Fred has indeed lost his investment; but what is most unfair is that Caleb Garth will have to cover for this foolish boy if he cannot take care of himself. The horse that Fred buys is a symbol of his foolishness, and his inability to hold onto his money, and the affair proves again that Fred is irresponsible and needs to assume financial responsibility for himself.

Chapter 24: Summary:

Fred finally feels very sorry about his debt, and the fact that he has only fifty pounds and five days to pay up. Fred is most sorry because Mary's father is going to have to pay, and he feels this will jeopardize his chances with Mary. Fred goes to the Garth household to tell Caleb Garth, whose wife is very fond of Fred, but probably will not be after he tells her. Mrs. Garth is teaching her children their lessons in the kitchen, and Fred sits down and tells her and Mr. Garth the news. Mrs. Garth will have to give up the money she was saving to send her son to school; Fred feels terrible, as he should, knowing that his irresponsibility is costing them so much. Mr. Garth knows then that he was a fool to trust Fred, and they believe that there is little chance Mary will regard him so highly when she finds out.

Analysis:

The theme of the importance of money resurfaces again, as the Garths find themselves hard-pressed to pay for their trust in Fred. Although the Garths work very hard, they have little money because Mr. Garth does not like to charge much, if anything, for his work. However, in this case, money does not mean happiness; the Garths are very happy, certainly much happier than people like Dorothea and Casaubon who have plenty of money.

How ironic that responsible, hard-working people are forced to pay the debt of another person. In comparison with the Garths, Fred appears even more irresponsible, flighty, and lazy; in order to win Mary's affection, he will certainly have to work very, very hard. It is a good thing for Fred that he is very sorry for what he has done; perhaps it will teach him some lessons in responsibility, and he will be able to win back Mary's regard by working hard and repaying his debt to her family.

Chapter 25: Summary:

Fred goes to Stone Court to tell Mary the news; he is not as repentant as he should be, and wants comforting words from Mary about his irresponsibility. He still doesn't see the entire magnitude of what he did; he tries to rationalize things with his good intentions, and by claiming that he is not so bad, compared to what other people do. Mary is upset, and says that she cannot trust him, and that he should be more sorry for what he did. Caleb comes later, to ask for whatever she has saved up; Mary gives it gladly. Caleb Garth is worried that his daughter has some feelings for

Analysis:

Mr. Garth makes a good point about marital relations: "a womanŠ has to put up with the life her husband makes for her" (257). The statement is a very accurate piece of social commentary, and certainly demonstrated as a valid theme within the book so far. Dorothea has been suffering because the life her husband has made for her is very lonely and gives her little of value to do. If Mary does decide to marry Fred, she will have to bear the brunt of his irresponsibility and spendthrift qualities; since women are economically and socially dependent upon men, and divorce is out of the question, women are forced to put up with the personalities of their husbands and the living that they choose to make. A woman's decision to marry was something she could not afford to think lightly of, as her future would be almost entirely determined by the match she made.

Another good bit of advice, which Dorothea would have benefited from hearing, is Caleb Garth's observations on how a relationship changes from courting to marriage. When couples first dream of marriage, "they may think it all holiday but it soon turns into working day" (257). This truth is one that plagues Dorothea and Casaubon's marriage, as their idealistic views of their union have failed to prepare them for the realities of marriage. Caleb Garth may be too trusting of his fellow man, but he is a great source of wisdom and sense in the book.

Chapter 26: Summary:

Fred is foolish enough to go back in search of his old horse, and ends up with an even worse one. He soon becomes ill, and after their regular doctor tries to help and fails, Lydgate is brought in and says he has scarlet fever. Mr. and Mrs. Vincy get angry at their regular doctor, Mr. Wrench, for failing to catch such a serious illness; Mr. Wrench is in turn angry at Lydgate for interfering, and very uncivil to the new doctor. Rumors spread about the confrontation between Mr. Wrench and the Vincys, and between Mr. Wrench and Lydgate. Various opinions and stories surface about the alleged scuffles, leaving everyone worse off as subjects of untrue gossip.

Analysis:

Mrs. Vincy proves to be as overprotective a mother as previously shown; upon Fred's diagnosis by Lydgate, she becomes like "Niobe," overly full of tears and sorrow. The allusion shows how much Mrs. Vincy dotes on her oldest son, which cannot be healthy, regarding his irresponsible and selfish nature. Although Fred's faults are his own, he cannot help that these traits were bred into him through his upbringing; he has the difficult task of leaving his parents' protection and becoming independent, a struggle which is as much his own fault as it is his parents'.

The medical profession in Middlemarch seems to be more political than politics, even; people take Mr. Wrench's side because Bulstrode swears by him, or like Lydgate because the Vincys and others do, and Fred's condition is manipulated and exaggerated by hearsay fueled by what people think of the parties involved. It seems that the livelihood of Middlemarch doctors is made or broken by what people say and think about them; and the greatest irony is that they are not judged by their skill, but by whether people say good things about them.

The Wrench/ Lydgate situation parallels the machinations of the Tyke/ Farebrother debate; people align themselves with either party due to who they feel they must align themselves with, who they might have a personal grudge against, and based on what embellished news they have heard about either of them. The real issue, of who is a better doctor, seems to have no place in this debate; again, Middlemarch comes off as looking like the most backward of backward towns, more concerned with squabbles among townsfolk than obtaining good health care and better doctors.

Chapter 27: Summary:

Mrs. Vincy becomes completely consumed by Fred and his illness, to an unhealthy extent; Lydgate is around the house frequently, and sees a good bit of Rosamond as well. Lydgate's attentions to Rosamond are causing some resentment in the neighborhood, as rivals for her affection become jealous of him; Rosamond continues to believe that Lydgate is in love with her and intends marriage, while Lydgate merely enjoys her pleasant company. At the end of the chapter, Lydgate receives a summons from Sir James Chettam, who he has not attended to before.

Analysis:

Eliot's extended metaphor of Rosamond's luck to scratches in a pier-glass is an apt one; Rosamond does believe herself to be lucky and served by fate, and events do seem to happen by chance that further her designs. It is another good thing that Rosamond recognizes a good chance when she happens upon it, and so takes advantage of the opportunity to become closer to Lydgate. Rosamond, for all her flaws, is a very canny girl, and able to use situations to her benefit.

The vanity of Middlemarch men becomes apparent, as they all begin to resent Lydgate for gaining Rosamond's attentions. They prefer to blame Lydgate, though it is Rosamond who is responsible, and they are loathe to admit that maybe she just isn't interested in them. Skins are rather thin in Middlemarch, and it seems that people try hard to blame other people, rather than to realise a truth that might hurt them.

Unfortunately for Lydgate, not only is he making enemies, but he is failing in his attempts to get close to Rosamond, yet keep marriage at a distance. Eliot compares the plight of Lydgate's plan to a "jellyfish which gets melted without knowing it"; the metaphor reinforces the danger that Lydgate is in, of being pushed into a relationship which he is in no way ready for.

Chapter 28: Summary:

Dorothea arrives at Lowick with her husband in January, after their honeymoon. Dorothea, who had been so dejected during their honeymoon, feels revived by being home, in familiar surroundings. However, she is still haunted by the knowledge that her vision of marriage is yet unfulfilled, and the depressing atmosphere of Lowick. Her sister Celia finally arrives, brightening up the place with her presence; Celia tells Dorothea of her engagement to Sir James, and Dorothea is very happy for her sister.

Analysis:

The many images of liveliness in Dorothea's appearance convey her change of heart, how she feels renewed and hopeful at her future again; the irony of these feelings is how false they are, and how they do nothing to prepare her for what she will have to endure. Perhaps Dorothea is trying to falsely reassure herself that everything will be alright, now that she is in Middlemarch again; but the same problems that dogged her in Rome have not gone away so easily, and she will find her married life very difficult. The "ghostly stag" that appears in her room is a symbol of Dorothea's married life; both are trapped, flattened into decoration, and live in the same "chill, colorless, narrowed landscape".

"Each remembered thing in the room was disenchanted, was deadened as an unlit transparency," to Dorothea; Eliot's metaphor conveys Dorothea's despair, and the lack of colour in her life. In her new situation, Dorothea feels that there must be parallels between her and Julia, Will Ladislaw's grandmother, who was doomed by a bad marriage. She finally sees that her match was also badly made, and that the same consequences and unhappiness might be in store for her.

Chapter 29: Summary:

Mr. Casaubon's beliefs about marriage are reiterated; he wanted to marry someone young and impressionable, so that she would be pleasant and able to help him with his work and be taught by him. He also believed that marriage would make him happy for the first time; but marriage could never instantly change his disposition, and his hopes for his union were too high, as were Dorothea's. Casaubon and Dorothea have a bit of a tiff, as Casaubon tells her that he does not want Ladislaw to visit, and Dorothea resents the condescending and mean-natured tone he takes with her. Casaubon is weakened, and Dorothea strengthened by this altercation; it seems like this relationship is going to make her stronger, though it will definitely not work out.

Analysis:

Here, Eliot foreshadows the outcome of Casaubon and Dorothea's relationship; though, with every clash Casaubon feels weaker and more vulnerable, Dorothea only learns how to defend herself and becomes more confident. The tables have just turned, and it is unlikely that their relationship will be able to last any significant amount of time. Casaubon's dearest fantasy, about marriage bringing him perfect contentment and filling the gaps in his life, is falling apart, and he is faltering along with it.

Sir James' misgivings about Dorothea's union prove true; the question is, will the problems in her union resolve themselves, or will she just be trapped? Dorothea does not deserve to pay such a penance for anything she is done; it comes down to whether fate is kind to her or not as to what happens, and how her story ends.

Chapter 30: Summary:

Lydgate comes to check on Casaubon, and cannot find anything immediately wrong; he asks that Casaubon give up his studies for the time being, and focus on leisurely pursuits. Dorothea is informed as to the details of whatever ails Casaubon; Lydgate says that he must be kept from any stresses, or else his condition might be aggravated, and his life cut short. Dorothea is sad, but not sure exactly what to think; Ladislaw is supposed to be arriving there in a few days, and she asks Mr. Brooke to write Ladislaw a letter saying that Casaubon is ill, and not to visit. Mr. Brooke does write a letter, but the contents are nothing like Dorothea intends; Mr. Brooke invites Ladislaw, and also proposes that he might work for Mr. Brooke's newspaper, since Mr. Brooke has been favorably impressed with what he has heard.

Analysis:

It is ironic that the very thing which Dorothea wants Ladislaw to know is the opposite of what is communicated to him; Dorothea would, because of Casaubon's condition, have Ladislaw anywhere but near them, yet providence seems to have arranged that Ladislaw is going to live and work in Middlemarch with Mr. Brooke. It seems that Casaubon's wishes are being thwarted once again, and he is destined for aggravation; this situation will do nothing to extend his life-span, and seems to be arranged in order to cause Casaubon more illness. The tone of Lydgate's message, and the content of what he says, is a definite foreshadowing of Casaubon's coming illness. Lydgate does say that Casaubon could live for some time if he is not aggravated; but, with all the unpleasant surprises in store for him, compounded with Lydgate's harsh warning about what could happen, mean that Casaubon is in for trouble.

Chapter 31: Summary:

Lydgate and Rosamond become closer, as Lydgate is about to be sucked into a relationship which he is unprepared for because of the nature of Middlemarch society. Mrs. Bulstrode and Mrs. Plymdale gossip about Rosamond's pride, and how Lydgate might suit her; Mrs. Plymdale thinks that the match would be unwise for Lydgate, since Rosamond has expensive habits, and Mrs. Bulstrode goes to speak to Rosamond out of concern.

When Mrs. Bulstrode sees Rosamond and her fine garments, she knows that Mrs. Plymdale was at least right about that one point. Mrs. Bulstrode speaks to her, telling her that if she marries Lydgate, she will not be able to keep her expensive habits; Rosamond admits that he has made no offer of marriage to her, and seems intent on ignoring her aunt's good advice. Then, Mrs. Bulstrode approaches Lydgate, and tells him that he should not press his advantages as a romantic-seeming outsider with the Middlemarch girls; Lydgate sees that others believe him to be engaged to Rosamond, and wants to avoid marriage at all costs.

However, Lydgate ends up going by the house after an absence of two weeks, to deliver bad news about Mr. Featherstone's health; Rosamond cries when she sees him again, and this display of affection touches him enough to abandon his plans and reasonable thinking, and propose to her. Rosamond accepts, and they are engaged.

Analysis:

Rosamond's first priority in all things seems to be "playing the part prettily," as she is in Mrs. Bulstrode's frank discussion with her. Rosamond refuses to take good, practical advice, even when it is offered to her in a sincere way; she is stubborn and wants to hold onto this stubbornness, and proves vain about more than just her looks. Vanity is a key issue that Rosamond needs to overcome; not only does she pride herself on looking and acting beautifully, she likes to think that her ideas and manner of living are above reproach, and her character needs no correction.

Lydgate's pride is his failing, and his own issue to get over; he blames Mrs. Bulstrode's diction for his stung feelings when she speaks to him about Rosamond, rather than his own character issues. However, Lydgate, unlike Rosamond, is not too vain to think that his character and his perception are beyond reproach; he takes Mrs. Bulstrode's talking to him to mean that Rosamond is set on him, and others expect them to marry, and decides to serve his original intention of remaining single. Lydgate had not previously realized the power of other people's expectations, another theme in the novel.

He wants to disprove that his situation is metaphorically akin to being tempted by a siren, as Farebrother states that Lydgate's situation might be; the allusion particularly upsets Lydgate, as he realizes that the sirens, whom Farebrother alludes to, might stand for the expectations and ideas of those around him.

Rosamond seems to be more in love with the way Lydgate compliments her and flatters her vanity, more than Lydgate as a person. She is a rather mild version of Ariadne, Eliot says, with the allusion emphasizing Rosamond's relatively shallow feelings and the sometime ridiculousness of her expectations. Lydgate proposes to her out of his great weakness, pride; he is somewhat proud of the fact that Rosamond is unhappy without him, for the brief period of time that he avoids her home.

He sees that Rosamond looks up to him and has some feelings for him, and this cements their engagement. Since Rosamond and Lydgate's relationship is based on their mutual need to feed their flawed natures, it is doomed to fail; there are greater considerations for marriage than the fulfillment of pride and vanity, and intellectually and ideologically, they are ill-suited.

Chapter 32: Summary:

Mr. Featherstone's relatives begin to pop out and appear, and all expect that he wili die soon, and will leave them some bit of money, since he is their rich relation. They all expect that he should do something for them, that he owes them money because they are relatives; they do not consider that they have done nothing for him, but are like vultures circling, waiting to pick up his money once he dies.

Mr. Featherstone wants to see none of the greedy, crowding relatives; Mary Garth has to try and turn them away, but doesn't have the heart for the task. Mrs. Vincy hovers around, sure that Fred will receive most of the property and money anyway, as Featherstone regards and treats them so much better than his other relatives. Trumbull, an auctioneer and assistant to Featherstone in business matters, is the other person who Featherstone shows any regard for; on the basis of behaviour alone, it would seem that these people would receive most from Featherstone's will. Mary Garth must put up with the various visitors and their varying degrees of rudeness, but manages to stay calm and make the constant crush of daytime visitors as comfortable as she can.

Analysis:

The theme of family and family obligations comes to the fore once again as Mr. Featherstone is dying; Featherstone, being the mean-hearted, always distempered person that he is, feels no kinship or kindness for family members, while others only pretend affection for him thinking that he will leave them money. People's conceptions of blood ties and what they entail vary widely; Mr. Featherstone disregards them entirely, some relatives believe it entitles them to gifts in Featherstone's will.

Fred and the Vincys believe that the fact that they are closely related to Featherstone means that they will gain the bulk of the money in the will, and regard Mr. Featherstone as a benefactor. There is a great deal of hypocrisy in people's conceptions of family, especially with the herds of distant relatives who believe that they are owed money simply because of being related, and not because they have done anything nice or been well-acquainted with Mr. Featherstone. It is a good thing that Featherstone sees through these attempts to flatter themselves into money, but a shame that he regards nearly everyone with great suspicion and meanness.

It is interesting how impressions of Mary Garth vary according to the personality of the person appraising her. Mrs. Waule, a naturally suspicious person, regards Mary as tricky because of her potential influence on Mr. Featherstone, and because she appears shy and intelligent; this view is ironic, since Mary is both of those things, but that Mrs. Waule loads these traits with such negative baggage. Mr. Trumbull compliments her and is very polite to her, because he is a person who regards his own social graces highly; others regard her kindly merely because they are looking for some way to get into Featherstone's will, and think that she is trustworthy enough to help them with that.

Mr. Trumbull makes a point worth noting at the end of the chapter, about marriage; "a manŠshould think of his wife as a nurse," he says, and "some men must marry to elevate themselves a little". The first point is most applicable to Casaubon, who believes that Dorothea is responsible for curing all his ails, mental more so than physical; but it does no good to regard your wife as a nurse when you refuse to tell her what you need fixed, especially when it is something that only a person can fix for themselves. It seems that Lydgate is about to marry to elevate himself, in terms of style, breeding, and refinement; but it is still to be seen whether this will work. Mr. Trumbull's remarks aren't directed at any situation in particular, but his words put an interesting frame on a few of the relationships in the novel.

Chapter 33: Summary:

Mary Garth is sitting with Mr. Featherstone at night, as she usually does, reflecting on the events of the day, and sitting in silence, for the most part. She figures that the issue of Featherstone's will shall disappoint everyone involved. Mr. Featherstone suddenly tells her to open the chest with his will in it, and burn one of them; Mary refuses, even when she is offered a sizable amount of money to do so. Mary is scared of his sudden energy, and does not think that he is in his right mind; Mr. Featherstone drifts off to sleep, and by the morning he is dead.

Analysis:

Mary is quite a paradox; she is sweet, modest, and uncomplicated, yet she has a great deal of wisdom about human nature, and a keen sense of humour, neither of which can be guessed from her day-to-day dealings. She seems very plain, but inside she is anything but; few people in the book suspect that this difference between what Mary is in her common interactions, and what she is to herself, which makes their judgments of her particularly laden with irony. Mary also has a great deal of foresight, which few people have seen in action; she knows that everyone will be disappointed by Featherstone's will, though there is more to be decided on this issue still.

By the end of the chapter, whether Mary has done or not done the right thing is a pressing question. Mr. Featherstone's frantic tone must have put her off; he is acting "like an aged hyena," the simile denoting his nervous energy, and his uncharacteristic behaviour. Mary did manage to avoid the temptation of money, which is the weakness of many in the book, especially Fred; and, she also did nothing that could have haunted her later, or made suspicion fall on her, which was also a good decision. But what the repercussions of Mary's upright behaviour will be, is soon to be seen.

Summary and Analysis of Chapters 34-44

Chapter 34: Summary:

Mr. Featherstone is finally buried, with many relatives whom he did not like there; the occasion is a rather expensive one, for although Featherstone was miserly in many respects, he liked to show off his money when it could impress many people. Dorothea and Celia, along with Sir James, watch the proceedings from their house, as he is being buried at the church that is on Casaubon's land. Will Ladislaw appears again, and Mr. Brooke reveals that Will is his guest, and has brought the picture that Casaubon sat for in Rome. Casaubon is shocked and upset, and Mr. Brooke explains that he wrote to Ladislaw when Casaubon was ill, not Dorothea; Mr. Brooke continues to speak of his fondness for Will, as Casaubon tries to hide his displeasure, and Dorothea becomes alarmed.

Analysis

Money is a theme of importance in the book, and means very different things to different people. To someone like Fred, money is something that appears when he needs it, and is not something of terrible consequence; to the Garths, money is a precious commodity, and is saved carefully for worthwhile causes. Featherstone's character is illuminated by the way he regards money; he uses money to gain power over people, like Fred, and to show off the power and advantages that having money gives him.

In Eliot's explanation of the significance of Featherstone's funeral to Dorothea, we are introduced to another theme of the novel; the unity of people in Middlemarch, through events that they share in. Dorothea might not be at the funeral, nor did Featherstone mean anything to her in particular; however, it is times like this one that become associated with moods and feelings, and so become important in the memory. The funeral "mirror[s] that sense of loneliness" that is part of Dorothea's nature, and so becomes significant to her.

Chapter 35: Summary:

The funeral is over, and people are waiting anxiously for the will to be read and the sums they are to receive to be announced. There is a stranger among them, though, who makes them nervous; his name is Rigg, he is in his early 30's, and no one is quite sure of who he is or where he comes from. A lawyer is there, named Standish, who went through the will with two witnesses; he reads through the two wills that Featherstone left, regarding the last one as the most correct.

Mary Garth is nervous, and somewhat excited, since her refusal to burn one of the documents has led to this outcome. The first leaves Fred a good bit of money, and gives something to most of the relatives; the second, which is considered the correct one, gives everything to Mr. Rigg, who doesn't seem surprised.

Upon hearing this, many of the relatives start complaining about the expense of traveling to the funeral, and how they should not have come if they were to get nothing. Mrs. Vincy cries, and Fred seems upset as well, to have a large bequest announced, and then taken back. No one seems very fond of Mr. Rigg, who takes the name Featherstone as requested in the will. But, it seems that all the greedy relatives, and the expectant Vincys, have all gotten their just desserts; the Garths could have been better served, but overall, people do get exactly what they deserve.

Analysis:

Eliot compares the procession of different relatives at Featherstone's funeral to the line of different paired animals onto the ark, and says that in both cases, it might have been thought that the sheer numbers would decrease rations, and that it was better to have fewer there. The parallel between the situations is clever, and it is certainly a fair description of the situation at the funeral, and before the will is read.

Money is said to bring out the worst in people, and here it does. With money present, people forget their shows of politeness, say rash and uncomplimentary things, are greedy, and jealous as well. When the theme of money is introduced in the novel, it is usually to show people at their basest, or illuminate their flaws; and here, when money becomes an issue in the plot, it does exactly this.

Chapter 36: Summary:

Fred is sorely disappointed with not getting any money; he expected that he would get a large amount, and would not have to work. Now, he will likely have to join the clergy, or find some form of work; he will finally have to stop being idle, as his father will tolerate his idleness no longer. Mr. Vincy also says that Rosamond will have to postpone her marriage, until the family are in a better position to pay for it; Mrs. Vincy, Fred, and Rosamond are all spendthrifts, expecting that the money they need will somehow drop into their laps. Rosamond takes the issue up with her father, and he caves in; Mr. Vincy doesn't have the heart to stand up to his daughter, though she clearly needs some reasonable advice on the subject of her marriage.

It seems that only Mrs. Bulstrode knows better on the subject of Rosamond and Lydgate's engagement; she knows how difficult it will be for Rosamond to live on little money, and how extravagant she is, and how ill prepared Lydgate is to live with a flighty girl like her. However, no one will listen to her; her advice, though it will prove correct, is unheeded.

Rosamond tells Lydgate that her father wishes their marriage to be postponed; Rosamond says that she refused, not so much out of love for Lydgate, but out of stubbornness. Lydgate urges her that they be married soon; Rosamond agrees to six weeks, and manages to convince her father. Lydgate soon starts buying new things for the house, though he has little money to do so; already, he is spending beyond his means, a dangerous habit. They will go to his uncle's estate for their honeymoon; he is a baronet, and wealthy, which boosts Lydgate's hopes for a better position.

Analysis:

Eliot compares Rosamond and Lydgate's love to a "gossamer web," and indeed, the metaphor describes the relationship well, being based on tender moments together, delicate feelings, and easily dashed hopes. At the same time, the relationship is anything but solid, and certainly not based on genuine compatibility either; it is also ironic that Lydgate hurries forth with the relationship, after getting burned before by love, and the difficulty of his present circumstances.

Eliot's tone becomes slightly mocking, and shows the ridiculousness of Lydgate and Rosamond in their considerations of marriage. Rosamond's mental faculties are belittled, as becoming "slightly meditative," quite a feat for her, amounts to no more than thinking of how long it will take for her marriage clothes to be made. That Lydgate and Rosamond consider everything in deciding to get married but whether they love each other and are compatible is an irony that dooms their relationship from the start. The demise of their union is foreshadowed by their consideration of only inconsequential things, and their inability to act outside of the confines of their pride, vanity, and stubbornness.

Lydgate too believes in the preconceived notions of the day about gender relations; the "goose and gander" model, as Eliot calls it, is his ideal. Indeed, Lydgate wants a woman who is unassuming, attractive, knows the appropriate arts and flourishes, and will obey him. Rosamond is all of these; but what he does not foresee is how little economy she has, how silly she really is, and how basically unsuited they are. Lydgate is misled by society's ideals of women, and of marriage; and in searching blindly after these ideals, he will make a marriage that will not be beneficial for him, an be very disappointed in the life he will have to live with Rosamond.

Chapter 37: Summary:

Middlemarch politics assert themselves once again, in the rivalry of the two papers of the region. It is revealed that Mr. Brooke has bought one of the papers, The Pioneer, and has inserted his unorthodox political views into it. Will Ladislaw has been hired to head the paper, and Mr. Brooke is very pleased with his work, and his coverage of the Middlemarch political situation. Casaubon continues to resent Will, and Will grows more angry that Casaubon married someone as young and naïve as Dorothea, dragging her down into Casaubon's dull, dry world of academia. Will's affection for Dorothea continues to grow, and Dorothea becomes more and more fond of Will in return.

Will goes to Lowick to sketch; luckily for him, it begins to rain, and when he takes refuge in the house, he finds only Dorothea at home. They begin to speak as they did in Rome, very happy to be alone in each other's company; Dorothea becomes more aware of her husband's failings, but also learns of his generosity toward Will's family. Will tells Dorothea that he has a job at Mr. Brooke's paper, if he wants it; Dorothea says she would like him to stay in the neighborhood very much, but then realizes that Casaubon would disagree with her.

Dorothea tells Casaubon, who of course is not in the least supportive. Casaubon writes Will a letter, telling him he should not take the position, nor should he call at the house any longer. Casaubon's letter seems to be motivated not out of embarrassment for having a relative of lower status nearby, but out of some jealousy perhaps for his friendship with Dorothea. Dorothea becomes consumed by the case of Will's grandmother, and her unfair disinheritance when she married; she believes that Will is owed a good part of what Casaubon has because his family was impoverished unfairly, and wants to bring that up to Casaubon, though it will upset him.

Casaubon is not suspicious that Dorothea is being influenced by Will, but he thinks that it might happen; his insecurity and jealousy lead him to contrive secret hindrances for Will. He dislikes his cousin more than ever, because he imagines that Dorothea would like Will more than she likes him.

Analysis:

The issue of propriety would have Mr. Brooke take no part in papers, or in politics in general; also, the theme of social position plays a part in how neighbors and relatives regard Mr. Brooke's new venture. It seems that the newspaper business is regarded as too lowly and common a pursuit for a gentleman of money like Mr. Brooke; also, Mr. Brooke's airing of his political views in such a public forum is also considered distasteful. It is quite a paradox that politics in Middlemarch are decided through the influence of wealthy gentlemen like Mr. Brooke, yet to have these men publicly declare their opinion in politics is taboo.

The theme of social position is also very important in Casaubon's situation; he believes in a well-defined social hierarchy, especially since it gives him a position of superiority over people like Will Ladislaw. However, once Will stops accepting money from him, and establishes his own place in

Middlemarch with Mr. Brooke's newspaper, Casaubon feels that his position over Will has been diminished, which he resents. Casaubon's feelings about social organization are not unorthodox in the Middlemarch community; there are others who feel the same as Casaubon does, like the Vincys and the Bulstrodes, who like people to know their place, and act accordingly.

Will's inner declaration of loyalty to Dorothea shows how his affection for her is continuing to strengthen; and the fact that she regards him highly as well foreshadows a romantic relationship between them in the book. Eliot is building up the romantic tension between them, as their feelings become stronger and more intense; they will have to come to terms with their mutual affection at some point in the book, and hopefully all turns out well. With Eliot's metaphor comparing them to "two flowers which had opened then and there" when they get in each other's presence, and describing Will as "fresh water" to Dorothea after the stagnation she bears in her marriage, it is unlikely that the two can be easily separated.

The changed tones of voice which Dorothea and Will use in each other's presence testifies to their being suited for each other; Dorothea only seems to shrug off her melancholy, and the careful, depressed tone she uses around her husband when she is talking to Will, and Will sheds his usual sarcasm and becomes more gentle and thoughtful in his tone and speech.

However, at the same time, "tongues are little triggers," and Will cannot help but display this metaphor at work. Dorothea becomes conscious of her husband's failures when she speaks to Will; Dorothea pours forth the reasons why she married Casaubon, which Will could not have guessed. But jealousy is a theme in the novel that comes about because of this relationship; Mr. Casaubon is anything but pleased that his wife and cousin are friends, and fears that Dorothea could like Will better than he, which she does. Casaubon pretends to act out of concern for social hierarchy, another theme of importance in Middlemarch life; however, his real intent is hidden beneath, and is a function of his insecurity about himself. The end of the novel, and the brief mention of

Casaubon contriving obstacles for Will, foreshadows some great plot of his, some act of spite to come.

Chapter 38: Summary:

Mr. Brooke is making enemies through his advocacy for the Whig party, when Middlemarch is a predominantly conservative, Tory area. Bulstrode is allied with Brooke politically, but many of the neighbors disapprove, including Sir James. Sir James, Mrs. Cadwallader, and others are gossiping about Brooke and Will Ladislaw, Brooke's need to take care of his parish and other subjects. Brooke comes by, in the middle of being discussed; they inquire about the state of his tenants, attacks that have been made on him, etc.

Brooke, however, does not wish to enter into any arguments, or listen to see if they do have any valid points to make amid the rumors they are discussing. Brooke runs out quickly, and the others wish that maybe he could see if he was doing something wrong, and act on that.

Analysis:

Middlemarch politics seem very modern, for all the wrangling an dealing that goes on; Sir James mentions that dirt will be dug up on Brooke, to discredit his opinions, a practice which is regular in today's politics. However, the enmity between the conservative Tories and the liberal Whigs is something that is a little uncommon; people seek to squelch minority opinion, something which is not as common today. Snobbery and social standing also have a great deal to do with political opinion, which is not as true now as it was then; the wealthy are mostly conservatives, and those who are not, like Mr. Brooke, are shunned. Middlemarch has its own "liberal," Whig-leaning media in the form of its papers, plenty of political haggling, dirt-digging, wild rumors, all kinds of things which are still parts of politics today, which might be surprising, regarding the time period.

In Middlemarch, rumors are almost as good a currency as fact; this intermingling of rumor and fact and how each works compared to the other, is another theme. Brooke especially sees that insinuation can do as much damage as fact; when Sir James and his company are talking, hearsay is treated as fact, even as having more weight than Brooke's denials or explanations.

At the same time, Brooke could benefit from listening to the more mild, objective criticisms, and perhaps acting upon them; although he is politically liberal, it is his unique paradox that he is conservative when it comes to his own tenants and social improvements. Brooke would be better off if he did try to reconcile his public beliefs with his private actions; and his reluctance to do so foreshadows his downfall if he runs for office, especially since it is an idiosyncrasy that is well-known in the neighborhood, and much disputed.

Chapter 39: Summary:

Sir James becomes more judicious in his appraisal of Brooke's situation, and decides that Brooke needs to invest in improvements for his tenants if he wants to evade the scathing criticisms of the other Middlemarch paper, The Trumpet. Dorothea is the key to convincing him, figures Sir James, since she is a great advocate for improvements.

Dorothea goes to visit her uncle, and Will Ladislaw turns out to be there; she tells her uncle that Sir James told her that Tipton was to be managed by Caleb Garth, and improvements made. Dorothea is very passionate that this should be done; however, her uncle will not commit. She and Will find a moment alone, to explain a bit more of themselves; Will seems to be falling in love with her, as their relationship becomes stronger. Mr. Brooke goes to visit a tenant whose son has been poaching on Brooke's land, and is chastised by the tenant. Brooke, who liked to fancy himself a favourite of his tenants, is shocked; also, the house looks worse now that Dorothea has made her criticisms. It looks like Mr. Brooke will give in, and turn the management of the estate over to Mr. Garth after all.

Analysis:

When Dorothea speaks of improvements to be made on the property, to help the tenants, she is filled with passion for the first time in a while. Social reform is Dorothea's true passion; she is a woman who needs to be doing and achieving, which makes her match with Casaubon particularly ironic, and also strange. Dorothea in this scene becomes a complete dramatic foil for Casaubon; where he is cold and meticulous, she is passionate and impulsive. Casaubon's work is in his mind, and not result-oriented, whereas Dorothea wants real progress made, for the benefit of real people. As Dorothea becomes wiser about Casaubon's nature and about their marriage, the juxtaposition between the two of them becomes even more start; for Dorothea cannot stifle her true personality and self any longer to spare Casaubon's insecurities and feelings, and it just so happens that everything that Casaubon is, Dorothea is not.

The change in Dorothea's tone when she speaks about something for which she has so much interest is very marked; there is a great contrast between the brief, strained tone she uses with her husband, and the emotional, image-laden, eager tone that she adopts here. Self-expression is an issue that has dogged Dorothea since her marriage, and finally she is finding ways to express her feelings and desires. The irony is, where her marriage was supposed to broaden her knowledge and fulfill her desires, all the knowledge and fulfillment she has gained are from outside her marriage‹like Sir James and Will. Also, Dorothea's expression is quite apart from the appropriate modes of women's expression, which startles Will and reduces Mr. Brooke to stammering; this tendency is not looked upon kindly in society as a whole, and Dorothea continues to be very unconventional in nature compared to what women were expected to be.

The lancelet that the boy kills can be taken as a symbol of how Mr. Brooke is mistaken; he believes that the boy should be punished for killing the animal, just as he believes that his tenants should, and do, bear him some amount of affection. He actually finds out that things are very much the opposite; and Mr. Brooke is not such a hard man that suggestions from his neighbors and his niece, compounded with an outburst from a tenant, does not move him. Mr. Brooke realizes the irony that has dogged his position as landlord; he thought that everything he did as a landlord, including taking over the operation of his land, was positive and good, when in fact he was messing things up beyond what he could have expected.

Chapter 40: Summary:

Focus moves to the Garths, who are gathered at the table, reading letters. Mary is looking for another position, and has decided to take a place at a school in York, though it does not please her, or her parents, too well. However, Mr. Garth reads a letter from Sir James that asks him whether Mr. Garth would start managing Freshitt, and mentions that Mr. Brooke might want his services again as well. This would double the Garths' income, and means that Mary can stay at home; but Mr. Garth will need an assistant, and none of his sons are in the position to do so. The whole family is happy, Caleb Garth most of all because he will be able to do good work to help even more people.

Mr. Farebrother comes to visit; he has some interest in Mary Garth, and also likes to visit and spend time with the family. He has been talking to Fred Vincy, and informs them of Fred's situation, telling them Fred is going back to study, and still cannot pay off his debt to them.

Analysis:

Rosamond and Mary Garth are dramatic foils in every possible way; Rosamond is vain, naïve, materialistic, whereas Mary is intelligent, modest, and frugal. Although Mary and Rosamond are friends, Mary thinks nothing of pointing out Rosamond's ridiculous insistence on certain clothes for her wedding; "she can't be married without this handkerchief," Mary says, her playful tone bringing attention to Rosamond's folly.

The boys' reaction on hearing Mary say that she will have to teach at a girls' school exposes a bit of the difference between the education that boys receive, and the education that girls receive during this time. Most girls' schools were the equivalent of charm schools, like the one Rosamond went to;

little is taught besides basic knowledge, social skills, and a little art and music. Girls are also not allowed to play like boys, as Jim points out; boys are given far more freedom and learning in their education, but girls must settle for a window-dressing equivalent.

Money, which is so important to so many others, is an issue of lesser importance to Mr. Garth. His first love is helping people, improving the land, making others' lives better through his work. Although the situations of Mr. Garth and Dorothea are quite different, there are parallels between the two because of their lesser regard for money, and their passion for social improvement.

The social standing of the clergy is a quirk of the English class system that is in place in Middlemarch; whereas most people are judged according to birth and family first, and according to wealth and landholdings next, clergymen, who are poor and have little property, are given far more respect and latitude than someone else of similar social, but different professional, situation. At the same time, the clergy is not for everyone; it certainly does not seem suited to Fred, though it is a profession that wayward sons and men with few prospects are dumped into.

The clergy, however, would not be an unrespectable field for a young man of good family, like Fred Vincy, to enter into; however, manual work, like Caleb Garth does, is considered beneath him. This is another place where social hierarchy intrudes upon Middlemarch life, attempting to hinder people for the sake of "respectability." At the same time, the Industrial Revolution is beginning to change English society, and notions of "respectable" occupations according to class; social mobility is becoming more common, and business and commerce are finally seen as decent occupations, as men like Mr. Vincy and Bulstrode are not looked down upon for their commerce-funded livelihood.

It is quite a paradox that Mary thinks well of Farebrother and is harsh on Fred, but loves Fred and is just friends with Farebrother. Mary's particular concern for Fred, especially for his prospects, foreshadows that they will become a couple;

indeed, Fred is not one to learn from doing foolish things, but when he costs the Garths a good deal of money, he is more sorry of that than anything he has ever done. Family expectation is one of the guiding themes of Fred Vincy's life; he does try to please his parents with his choice of profession and his study, but at the same time, seems ill-suited to the academic and business pursuits they would have him enter into. Will Fred defy his parents' wishes, and society's unwritten rules, about the occupations he should hold according to birth and family position? Fred is unable to excel in anything he does not enjoy, so knowing him, if he wants to work for Caleb Garth, that will be all he will be able to do.

Chapter 41: Summary:

It is not long since Mr. Rigg Featherstone has gained the estate of Stone Court, and already there is word that he wishes to sell the place to Mr. Bulstrode. It is revealed that Mr. Rigg is Featherstone's illegitimate child, who was brought up far away from Middlemarch, with very little money. Someone named John Raffles is there, his mother's new husband; he wants money to start a tobacco shop from Mr. Rigg's new-found fortune. Rigg refuses, because Raffles, he alleges, was very cruel to him as a child, took money from his mother, and left them poor and miserable. He says that he will continue to send his mother an allowance, but will give Mr. Raffles nothing. Rigg gives him money to get back home, and some liquor, but not before Mr. Raffles makes use of an important paper, signed by Mr. Bulstrode, to keep his flask from falling apart.

Analysis:

It seems that Mr. Rigg has inherited more from Mr. Featherstone than just a name and some property; he has inherited Mr. Featherstone's coldness, whether deserved or not by the person on whom he bestows it. Mr. Rigg, like Featherstone, is the kind of person whom flattery cannot sway, nor belated kindness persuade; neither have much regard for their relatives if they are of no good account, but at least Rigg is less mean with his money when it comes to supporting his mother. However, Rigg's constitution also differs from Featherstone's; he is more quiet, less liable to taunt or try to impress people with his money, though it is newly come to him. Rigg is a man of greater stoicism and stiffness, and seems less likely to give people trouble if they deserve none.

Chapter 42: Summary:

Lydgate is at least back from his honeymoon with Rosamond, and is immediately called to Casaubon, whose health seems to be getting worse. He is also haunted by the idea that he has never been given credit for his studies, and that the Key to All Mythologies will never be finished; he is starting to admit that he has failed in his life-long project. Casaubon is disappointed also with Dorothea; she does all her duties as a wife, but he suspects that she is critical of him secretly, and this disturbs him a great deal.

Casaubon's vitriol against Will, and against Dorothea's suspected affection for Will, takes him over; he concedes to write a passage into his will "protecting" Dorothea from marrying eager, potentially deceptive suitors like Will. Lydgate finally arrives, and Casaubon asks that he be told exactly what his condition is. Lydgate tells him that he has a heart ailment, but cannot be sure that it will cut his life short, or have any immediate effect. Lydgate goes once Casaubon has heard enough, and Dorothea comes out to fetch him; he withdraws from her, and soon she becomes angry at him for treating her so. Dorothea realizes that she has reduced herself in order to try and please him, but he seems to be satisfied with nothing; she is tired of not being herself, and resents him greatly. However, when he says that he needs her help, she forgets her anger, and goes to join him.

Analysis:

The theme of gender roles and accepted notions of gender comes back to haunt Casaubon; he has been led to believe that women are supposed to be self-sacrificing, supportive, emotionally giving, etc., and no different from the flat, narrow stereotype of the typical wife. Ironically, he believes that Dorothea is a woman, but does not believe that this makes her a person; the idea that she might have opinions about him, a mind of her own, or the ability to make her own decisions disturbs him, as if she should lack these basic human qualities because she is a woman.

The Key to All Mythologies becomes a symbol of Casaubon's failure as a scholar, and as a human being; his life's work has finally come to an unpublishable heap of meaningless papers, and his obsessive devotion to these papers has cost him any real relationships he might have had. Casaubon's life among moldy books has gained him nothing, in the end; he has gained no recognition, because he cannot seem to distill his learning into anything of practical use. He is too involved in his directionless studies that he leaves no time to get to know his wife, or form any friendships with neighbors, or with family like Will. He is socially insecure and more than a bit jealous of people, like Will, who are able to operate in society in the ways he cannot; this is another hindrance to him, in finding and making acquaintances.

Casaubon's tone, as he speaks of "protecting" his wife and of the potential influence Will would have on her, becomes bitter, informed by suspicion, and prone to justify invention with a gloss of rational-sounding diction. His thoughts are structured like a lawyer's argument, the diction stiff and sometimes precise, though the sentiments contained within, and the presumptions of character, are mostly the stuff of Casaubon's paranoia.

However, the fact that Casaubon is putting a formal hindrance in Dorothea and Will's way foreshadows that they will finally become a couple; such a mean-spirited, vain attempt on Casaubon's part must be proved as wrong as the spirit in which it was written.

Eliot's personification of death adds drama and immediacy to Casaubon's situation; it also foreshadows that something is to happen to Casaubon soon, and that his illness shall not be drawn out by any means. The subdued, solemn images and surroundings are also conducive, and sympathetic, to some dramatic event. Dorothea being described as being possibly a "heaven-sent angel" is also further hint about Casaubon's fast approaching fate; the metaphor is correct in characterizing her as a kind of loving, sympathetic creature, but not even Casaubon is his state will accept her affection.

This chapter sees Dorothea finally come close to revolt; she has shaken off her naivete about the marriage, and settled into anger, rather than pity or self-consciousness. If Casaubon has been displeased with her so far, he in unlikely to find any satisfaction; she knows that she has been trying hard to suppress herself, in order to please him, and can no longer do this. However, she sinks into her old ways once again, when he comes to get her, and asks for her help. Dorothea is so affection-starved that she will continue to distort herself in order to please, but in light of her realization, this tendency might not be long-lived.

Chapter 43: Summary:

Dorothea decides to seek out Lydgate, and ask him if there has been a serious change in her husband's condition, or else why he has been so troubled since Lydgate's visit. She goes to his house, and finds Rosamond there; but Will is also there, which makes Dorothea panic, and she immediately leaves to find Lydgate at his hospital.

Will fears that Dorothea will think badly of him because she has found him in the company of another woman, and not totally devoted to her; but she acted the way she did because she likes him, and knows that her husband doesn't approve of the friendship, and that it is some kind of betrayal as well.

Rosamond begins to get ideas about perhaps attracting other admirers, in order to appease her vanity, and allay her fears about Lydgate's fondness for her growing weaker. It seems like she might try to win Mr. Ladislaw's affections, and seems a little jealous that he likes Dorothea rather than her. She also seems to suspect that maybe her husband has a soft spot for Dorothea, and that might have been part of the reason she was searching for Lydgate.

Analysis:

Eliot juxtaposes Rosamond and Dorothea in appearance in order to show a corresponding difference in their character. Whereas Rosamond dresses in a showy, fashionable way that plays to her vanity, Dorothea is attired in a way that suggests her piety, modesty, and humility, which are especially plain to see in contrast with Rosamond. Eliot's allusions to Imogen and Cato's daughter convey the almost theatrical dignity with which Rosamond composes herself; she is all for show, and acts the part, even at home.

Will feels that being seen at Rosamond might convey to Dorothea that he doesn't think exclusively of her; he fears it has made a bad impression on her, and that Casaubon has poisoned her against him. He feels that his dilemma lies in having to make acquaintances in Middlemarch in order to get ahead professionally and socially, versus devoting himself completely to his admiration for Dorothea. Will compares his situation to "the situation in which Diana had descended too unexpectedly upon her worshipper". The allusion to Diana confirms Will's high regard for Dorothea and her virtue, and the parallels between Will's conception of the situation and this example highlight his wishes to please her, and to convey his love to her.

Dorothea is torn by the theme of loyalty vs. desire; she wants to be in Will's presence, but on the other hand, this will be directly against her husband's wishes. Dorothea is not sure at all what she should do in this situation; she knows now of her husband's fallibility, and something of his prejudice toward Will as well. If she were to be herself, as she wishes, she would merely go to see Will, and think nothing more of it; but Dorothea is too faithful a creature to be dishonest, and must continue to struggle with her feelings, as Will is with his.

Chapter 44: Summary:

Dorothea finally talks to Lydgate, and Lydgate tells her that Casaubon now knows about his condition, and he is probably upset by it. Lydgate turns her attention to the new hospital; Bulstrode has been one of the few supporting it, and so many are against the hospital because they do not like Bulstrode. Dorothea says that she would like to do something for such a good cause, and pledges money from her yearly allowance; she is happier that she is able to make a significant contribution, but still her husband's illness and behaviour bother her.

Analysis:

The theme of politics becomes prevalent once again; it seems that political maneuvering is more important than the health of the community, a stance that is both ironic and counterproductive. Political ties seem to trump almost any other kind of consideration in Middlemarch, including friendships and social duty. The amount of strong dislike for Bulstrode is not a good omen; it foreshadows his downfall if he attempts to overstep his bounds, as people are already poised to attack as things are.

Dorothea is down to her last avenue for joy, which is social improvement; it seems that she has given up any hopes for happiness in her marriage, or any idea that she might be able to please her husband as well. Since her husband's talk with Lydgate, Dorothea has settled back into her usual dejected tone, and pious understatements of her unhappiness. It is unexpected that Dorothea would be back to her old self after having her epiphany about Casaubon's behaviour, the state of their marriage, and her uselessness in the union.

She is resilient in a way that is not necessarily healthy for her; she is getting more knowledgeable about her situation, but needs to snap out of her almost masochistic attraction to misery, and make some changes in her life. At this point, it is clear that Dorothea is not a prisoner, that she does have some power over her situation; however, she perversely refuses to use it, and makes herself into a kind of martyr, which suits the more perversely pious aspects of her personality.

Summary and Analysis of Chapters 45-55

Chapter 45: Summary:

Lydgate's practice seems to be at the mercy of rumor,

hearsay, and general sentiment; people go to him because they have heard about "miracle cures" that he has done, or stay away because they have heard he is newfangled, and they like their present practitioner just fine. The backward Middlemarch way of doing and deciding has helped Lydgate's reputation and practice to spread, but opinion could turn against him just as rapidly, and dry up his practice. Lydgate is unlucky enough to come into Middlemarch at a time when old ways are becoming contested in other regions, and reforms have started to creep into Middlemarch as well; a few believe that maybe his way is best, but others have been roused to defend the old, and are more militant about this point than usual. Lydgate is also disliked because he has taken on cases from other doctors, given a different diagnosis, and been able to cure them; this wounds the vanity of the old-guard doctors, and increases their personal dislike for Lydgate.

Mr. Bulstrode is on the side of progress, with Lydgate; this means that many prominent, wealthy citizens, who dislike both Bulstrode and innovation, refuse to donate to the new hospital. Lydgate is becoming too closely tied to the widely disliked Bulstrode that his reputation is beginning to suffer; Farebrother tells him so, and hopefully Lydgate will distance himself some. Farebrother also warns Lydgate against having too many debts.

Lydgate thinks that he might be among the great innovators of medicine, and this necessitates making enemies, and having opinion turn against you; in this, he is a little conceited, since there is no way he can claim an advance as great as those of his hero, Vesalius. It is fine for Lydgate to try and change the outdated medical practice around him; but his egotism and his visions of greatness could easily hamper his progress, and get him into even more trouble with his peers and patients.

Analysis

Tradition seems to be the strongest force in all of Middlemarch; and it is tradition that is a major hindrance to Lydgate's attempt to innovate and streamline medical practice.

It is a paradox that tradition isn't heeded because it is tried and true, or even the best way to do things; tradition is important because people are used to it, even if it is backwards and better things have since come along. Either Lydgate will have to give in to the usual way that surgeons practice in Middlemarch, or struggle very hard to get people to accept him; either way, the pull of tradition will be a theme in the novel with which he shall have to contend.

Prejudice is also another theme that Lydgate will have to fight; people are distrustful of him because he is new in the area and trying to make advancements, and this colors their ideas of his character, and of his medical practice as well. People who have not met Lydgate decide their opinion of him as a person by the tone of voice in which he is discussed; if people they know are expressing disdain, they assume that Lydgate must be an arrogant fellow, and hold that as their truth. It seems that there isn't any way for Lydgate to win; even when he does succeed with patients, like Fred Vincy, he gets no credit for his advice, and is even more cursed for his medical opinions.

However, social change is beginning to touch Middlemarch with regard to medical practice, and stubbornness will not be able to win out over the onslaught of progress. Luck has aided Lydgate in his cause, helping him impress people with the idea that the new way is the right way; it is clear that the Middlemarch ways of practicing medicine are counterproductive and less than useful, so it will take an enormous deal of blind stubbornness to keep traditional methods at work.

Lydgate is disliked by every other doctor because he is an upstart threat to him, and their opinions about him can damage his reputation; Lydgate does not deserve such ill-treatment, but at the same time, he is not a man who knows politics very well. It is fine to refuse to play games or manipulate people; but to stay afloat in Middlemarch, as Farebrother knows, one has to make certain concessions and try not to make too many enemies, as Bulstrode has. Granted, that Lydgate's enemies are all petty, piddling people who insult him for their own gain, or pleasure; but Lydgate must make a living among these people, so he must tread carefully.

Unfortunately, Lydgate seems to have little concern for the debts he has been making; he has little money, and Rosamond, who has expensive taste, could get him into trouble. Both Farebrother's careful warning, and Lydgate's refusal to really heed it, foreshadow the trouble Lydgate will be in when his debts catch up with him; he needs to keep it in his mind to be careful with money and how much he borrows, or else he will find himself in great trouble.

Lydgate seems to be an upstanding fellow in every sense but one; his idea that he might be a great man of medicine, like Vesalius or the like. Lydgate is a good doctor, but has shown no signs of being a brilliant one; and this opinion, if it is wrong, will continue to damage his reputation in Middlemarch. Maybe Lydgate will be able to make some difference in medicine, but as long as he continues to pretend that he is a genius to be extolled, he will be unable to set aside his ego and make any real medical progress.

Chapter 46: Summary:

An issue of reform is coming before Parliament, which Will supports, and Brooke decides to as well. Will seems to have a good deal of insight into British national politics, as he can make sense of issues and candidates, and make a convincing case for his opinion. Mr. Brooke, however, doesn't seem to be able to put his thoughts in a convincing argument; he is rather flippant in setting out his opinion, and is easily swayed by Ladislaw's better-formed opinions. Will is not winning any fans because of his unconventional behaviour and views, as most people dislike his speeches and his writing because they are different.

Will wants Mr. Brooke to be elected to Parliament; however, with the uncomplimentary way in which Mr. Brooke is regarded in much of the neighborhood, this is unlikely. Will is perhaps a bit idealistic in believing that Mr. Brooke could actually win; he might assume that the citizens of Middlemarch are more sensible than they really are, in which case his plans would fail. Lydgate makes some points about area politics that perhaps he should take into account regarding his own situation; the two argue for a bit about these political issues, then Ladislaw leaves after they have tried to patch things up.

Analysis:

Although Will has a settled position in Middlemarch, he is still the same wandering, dilettante- like figure he has always been. He is at the newspaper for want of anything else to do, and actually finds it rather interesting; his interest in Dorothea, of course, also helps to keep him there. Mr. Brooke and Will are a sort of interesting juxtaposition; Mr. Brooke is absent-minded, rather eccentric, and very inarticulate, while Will has a more intelligent mind, is able to set things down intelligibly, and is less unexplainably odd. Will has good reasons for everything he does and says, unlike Mr. Brooke; he is unlikely to hold a prejudice even if it is completely incorrect, like Mr. Brooke's ongoing, and very foolish, prejudice against women.

The themes of social position and conformity struggle to defeat Will; many dislike him because they cannot fit him into any particular class, and also because he is of a lower rank than they, yet is politically vocal. Will is also disliked because he is a gypsy-like figure, defying classification, and also defying Middlemarch's desire that everyone conform to a certain mold. His situation is parallel to Lydgate's because they are both being told by Middlemarch to be traditional and regular, and are being scorned for refusing; however, it is Will's personality and personal views which are the object of spite in his case, whereas with Lydgate, it is a question of professional practice.

It is brought to Will's attention that his relation with Mr. Brooke, like Lydgate's with Mr. Bulstrode, might be harming his reputation; Mr. Brooke, though he is kind, is seen publicly as a scatterbrain and a fool, which is somewhat true. Will is seen as Mr. Brooke's pawn, a view which belies his intelligence, and dishonors his position at the paper. Both Will and Lydgate will need to sort out their alliances, if they want to correct the incorrect assumptions that their alliances have been spreading about them.

Chapter 47: Summary:

Will, who cares little what people think, stops to consider how his employment with Mr. Brooke, and his involvement with Mr. Brooke's politics, might be hindering him and making him look foolish. Even more important is whether he really is a fool for following along with Brooke; Will does think that the relation has cost him some of his dignity and individuality. All the same, he wants to stay in Middlemarch, at that position, in order to be near Dorothea; but he considers whether he is a fool with her too, and his hopeless devotion will amount to nothing if he gains no proof that she shares his affection.

Will has also become aware of what his cousin Casaubon thinks of him being friends with Dorothea; he knows that Casaubon might think that Will means dishonor in his interest in her, but Will really does not. Will decides to go to Lowick church to see her, aware that Casaubon will be upset. However, his doubt is only reinforced; Dorothea shows no happiness to see him, instead seeming pained; Will is saddened by the whole affair, and seems close to calling it quits on the whole affair.

Analysis:

For the first time, Will is saddled with the concerns of ordinary, settled, and employed citizens; although the work at the paper does suit him, he must ask whether he is compromising himself too much with his work there. The Pioneer has become a millstone to him, a symbol of the loss of his freedom and his sacrificing his real interest in art. And Dorothea is beginning to seem not worth the sacrifices that Will is making, because he can rarely see her; Middlemarch is quickly losing its charm, as Will's reasons for staying are diminishing.

Will cannot deny that he is a romantic, not a rationalist, at heart; he looks to nature to decide whether he shall go to church, and when the images he sees around him prove cheery, he determines to go. Will is no blind fool, he can see what is set before him plainly; at the same time, he is ruled mostly by his heart, especially when it comes to Dorothea. However, even

Will needs signs and encouragement to go by; when he gains neither from Dorothea at the church, he cannot rationalize his being in Middlemarch merely for her sake any longer. Either Will is going to need some sign from Dorothea that she wants him to stay, or it is likely that he will leave Middlemarch sometime soon.

Chapter 48: Summary:

Dorothea is actually happy that Will showed up at church, and wishes for his company, since she is often alone at home. Dorothea is not allowing her husband's disapproval to stifle her feelings for Will, though it will be difficult for her to see him. Casaubon is, all of a sudden, requesting Dorothea's help with his studies, and being kinder to her; perhaps this is a result of his talk with Lydgate, and he wants to get his work in order finally, and be on better terms with his wife, in case he dies suddenly. However, Casaubon next asks her if she will follow his wishes for her after he dies, whenever that is; Dorothea has to consider, since she is reluctant to promise to do something, when she does not know what it is. She secretly suspects that it may have something to do with Will, but consciously considers that it has to do with finishing Casaubon's work, which she does not want to devote years to.

However, before she can make an answer, Casaubon dies. Dorothea is at first in denial, and tells Lydgate everything, and to tell her husband that she has an answer. It might be a good thing for her that she does not have to hold herself to any answer she made; but she still does not know what Casaubon's wish was.

Analysis:

This is the first time that Casaubon has showed real care for Dorothea's feelings since they have been married; he speaks to her in a softened tone, and actually says that he likes her company, and her help too. This sudden change might foreshadow an overall change in Casaubon and Dorothea's relationship; or, it could be a sign of his mortality, and this is his opportunity to set things right again. However, this represents a big step forward for the pair, and hopefully marks the beginning of cordial relations for them.

Ironically, Casaubon's kindness seems to be a prelude to asking her if she will obey him, even in death. His will in this area is not kind, and Dorothea knows it; she is aware that it probably has something to do with Will, and shall be unpleasant. Though Dorothea still defers to her husband, she is aware that he is a flawed being as well. The theme of faithfulness is one which Dorothea's story has been guided and shaped by; however, she has to decide whether she can bear to be faithful to a man she does not love after he has left, especially if his wishes might be marked by suspicion and ill-will. Dorothea tries not to admit to herself that his wishes might be darker than just completing his work; however, this idea is swimming around in her mind, and creating a great sense of dread in her.

The Key becomes a symbol to Dorothea as well; her other thought is that his wish will have something to do with completing his life's work. Dorothea begins to see the Key as enslavement in cryptic, unpleasant things; she wishes to learn, but she sees this task as being buried under mounds of paper, being prisoner to things that she does not understand. The Key seems to also be a symbol of her marriage; both are troublesome to Dorothea, threaten her with the loss of her freedom, and are impossible for her to gain any knowledge over.

Although Dorothea wants, in some capacity, to deny her husband, she also fears what her denial might do to him; he has her in a corner on this issue, and she feels that all she can do is accept, however little she wishes to. But, as it turns out, Casaubon's request for her promise foreshadowed his coming death; there is great irony in the fact that he died before he could receive an answer to the one question which had plagued him for some time. It might prove good to Dorothea, however, as she will not have to live knowing that she had made a promise one way or another; her conscience has been spared, and now she only has to wait and see what the request actually was.

Chapter 49: Summary:

Sir James and Mr. Brooke are supposedly discussing Casaubon's last wish; they decide that whatever was in the will should be hidden from Dorothea until she is strong enough to hear of it, and until then she should be with her sister and her new baby. Sir James wants Will sent out of the country, which means that he had something to do with Casaubon's last wish; Mr. Brooke refuses to act so hastily, since Will has done very good work for him. They reveal that Casaubon added a codicil to his will, saying that if Dorothea marries Will, she will forfeit the land and money that Casaubon has left to her. The whole thing looks very bad, as if there was something sordid going on between Will and Dorothea. Sir James and Mr. Brooke come to the conclusion that if they sent Will away, it would make the situation look worse, and that they could not make him go unless he wanted to. Sir James is bent upon protecting Dorothea now however, as he could not do with her first marriage; she will be sent to Freshitt to live with Sir James and her sister for a while, and then more will be decided later.

Analysis:

At this point, Sir James is embodying the theme of prejudice, which is prevalent in Middlemarch when it comes to outsiders like Will. It is not that Sir James knows Will personally, or has much grounds to dislike Will. Since Casaubon's will speaks ill of him, Will is of inferior social standing, and much public opinion is against him, Sir James assumes that Will is reprehensible, and is no good for his sister-in-law, Dorothea. This stance is ironic, given Sir James' misgivings about Casaubon; he does not consider what Dorothea, whom he cares about, might feel in the matter, nor what Will is really like.

Uncharacteristically, Mr. Brooke is more right-on about this situation than Sir James; he has far more information on which to make a decision, and knows the people concerned more personally. It seems that Sir James and Mr. Brooke are almost switching places in this one debate, still representing opposing positions. However, Mr. Brooke would be more expected to act on prejudice, and Sir James to be reasonable, according to their behaviour up until this point.

Casaubon's will becomes a symbol and an embodiment of his bitterness, suspicion, and spite; it is as if he was not content on making Will and Dorothea miserable enough when he lived, that he had to leave a secret document that amounted to slander on both of their characters. This is the last impediment to Dorothea that Casaubon has left; at least she is free of him, her misery when she was around him, and her lonely imprisonment at Lowick. Hopefully, she will be able to shed the perverse, martyr-like, self-sacrificing qualities that led her to Casaubon in the first place, and be able to shed his miserable influence, and finally be happy.

Chapter 50: Summary:

Dorothea is at Freshitt, but not a week has passed before she is interested in the will, and what she will do with Lowick. She insists on going to Lowick, to look after the papers; after Mr. Brooke tells her she cannot, Celia finally tells her about the codicil, and tries to soothe her. Dorothea realizes how her life is changing, and wants to be with Will even more.

Dorothea still has the problem of what to do with Lowick, and the vacant position at the church; she thinks of giving it to Mr. Tyke, but Lydgate recommends Farebrother, and says to ask Will about his character. Dorothea decides to give him a try, and wonders how Will is faring through all of this.

Analysis:

In this Chapter, Celia and Dorothea are juxtaposed not only through their personalities, but through their dress as well. Celia is lighthearted, dressed in white, very happy, and does not see why Dorothea should mourn a husband of such a foul temperament, who made her so unhappy. Dorothea is in black, and far too sorrowful for the situation she is in; she is her usual tragic self, touched with melancholy, a foil in character and looks to her sensible sister.

How ironic that everyone who knows of the codicil thinks

that Dorothea and Will have no connection at all; they assume this because of social status and general dislike of Will, but do not consider for one moment why the codicil was written. It is painful for Dorothea to hear her sister say that she would never marry Will anyway; Dorothea knows how untrue this is, and to hear a man who just might be her soul-mate talked of so casually is a blow to her. Dorothea is finally allowed, however, to think of Will without considering her husband's dislike; she admits her longing for Will, and thinks for the first time that they could be lovers, which seems to comfort her.

Despite her husband's death, Dorothea remains very much unchanged; she is hard-pressed to flout her husband's last wish, still is interested in social improvements, and stays concerned in the matter of Will's rightful inheritance. Little about Dorothea seems to change, other than her daily company and employment; she is less cut off from people than she used to be, and no longer has to toil at academics, but otherwise her position is very much the same as always. Perhaps Dorothea's continuing regard for Will, and her wishes to be with him, foreshadow that they might get together sometime soon.

Chapter 51: Summary:

Will is upset, because Mr. Brooke is no longer inviting him to the Grange, and he feels that maybe he is being avoided out of concern for Dorothea. Still, he has heard nothing about the will yet. Will believes that he and Dorothea are divided forever; still, he cannot leave Middlemarch, because he needs to help Mr. Brooke get ready for the coming election. Mr. Brooke is running for the Independent party, and needs Will's help if he is able to have a chance.

However, Mr. Brooke's main speech goes terribly; he is mocked and egged, hung in effigy, and is disgusted so much by the whole thing that he quits the election. He also decides to quit the paper too, and urges Will to do the same. However, Will has been thinking on his future; he will become a political writer, raise himself up, if he knows that Dorothea would marry him after he achieved these things. He decides to seek some sign from her, and in the meantime, stay at the paper.

He has some idea that Mr. Brooke and others are trying to get rid of him for Dorothea's sake, but will not go unless she doesn't care for him.

Analysis:

A bit more about English politics is revealed here; unlike in the U.S., there are any number of parties in Parliament, and more than two candidates for one position as well. Political voting is not as polarized in Middlemarch as it often is in the States; people do vote for different parties, according to which candidates they like. But, some also do vote straight-ticket, for the whatever representative of the party which they prefer.

Mr. Brooke and Will have the difficult task of convincing people to vote for reform, when the outcome of this vote is uncertain. People in Middlemarch, as elsewhere, "vote their pocketbooks," meaning that Mr. Brooke and his platform of change will be a hard sell with people like Mr. Mawmsey, who can ill-afford reform if it means less money for them. Mr. Brooke's thinking on such issues seems to be getting a little more lucid, at last; however, Will sees that Mr. Brooke can remember nothing complicated, unless it is all he has in his mind.As in the U.S. also, politics are often dirty, decided by ridicule, rumors, etc., rather than facts and truths. Politics seems to be the opposite of science, especially in the hands of simple Middlemarch citizens; Mr. Brooke proves unable to put a positive spin on his situation, and so must drop out of the game. Will, however, knows that he has some aptitude for writing politically, though in support of a candidate like Mr. Brooke, nothing he could do would help. It seems that Will has been completely transformed by his love for Dorothea; he has settled into a job, and would even embark upon a celebrated career, if it meant winning her. Dorothea's influence has been more powerful than she can guess, and hopefully, she will be able to talk to Will, and let him know what is going on in her life.

Chapter 52: Summary:

Farebrother finds out that Dorothea has given him the

living at Lowick; he is glad since this will increase his income, and give him more freedom in his living. His sister will now be allowed to marry, as they can afford a dowry, and Farebrother too can afford to have a wife. However, the only woman he wants to marry is Mary Garth; and Fred in newly back from finishing college, and wants nothing more than for Mary to love him. Farebrother, as Fred's confidant in this situation, does a very good job of being impartial, giving fair advice without the prejudice of his own heart. However, it pains Farebrother that the only woman he would like to marry is marked for someone else, who is less stable and responsible than he. Fred thinks that he might have to go into the clergy, since he can think of no other profession to join. However, he knows that Mary is against this; so, he recruits Farebrother to go and speak to her about all of this, so that he might know what he should do. Farebrother does, and speaks to her plainly, and fairly; Mary says that it would be wrong of Fred to be in the clergy, but she would marry him if he found another stable profession. Mary says that she will remain single for Fred, and loves only him; Farebrother's hopes are finally dashed, of which Mary is sorry, though she has told the truth of her heart.

Analysis:

Fred and Will seemed similar in their flightiness and unwillingness to settle into a profession; now, both of them have been changed by love for the better, and are becoming good, stable workers to impress the women they love. Both of them are trying to prove themselves worthy, and have their love requited. The theme of unrequited love has run through their stories before this point, and has not cheered them any; still, they are both models of young, hopeful lovers, and have decided to try their hardest before they will surrender.

How sad, though, for Farebrother, that unrequited love must be the main theme of his part of the story; he is able to act with honor despite how pained he is that Fred and Mary are to be together, which is admirable. Farebrother's situation is parallel to those of Fred and Will, because he too is tested, and changed, by the force of unrequited love; he becomes more mature, more placid, and a better friend as well because of his pain. However, unlike with Fred or Will, he has no chance of winning the one he loves, since she loves another; but, Farebrother proves his worth and his good character through his admirable dealings with both Fred and Mary.

It is ironic that Farebrother is chosen to try and join Mary and Fred together, when he is the only other man in Middlemarch who loves Mary. Mary, proving the powers of her perception, senses Farebrother's affection for her, and his pain that she must declare her affections for Fred. Now that Mary has said she will accept Fred if he is worthy, Fred must come around; Mary's statement will probably provide enough fuel for Fred to get a profession, and foreshadows their eventual marriage, and the beginning of Fred's industrious years.

Chapter 53: Summary:

Stone Court has finally been transferred to Bulstrode, Rigg having relieved himself of the estate and grounds. Bulstrode is not pleased that Farebrother, rather than Tyke, is the new preacher at Lowick, but can do nothing about it. Rigg's fate is not at Middlemarch, and so he departs with little ceremony. Raffles comes to Stone Court, looking for Bulstrode, an old acquaintance; he found out that Bulstrode took his stepson Rigg's place at Stone court by the crumpled paper he took, and so has sought Bulstrode out there. Bulstrode is displeased to see Raffles, and doesn't want anyone to know that he is there, or the real purpose why. It seems that Bulstrode and Raffles had some shady dealings a while back, that Bulstrode does not want discovered. Bulstrode's family connections are questionable as well, as Raffles knows; Raffles takes advantage and asks Bulstrode for money, on threat of exposing him to general knowledge. Bulstrode pays him off, and Raffles remembers that Bulstrode is related to someone named Ladislaw whom he has not seen in years‹but Raffles does not know who Will is, and also does not tell Bulstrode.

Analysis:

Fate has caught up with Bulstrode, as it is wont to do;

and right as he is beginning to enjoy his station and his wealth too, which is the ironic way that fate likes to work. It seems that no one has the right to commit grave sins in his past, or those sins come back and take him down; this is really only fair that people like Bulstrode are destroyed by their treachery, of no one's doing but their own. At last, Bulstrode's great pride and power-mongering are stifled by the fact that someone else has power over him. But will Bulstrode be able to keep his place in Middlemarch society, or will the facts leak out and undo him? It would only be just if Bulstrode, after his pompous behaviour in society, his manipulating of people, and his attempts to control Middlemarch politics and policies, was taught a lesson about his behaviour. For the moment, Bulstrode may have gained a reprieve, but this does not mean that he is yet free of the lessons fate has to teach him.

Chapter 54: Summary:

Dorothea is tired of staying at her sister's, having nothing to do but stare at Celia's baby, whom Celia worships, but Dorothea couldn't be more indifferent to. She longs to get back to Lowick and set things in order; her sister and Sir James do not believe she should go, but she is determined to, because she can stand Celia's no longer. Others also wish that Dorothea go to live with someone, so she should not be lonely, but she refuses. She also refuses to finish Casaubon's work, since her interest in it has been obliterated by his death, and before that his behaviour toward her.

Will finally does visit her, to see if she does have some affection to encourage him with. Their meeting is heated, however, with both of them being frustrated by not being able to admit their affection, and then their pride clashing on the subject of their division from each other. Will leaves, with Dorothea trying to show little emotion, especially because Sir James is there, and disapproves of the whole relationship.

Analysis:

At many points in the novel, Celia seems like the more sensible, likeable of the two Brooke girls; however, even Celia has her flaws, and can make her sister look very deep in comparison. Upon her baby's birth, Celia tends to discount everything that is going on around her; she assumes that her sister's interest, like hers, must all be in the baby. She also takes a rather flippant view on Casaubon's death, insisting that her sister cannot feel any grief for it, because he was dull and mean, and that was it. Celia is a good foil and counterbalance to Dorothea, but she can be just as flawed and silly too, although their flaws are quite opposite, and tend not to overlap.

After Dorothea is widowed, conceptions of gender once again intrude upon her life, and try to influence her course of action. Since it was not considered fit for women to live alone, without companions or guardians, she is entreated to move in with an older, widowed woman, or secretly people wish for her to marry again. Of course, Dorothea does not believe that she would be unable to get by without a man's help, or a wiser person's guidance; but still, gender roles play.into what is expected of her, and how she is told she must behave.

Dorothea has progressed in the sense that she is rejecting the life that her husband tried to force her into; she no longer has him to try vainly to please, and she begins to shake off his influence, and leave his life's work behind. Dorothea gets angry, in retrospect, at what went on in her marriage; and as she becomes more and more lonely because of Will's absence, Casaubon's memory and wishes lose their hold over her, a little at a time.

Dorothea only becomes her true self again when Will is finally back; but in their present states, nothing good can come of the meeting. Just as they need each other most, and should be speaking of their true feelings for each other, their communication becomes heated. Their separation shall be a major test of their relationship; if they can come to love each other sometime in the future, then they will surely remain together.

Chapter 55: Summary:

Dorothea seems more grieved at Will's departure than she was at her husband's death‹and rightly so, for she loved Will more than she ever loved her husband. She goes to Celia, where the company brings up the subject of marriage; it is openly suggested that Dorothea marry again, though that is the last thing Dorothea wishes. Dorothea decides to turn her attention toward public projects again, and will ask Caleb Garth's help in achieving her goals.

Analysis:

Once again, Dorothea is confronted with expectations of her gender; but yet again, she is able to resist, and do her own will rather than others. Dorothea realizes now that her ideas of gender roles, and of the duties of wives, did her no good in her marriage. She is not the kind of woman who can serve, and obey, and stay passive; she must follow her own will, and act freely, and make her own decisions, or else she will be as miserable as she was with Casaubon. Once Dorothea is able to act completely according to her own wishes, it is a good bet that she will be reunited with Will. Will seems to be the one passion that she has left, and she will only be truly happy if she is able to be with him.

Dorothea is finally returning to her old delights; her love for public improvements and helping others has become her chief concern, now that Will is gone. Youth is a resilient thing, that is another theme of this book; and though Dorothea has been widowed, lost her true love, and is besieged with suggestions about what a widow should and should not do, she is only twenty-one. Dorothea has already rebounded from the loss of her husband, and is not letting Will's absence weigh her down too much; Dorothea is of a much stronger, more resolute character than other women are acknowledged to be, and is proving herself to be a truly independent, different kind of woman.

Summary and Analysis of Chapters 56-66

Chapter 56: Summary:

Mr. Garth and Dorothea prove to be natural allies on the subject of improvements and social projects; Mr. Garth is very impressed With Dorothea's determination and her great mind, though Mrs. Garth is more concerned with her feminine virtues. Railroads are being built across England, and this becomes a topic in Middlemarch as the trains grow closer. Mr. Garth and Dorothea have nothing against them, and decide to sell an outer part of Dorothea's land to the railroads for a good price. Some men attack Caleb Garth and his assistant as they are doing some surveying for the railroad; they are as afraid of the unknown as anybody, but Caleb teaches them better.

Fred enjoys helping Caleb after his assistant is hurt; he asks Mr. Garth if perhaps he would be able to learn his business, though Caleb Garth believes that Fred is going to enter the clergy. Fred confides in him about his trepidation about entering the clergy, and his love for Mary and wishes to please her. Mr. Garth bears Fred no ill will about the debt he owes them, nor is he upset at Fred being in love with Mary; he decides to consult his wife about Fred becoming his helper, and about a possible match between Fred and Mary. Caleb decides to bring Fred into the business, and if he succeeds, then he is worthy of Mary as well. Fred tells his parents, who are disappointed at Fred's waste of education. They also lament Rosamond's marriage, which is seeming less attractive as Lydgate gets into more and more debt.

Analysis

Once again, the theme of progress vs. tradition comes into play for the citizens of Middlemarch, who are characteristically stubborn at first, but cannot hold out for too long. There is the typical huge outcry at the beginning of the debate; the few dissenters are condemned for their opinions, but opinion will have to change. Middlemarchers exercise their wonderful tendency to condemn something on only the most peripheral and sketchy of facts. But, as proud, foolish, and ignorant people, they will be proven wrong, as progress will not be ultimately hindered by the uniformed.

Caleb speaks against the ignorance and lies that have people up in arms about the railroad; he is too intelligent and discriminating to buy into any of it, though the masses are not. The group who attacks Caleb's assistant mask their fear with a show of aggression, just as others in Middlemarch hide their own trepidation with fighting words. It is a paradox inherent in the nature of everyone in the region; as they come to terms with the theme of progress vs. tradition, there is a great deal of fear to be faced and dealt with in ways that mask its existence.

Fred is finally proving good, thanks to his love for Mary; he is of a relatively honest, straightforward temperament, like Mary, and so their relationship has few of the troubles of Dorothea and Will's. Caleb sees Mary and Fred's courtship as being parallel to his courtship of his own wife. Though Fred shall not be rich, and is not completely deserving of Mary, he reminds Caleb Garth of himself, in his honesty, and his potential to become an industrious man. Their mutual love is also something that Caleb treasures; and once Caleb Garth has made up his mind that something should be done, it is.

Responsibility is a major theme in Fred's story, and it is something that he will have to learn if he is to have a profession, and Mary as his wife. But it is probably more like pride that is keeping Fred in his place with Mr. Garth; he cannot go to Mary and admit that he has failed, so he has to stick to his job, even when it displeases him. Pride is what allows him to tell his parents of his new job, without being crushed by their disapproval; and pride is why he has to stick to it, in order to prove that he is good for something.

At the same time, social divisions play into Fred's decision and his life; his father is upset because Fred is taking a position that is not considered suitable for one of his birth. Fred is somewhat disappointed at first too, that he will have neither the social standing nor economic standing that his parents had, and hoped him to have as well. Fred's marriage to Mary will also bring him down a little in the social hierarchy, which his mother laments; she believes she should marry someone of the same connections and money, but these are far from the only considerations that matter. Rosamond also made the same step, when she married Lydgate, who has few connections and little money; but where Fred can do without the money and the position, Rosamond cannot, and it will injure her vanity when she realizes she has to give up the living to which she is accustomed.

Chapter 57: Summary:

Fred has gone to the Garths, to consult them about his change in situation, and also to see if his wishes that Mary marry him are accepted by the family, and Mary as well. However, Mrs. Garth is still not assured of Fred's worth, and his character; yes, he means well, but he has never held a stable job or proven himself to be responsible. Mrs. Garth is still angry at Fred for the issue of his debt; but she cannot tell him directly, so she admonishes him for being unfeeling of others, and of having no regard for Farebrother's feelings for Mary too. Fred then thinks that it is very possible that Mary prefers Farebrother to him, and that Mary will become engaged to him; when Fred tells Mary this, Mary gets very upset at him. Mary thinks the allegation unfair, and scolds Fred for his jealousy; but, as many unpleasing qualities as Fred has, she cannot help but love him, and still plans to be married to Fred.

Analysis:

Fred and Christy Garth are indeed foils, as Eliot notes; while Fred displays all the signs of privilege, laziness, and irresponsibility, Christy is very much the opposite. Christy has all the qualities of industry and thrift that the Garths possess and respect; and Mrs. Garth's pride in her son, his achievements, and his character, show the kinds of qualities that the Garths treasure and find worthy. When directly juxtaposed with someone like Christy, Fred becomes less of an attractive prospect for a son-in-law to Mrs. Garth; he looks even less honorable and worthy than usual. The differences between Fred and Christy show the divide between Fred's upbringing, and the upbringing of the Garth children; there is much difference in their two families, which will give Fred some difficulty if he wants to prove worthy of Mary.

Mrs. Garth's metaphor for Fred's character and situation of "making a meal of a nightingale and never knowing it"‹shows her particular contempt for Fred's lack of responsibility. It is this thought which also begins to change her tone when she speaks to him; she becomes more bitter and fierce in what she says, trying to convey how Fred has hurt people like the Garths without feeling sorry for it, but without stating as much directly. At the same time, Mrs. Garth, like Fred's mother and father, has a soft spot for the boy; she soon relents, speaking with less accusatory words and a softer tone, though she wishes for Fred to still learn a valuable lesson.

The Garths' marriage is peculiar, especially when compared to other marriages in the book, like that of the Vincys, or of Dorothea and Casaubon. Mrs. Garth is allowed a great deal more latitude in making decisions for the household and guiding things along, and her husband is there as an occasional adviser and supporter. This system seems to work very well for the Garths, with Mrs. Garth intuitively knowing when her husband must be consulted on one matter or another. With the Vincys, Mr. Vincy is the official head of the household; when Mrs. Vincy wants things her way, she manipulates her husband into following her will‹not always healthy for a relationship. Casaubon and Dorothea were almost opposite of the Garths, with Casaubon assuming every responsibility, and dictating to Dorothea about what she should do, and how she should live. The Garths' marriage is definitely the healthiest found so far in the novel,and it is because both fulfill their duties and responsibilities, and do not overstep their unstated boundaries.

Fred, at this point, is still engaged in the process of becoming an independent adult. Though Mrs. Garth's suggestions that he does not think about other people really bother him, he is, foolishly, troubled more by the suggestion that Mary likes Farebrother best. It is ironic that Fred comes close to learning a lesson about being less selfish, and twists it around at the last to some sort of jealousy on his part. Fred still has much to learn, and he needs to have some faith in other people, rather than automatically assuming some sort of betrayal their part. Mary proves much more mature than Fred is at this moment; she has much that she can teach him, and probably will, since she loves him despite his failings.

Chapter 58: Summary:

She and Lydgate get a visit from his cousin, Captain Lydgate, which thrills Rosamond; Lydgate thinks his cousin foppish and stupid, and would rather him leave. Rosamond gets a little upset with Lydgate on this issue, though Lydgate insists he is not the only one who dislikes his cousin. Rosamond's baby is born premature because of an accident on a horse, and dies soon after; she would not have been riding if she had listened to her husband's advice, but stubbornly refused to listen to him. Lydgate is also troubled by his growing debt, especially since it was incurred buying things which he, though perhaps not Rosamond, could have done without.

Lydgate finally has to put up the furniture of the house as security against his debt; he tries to speak to Rosamond about keeping expenses down and buying less expensive things, but he is too soft-hearted to really tell her anything. Rosamond proves to be very silly and naïve, and even thinks to herself that she would not have married Lydgate if she knew he was to have little money, and that she could not have lived as she was used to. Rosamond decides to go and ask her father for money, against Lydgate's wishes; Lydgate is saddened that this issue will come up again and again, and he will have to struggle to keep Rosamond from wasting too much money.

Analysis:

Rosamond's favor for Captain Lydgate is based solely on her vanity. He flatters her, compliments her, and pays her a great deal of attention, which her husband seems not to do anymore; he fulfills Rosamond's need to be frequently attended to, increasing her contentment. Also, the fact that he is of higher rank and title means that Rosamond likes him even more for it; she is snobbishly proud of being visited by someone of higher rank than anyone she knows in Middlemarch. She still thrills in her husband's high connections and good birth, which also please her vain character. What made Rosamond love Lydgate in the first place was how he sated her vanity with flirtations, attentions, and compliments; but since this courtship behaviour is over, Rosamond might begin to feel that she doesn't care so much for him anymore, or that something is lacking in the union.

The other pillar of the union, Lydgate's pride, is also crumbling fast. He expected Rosamond to lavish her attentions and graces on him at all time, though that too was her courtship, and not her everyday, behaviour. He wants to feel that his wife honors and loves him above all, but her show of pleasantness toward Captain Lydgate, coupled with her less pleasant behaviour toward her husband, is quickly deflating his pride.

Also, the fact that she is making decisions for herself which are contrary to her husband's wishes, as when she goes horseback riding without his permission, is lessening his pride because he sees that he is not the real leader of the household that he suspected he would be. Once these two can no longer feed their flaws through each other's attentions and presence, the union will have nothing left on which to stand.

Mrs. Bulstrode's predictions about the union are coming true; Rosamond's expensive tastes have gotten Lydgate into trouble, and he does not know how to get her to stop. Lydgate is about as good with money as Fred is, but unlike Fred, he will not stoop to asking anyone's help with the matter. Lydgate had let Rosamond do as she wished with the household, trusting that she would do things sensibly, with an eye for their situation; however, Lydgate finds that Rosamond is an exceedingly impractical creature in more than one sense, which causes him great pain. At the same time, pride causes him to try and protect her from what is happening, and not to disappoint her too much in her new living.

Rosamond and her brother Fred are much alike in the ways they view money; money is something that they take for granted that they have, and they believe they should be able to afford anything they wish. Money is a major theme, and decisive element, in both of their stories, but Fred is forced to learn his errors, and Rosamond is not. Fred, as a man, has to try and make his own living, and is also forced to realise the consequences of his dependence on others to pay his debts.

However, Rosamond does not learn, because she is not a man; her husband makes the living, not her, and she has no conception of the value of money. Rosamond needs to see that her preferred way of living is getting her husband into deep debt, rather than be protected from her foolishness. But, Lydgate's pride, and his love for his ornamental bride, keep him from teaching her a very necessary lesson.

Lydgate chose to marry Rosamond because she was charming, beautiful, knew the appropriate arts and music, and had social graces; Rosamond is all the things that a proper young lady should be, and everything that society tries to force women to be. But, women who are near to the ideal, like Rosamond is, also have no capacity for anything practical or serious; it is as if society wants them to be helpless, and wants to keep them from being complete human beings.

Lydgate realizes that he might have been mistaken in choosing her, because the ideal in society is not necessarily the ideal for him. He thinks of Dorothea, who, though unconventional, would be intelligent, sensitive, and practical enough to be a good wife to a man like him. Rosamond too married Lydgate because he was an ideal‹attentive, intelligent, attractive, etc.

But though Rosamond and Lydgate are ideal models in many ways, this doesn't mean that they have any of the qualities necessary to make a life together. In searching out society's ideal, rather than someone who was a good fit for them personally, they have condemned themselves to a poor marriage, and a great deal of disappointment throughout their lives.

Chapter 59: Summary:

Gossip has gone around the neighborhood about the codicil in Casaubon's will; Fred finds out about it from the Farebrothers, and then proceeds to tell his sister. Rosamond is profoundly silly, and decides, unwisely, to tease Will about knowing something he doesn't, then make a joke of it all. Will grasps what she means to say, and gets the truth out of her; Rosamond still tries to spin the whole thing in lighthearted way, but Will is very upset, and perhaps understands more about Dorothea's behaviour.

Analysis:

Will's strong feelings on hearing about the will foreshadows another meeting, and perhaps the continuation of his friendship, with Dorothea. Finally, he has found out why she has acted as she has, and it is due to the influence of her dead husband, not her own wishes. The will, as a symbol of Casaubon's ill-motivated desires, is likely to fail very soon. Now that Casaubon is dead, Will and Dorothea's affection has far more force than his words in a document, and hopefully, they shall disregard the document entirely, and do as they are prompted by their feelings to do.

Chapter 60: Summary:

Mr. Larcher, one of the wealthiest people in Middlemarch, is auctioning off some furniture he does not need before he moves into a new, bigger, furnished home. The event is like a carnival, with everyone in Middlemarch in attendance; there is plenty of food and drink, drink especially so that people might make higher bids for things.

Not everybody buys things, but everyone is there for this social, outdoor occasion anyway. Will is asked by Mr. Bulstrode to go and acquire a particular painting for him; Will goes, though he is determined to leave the town soon. Still, Will does not want to leave without seeing Dorothea again, so his departure will have to wait on that.

A good many things are sold before the particular painting comes up; Will bids for the painting, and gets it for the Bulstrodes for a decent bit of money. Mr. Raffles turns up there, having found Will Ladislaw by inquiring somehow; Will is a bit put-off by him, and Mr. Raffles starts speaking of Will's family. Will cannot tell what Raffles' intentions are, so he gets away, and tries to forget about him; but it seems that Raffles has some less-than-desirable stories to tell about Will's family, which gives Will even more of a reason to leave, before stories like those could besmirch his name even more.

Analysis:

Though Will has been in Middlemarch for a good time, still there are prejudices against him, based on his social standing and his politics. Casaubon's will has not helped his situation any either, and as news of the codicil has spread around, people have assumed that Will must be out for Dorothea's money, or someone of no account. They do not consider that the codicil said more about Casaubon's insecurity or meanness than Will's character, simply because Casaubon had money, and had lived in Middlemarch for some time. Social prejudice is still a theme that has much bearing on Will's story at this point, though Will tries his best to ignore it and go about his business.

The re-emergence of Raffles means that his position as a threat to Bulstrode has not been avoided; his presence foreshadows a future importance for him, and perhaps that he might blacken Bulstrode's name a bit. But Raffles' possible intentions toward Will are something of a mystery; yes, Raffles knew Will's parents and something of his family, but why would this be so important that Raffles feel the need to track Will down? Perhaps Raffles means to blackmail Will with something too, though from his almost cordial demeanor, this seems unlikely.

Chapter 61: Summary:

Sure enough, Raffles has been back to Bulstrode's home, and refuses to go away until Bulstrode sees him. Raffles finds Bulstrode at the bank, as he tells his wife; but he is afraid to tell his wife much, lest she lose her confidence in him. It is revealed that Bulstrode married Will's maternal grandmother, after hiding from her that her daughter, Will's mother, was alive and had a son that the grandmother's riches were supposed to go to. However, Bulstrode prevented this from happening, for his own sake; and when the woman died, Bulstrode was left with the entire fortune, and Will and his mother with none. Bulstrode was also involved in various questionable trades, and these are the things that could destroy his reputation in Middlemarch. Bulstrode decides that he must do something to satisfy fate, and slow his own demise; he decides to speak to Will Ladislaw, and perhaps set things straight with him.

Will, however, is still unsettled by being approached by Raffles. He is shocked to discover the tenuous relation between Bulstrode and himself, and even more shocked when Bulstrode goes on to claim that he wants to be generous toward Will. Bulstrode tries to make it sound as if he is doing something out of generosity and his natural goodness, though it is more out of guilt and the thought that this good deed might save him. However, Will knows that Bulstrode made his money in a dishonest way, and is too proud to accept money from him, especially since that money is tainted by Bulstrode's wrongs. Bulstrode is saddened by the judgment on him, but is aware that Will won't tell anyone.

Analysis:

Unfortunately for Bulstrode, his troubles with Raffles are not quite over. Bulstrode is hardly a victim, however; he engaged himself in questionable business, including the selling of stolen property, so that he could gain money. But this, and the marriage and deception of Will's grandmother, Bulstrode tries to attribute to being God's wishes; he uses false piety as an excuse for the wrong things that he has done, and now he is going to pay. The lies and deceptions that have bound Bulstrode's sinful days to his honest ones in Middlemarch are coming apart; and, Raffles' continuing presence foreshadows a comeuppance for Bulstrode if he fails to appease Raffles.

Bulstrode and Will are juxtaposed in this Chapter, in both morals and attitude. Bulstrode's weak character and avarice are juxtaposed with Will's strength, honor, and disregard for money if he hasn't earned it. Both of the men present opposite fronts; Bulstrode tries his best to appear benevolent and generous, while Will is proud, curt, and merciless.

Just as Bulstrode once justified taking tainted money through piety, now he is trying to absolve himself by making a show of generosity and righteousness before Will. Bulstrode hasn't really changed; in both cases, he is trying to cover up his stark self-interest, selfishness, and greed by making a show of his goodness and justness. For Bulstrode to truly be absolved, he would probably have to confess his wrongs, and then try and live out his life. His trying to gain absolution through another self-serving act is truly a paradox, and backfires completely on Bulstrode.

Chapter 62: Summary:

Will sends a letter to Dorothea, saying that he cannot leave Middlemarch until he has seen her again. He already declared that he was leaving two months before, which is a point of suspicion with Sir James, who guards Dorothea jealously. Dorothea, however, is out when the letter comes, preparing for Mr. Brooke to come back to the Grange. She goes to Freshitt, to speak to her sister and Sir James, and Sir James tries to take the opportunity to dissuade Dorothea from seeing Will again. He and Mrs. Cadwallader make a few unkind remarks about Will, which makes Dorothea angry, and she goes home to find Will there, looking for some sketches he had left.

Will tells Dorothea that he knows about Casaubon's will, and Dorothea tries to reassure him that it had nothing to do with her wishes. Will gets angry at her about the whole thing, and says that everything prevents him from being with her. Dorothea realizes that he has acted honorably in every possible way, and is glad for this; but still, she is unable to show any signs that she loves Will, and he goes without this assurance.

Analysis:

Sir James' behaviour with regard to Dorothea is very odd; he is more jealous on her account, and more protective, than he seems to be with any matters regarding his wife. Perhaps Dorothea does need someone to guide and advise her, but why Sir James takes up this role without Dorothea's direct involvement, indicates something a little strange in his character. His animosity toward Will is almost as great as Casaubon's was, though it is based only on suspicion and no tangible reasons at all. It is ironic that Sir James is more possessive about his wife's sister than his wife, but then again,

Dorothea seems to be vulnerable in ways that Celia, with all her sensibilities, could never be.

With some irony, it is Sir James' attempts to keep Dorothea away from Will that only gain her anger. When Sir James and Mrs. Cadwallader speak of Will in condescending, scornful tones, it is too much for Dorothea; her love is still strong, and cannot bear their allegations. Dorothea is jealous when they gossip that Will and Rosamond are perhaps in love; her jealousy conveys how strong her feelings are, and her anger toward them at saying such things only confirms this.

Pride is a trait that Will and Dorothea both possess in abundance; and pride is the theme in the story which keeps them apart at this particular point. Will's pride keeps him from inviting more scorn from the community by staying with Dorothea, and from saying that he loves her because then she will have the upper hand if she does not. Dorothea is too proud also to admit her love for him, or to try and give him the financial support he deserves; she does not want to stoop to him, or lose her advantages, so she withholds her affections. However, Dorothea is also proud of Will, of his honor, and this strengthens her regard for him; pride is a thing of paradox in Will and Dorothea's relationship, at once conspiring to keep them apart, and then bring them together.

The strong feelings that persist after they part foreshadows a later meeting, especially since Dorothea is satisfied in knowing that Will is honorable and trustworthy. Their parting was not necessarily a friendly one, but it did not do great damage either. And, when love and longing begins to overpower pride on both of their accounts, it seems certain that they will end up together once again. Fate is a theme running through the book, that also seems to be something that is used to shape the narrative itself; and when fate is at work, a couple so suited to each other as Will and Dorothea cannot be left torn apart.

Chapter 63: Summary:

Farebrother notices some talk of Lydgate's practice declining, how his expenses much be more than he can really afford, and how he shouldn't have married a girl of such fine tastes. Farebrother really makes nothing of this talk, until he sees Lydgate again, and notices how nervous and strange his friend is acting. All are invited to a dinner party at the Vincys, and there seems to be some strain in Lydgate and Rosamond's marriage; she tries her best to ignore him, and they are not speaking at all. Even Rosamond's father is avoiding Lydgate. Farebrother, Fred, and Mary are all there, which means that Fred is worried about Mary liking Farebrother; Mrs. Vincy hopes that Farebrother and Mary will become engaged, because she doesn't want such a plain girl as a daughter-in-law.

Analysis:

In this Chapter, it seems that many different threads of the story and many different individual agendas become tangled up when so many different people are in one room. Eliot uses this Chapter to make clear how one person's actions can affect the fate of another; indeed, Middlemarch is such a small place, that any significant action has an impact on others in the community. This interconnection and interdependence is another theme of the novel, showing how individuals cannot avoid but be impacted by the community at large.

Various themes in the novel come into play at this simple dinner party; Lydgate's pride again hinders him from getting help from a trusted friend, and Rosamond's vanity prevents her from acknowledging the husband who has so lately spoken to her about money matters. Fred's jealousy over Mary and her possible regard for Farebrother rises up again; Mrs. Vincy's own pride prevents her from thinking of Mary Garth seriously, as a possible daughter-in-law.

Farebrother's geniality and good-will is spread around the room, but still, there are people who are reluctant to embrace him; most notably, Fred, because of the Mary issue, but Lydgate also becomes more distant when Farebrother offers help, and begins to speak about money. Many issues involving these people are waiting to be resolved; but when they are, it is likely that their decisions will affect other people in

Middlemarch, perhaps even the people they were around at the party.

Chapter 64: Summary:

Lydgate's money situation is certainly not getting any better, and Rosamond is very sour and inconsiderate whenever he mentions cutting down household expenses. He begins to resent the fact that she will not learn that they only have a limited amount of money, and cannot spend any more; she pouts like a sullen child, and acts like he has all the money in the world, he is only too mean to spend it on her. He decides that they should sell the house and the furniture, and move somewhere cheaper to live; Rosamond, of course, takes badly to this suggestion. Ned Plymdale is to be married, and Ned's mother rubs in that Ned has a lot more money than Lydgate, meaning that Rosamond was wrong to turn him down.

Rosamond decides to handle matters herself; she makes sure that the house cannot be sold to Ned Plymdale as her husband wishes, and writes his relatives for money without telling him. She tells her husband that she stopped the sale of the house, but not about the letters; Lydgate realizes that she will be unhappy if they move, and dreads that. He decides to apply to his rich uncle for money, not knowing that his wife has already done so.

Analysis:

One of Lydgate's problems is that he believes that life is more than everyday struggles, and attempting to make ends meet. His vision is that his life should be spent in curing diseases, making medical advances, and taking notable steps forward in his practice. Instead, he is greeted by the same backward patients, has to beg for balances to be paid in a timely manner, and worry ceaselessly about money, an issue on which his wife is less than sympathetic. Lydgate truly resents the issue of money because it is keeping him from what he thinks life is; life to him isn't worrying that your furniture will be taken if you default on a debt, or endlessly lecturing your wife about the need to cut costs. These ideas about life are part of the theme of greatness in achievement running throughout Lydgate's life, that Lydgate seems very unwilling to abandon.

The money problems that Lydgate and Rosamond are experiencing mark the start of the end of their relationship. Money is the one factor that can effectively set Rosamond's vanity and Lydgate's pride at odds with each other, thus hurting the two pillars of the relationship. Lydgate becomes almost like a thing, a strange symbol to Dorothea; he represents how her world is out of the order she wishes it to be in, and thinks that if she can just say the right thing, it will all be fine again. Lydgate, to her, is the originator and the source of all their money problems, a view that is both filled with irony, and not totally correct; he should work harder, he should ask his relatives for loans, according to her. Rosamond has never had to take responsibility for anything in her life, and if Lydgate tries to make her do so, he will become a symbol of even greater unpleasantness to her.

Eliot compares their marriage to a "delicate crystal," with that metaphor conveying the fragility, and marred beauty, of the relationship.

Rosamond begins to act out of bitterness and anger toward her husband; ironically, it is his behaviour which becomes inexcusable, though hers is all the more reprehensible. Her husband cares for her, though there are certain unpleasant things which must be done; Rosamond seems not to care for Lydgate one bit, as she tries to keep the house from being sold, and then defies his explicitly stated wishes. A more caring person would at least consult their spouse, and try to work out of the situation together; Rosamond's position is one of ruthless sabotage, of her husband's plans, and his pride as well. Rosamond's character is a good example of an appearance vs. reality theme at work in the book, and of the treachery that can come from greed and vanity.

Both Rosamond and Lydgate are finding out the terrible truth, that pleasant moments and occasional courtship have nothing to do with living together from day to day. Rosamond basically says to Lydgate that she married him because she imagined they would live well, with plenty of money, and be very happy that way. She dislikes almost every personal aspect of him; he is not nearly so harsh, though sometimes he can hardly stand the pressure she puts on him.

Chapter 65: Summary:

Lydgate finds out, from a letter written by his uncle Godwin, that Rosamond wrote him for money behind his back. Lydgate is enraged that Rosamond would do such a thing, and also because he was about to go to see his uncle, and may have gotten some money, rather than a complete denial. However, when Lydgate gets angry at her for deceiving him and playing him false, she does what she always does‹look pretty, shed a tear, and act with composure. Lydgate is weakened by this, meaning that he will always be in debt, and will allow his wife to be selfish, stupid, and vain, even if it means their financial ruin. Rosamond hits new lows of shallowness when she proclaims that she would rather have died in childbirth than have to give up her house and furniture.

Analysis:

Again, Rosamond displays the ironic view that she is to blame for nothing, simply because she has never lost her composure, and always expresses herself with the proper calmness. Rosamond is again shown as a creature of complete naivete, stupidity, and destructive stubbornness; why Lydgate prefers the desperation of financial ruin to correcting his wife's faults and thus healing the marriage, is an odd paradox which cannot be answered. Lydgate was very foolish in choosing Rosamond as a wife; and Rosamond has found someone she can manipulate and control completely, in Lydgate. Indeed, when she raves on, in a very ridiculous, self-important tone, about how he is making her life difficult, how he is responsible for their hardship, it is obvious that she is more to blame for the situation than anybody. However, Lydgate remains completely taken in, which means that he will soon be in a great deal of trouble, and the marriage will be in an even worse state than before.

Chapter 66: Summary:

Lydgate, out of desperation for money and foolish hope that some will come to him, begins to gamble. Usually this is something which he treats with contempt, but in the situation he is in, he decides to go to the Green Dragon and play billiards. He is very good at first, winning a good bit of money; Fred Vincy and a friend come in, and Fred is surprised, and displeased, to find his brother-in-law there. Fred has been working hard for six months and spending little, and figures he has a little bit to spare at gambling; but when he sees Lydgate there, he thinks better of it. Lydgate's luck changes and he begins to lose, and Fred is good enough to draw him away, and suggest that they see Farebrother, who is right downstairs.Farebrother is there to speak to Fred rather than Lydgate; he tells Fred not to slip back into his old ways, lest he lose Mary and his position with Mr. Garth. He says that he, too, loves Mary, and that if Fred messes things up this time, he is not sure to win Mary back. Farebrother does not mean that he will steal Mary, he is simply warning Fred that he should try to deserve her, and make her happy too. Fred takes the point, and hopefully will try to be more careful and more devoted to her.

Analysis:

It seems that Lydgate is falling into the same trap that Fred did, only with greater need and desperation. It is likely that he will end up in the same kind of situation as well; with such need and drive as he has, he is likely to go on betting more and more until he has finally lost it all. There are other parallels between Lydgate's situation and Fred's former one; neither truly know the value of money, preferring to have faith that chance will bring them funds where more respectable means have failed. Both are acting out of a great irresponsibility, Lydgate even more so; he is already deeply in debt and, unlike Fred, does not have anyone who could possibly afford to bail him out.Lydgate and Fred become almost reversed in this encounter; usually they are juxtaposed against each other, Lydgate as a more stern, responsible man, and Fred as a flighty youth. However, the circumstances of both men have changed greatly; they are still juxtaposed in this moment, but Lydgate has become fiercely excited, desperate, while Fred is the one who is reticent and responsible. It is ironic that the less responsible of the two would be the conscience of the situation, and that the one of them with more to lose is gambling more than he can afford. But, these reversals of fate are not unknown in Middlemarch, and will certainly happen again.

The interconnection of so many things in Middlemarch is a theme which again surfaces here; Fred's hopes and Farebrother's hopes are directly at odds for each other, and actions on either part might affect who ends up with Mary Garth. Farebrother seems to expose some of the contrary aspects of his personality; his tone becomes dark and threatening when he speaks of their conflict of interest, and how Fred could possibly foul his situation up. Mary becomes a symbol of righteousness and goodness to both of them, something valuable to be won and treasured; once Fred is reassured in this, he decides to be more considerate and disciplined so he can win her.

Farebrother seems something of a paradox for a brief moment; although he is a trusted advisor and friend to many, here he pretends that vicious self-interest has been threatening to prevail. Was Farebrother really so ready to betray as he pretends? It is not completely clear, though it is certain that Farebrother, though he is a good man, is certainly not a saint through and through.

Summary and Analysis of Chapters 67-77

Chapter 67: Summary:

Luckily, after losing at the Green Dragon, Lydgate feels no more desire to gamble. But, he is still in danger of losing his furniture because of his debt, and decides that he must apply to Bulstrode for money. Lydgate delays; and soon, Bulstrode has called on him to see to some health concerns of his. Bulstrode is feeling unwell probably because of the Raffles situation; but he also wants to speak of Lydgate about withdrawing his support from the hospital and moving away.

Mrs. Casaubon, he says, would take his place as major supporter, though it would be best to merge the old Infirmary with the new hospital. Lydgate objects, because he knows that the people who run the Infirmary dislike him. Then, he takes the plunge, and tells Bulstrode that he needs a thousand pounds to discharge his debts and keep himself going; Bulstrode says that it would be better to declare bankruptcy, which Lydgate resents. Lydgate is still left with no way out, and his debt to the town trades people is very nearly due.

Analysis

Lydgate is finally getting over his one major stumbling block‹his pride‹in order to do something about his debt. But pride, as the predominant theme of Lydgate's story and character, will not be so easy to overcome; how will Lydgate feel afterward if he has gotten the money? The debt has become a symbol of correction, for its sole purpose seems to be to rid Lydgate of his excessive pride, and get him to be more practical and straightforward. But, the irony is that Lydgate must apply to the one man he does not want to be any more beholden to; people wrongly consider Lydgate and Bulstrode closely allied, though they are not too much related. Another irony is that Bulstrode was one of the major causes that Lydgate's practice was much diminished; but, Lydgate chose to work with Bulstrode on the new hospital, so he certainly doesn't count as a victim in this case.

Lydgate does dismiss his pride, to the extent that he admits his situation to Bulstrode; however, it is still weighing him down, as he refuses stubbornly to allow the new hospital and the infirmary to merge, and also to declare bankruptcy, when that is what he should do. If Lydgate could focus on doing the right things to help his situation, maybe he could get through it and be fine. But then, there is the issue of Rosamond, who has also been like deadweight to him; he wants to make her happy, but when the only way to do so is to surround her with expensive things, he will surely fail.

Chapter 68: Summary:

Raffles comes again to Bulstrode's, and Bulstrode must

let him stay at the house for fear that he might go into the town and tell people about Bulstrode's story. Bulstrode tries his best to conceal who the man is and what he is doing there from his wife, but he still causes alarm throughout the household; his wife may not know exactly who Raffles is, but surely she has some idea that he is a friend from Bulstrode's less honest past. Bulstrode tells Raffles that he may get money from Bulstrode as long as he does not come back to Middlemarch; he takes Raffles to a nearby town, gives him money, and tells him to leave. He knows this might not be a permanent solution, but it is the best that Bulstrode can come up with at this given time.

Bulstrode tries to dispose of all his businesses and such, including the bank; he also gives Caleb Garth the management of Stone Court in his absence. Caleb, in turn, sees that it could be a good opportunity for Fred to learn more about the business, and gain his own experience; Mrs. Garth is a bit wary, but Caleb is decided. Fred is also allowed to live at Stone Court while he manages it, and hopefully will be able to afford to wed Mary sometime soon.

Analysis:

It seems that there is a growing paradox inherent in Bulstrode's situation; the more he is secretive and underhanded about his past, the worse he will look when the whole truth comes out. Mrs. Bulstrode, though she does not know the whole truth, already knows enough from her husband's behaviour to have some idea of what he is up to. Also, his attempts to cover things up and move away will probably look even more suspicious than if he had stayed. Either way, the harm to his marriage will be irreparable; and his feeble attempts to save himself cannot really stop what is coming.

Will Bulstrode be able to avoid the workings of fate? It seems that no character in the novel can escape without learning some lesson; even those who are mildly flawed, like Lydgate, find themselves in very trying situations. It is doubtful, considering the great trials that a good person like

Dorothea has had to undergo, that Bulstrode, with sins greater than almost anyone else's in the novel, could escape unscathed. Once again, fate is a major theme in the novel, and correction of flaws seems to be another related one; many of the characters in this novel have been placed in situations where it is certain that their faults will be tried, and hopefully, ironed out.

The only positive that seems to be inherent in Bulstrode's situation is that it will give Fred a chance to prove himself, with the management of Stone Court. Either Fred is going to fail miserably, or succeed admirably; and his performance with the Stone Court assignment will probably determine whether he ends up with Mary or not. Hopefully, Fred has heeded Farebrother's lesson well, and has succeeded in reforming himself into a more industrious, responsible person. It seems that Fred has done well so far, and perhaps marriage to Mary will be enough incentive to keep him going.

Chapter 69: Summary:

Mr. Garth comes to Bulstrode, to tell him that he found Raffles, very ill, near Stone Court; Raffles asks for a doctor, but also told Mr. Garth some things about Bulstrode. On account of these things, Caleb Garth says that he can no longer manage any of Bulstrode's property, and must give up the appointment to manage Stone Court as well. However, Caleb says, he will not spread around anything that he heard. Bulstrode then believes that all has happened with the aid of providence, and that Raffles might die, and leave him in peace.

Lydgate sees Raffles, and determines that though the case is grave, yet Raffles will probably survive. He decides that it must be a case of an alcohol-caused disease, and that Raffles must be an odd charity case for Bulstrode. There seems to be no escape from ruin for Lydgate; the furniture is about to be taken for his debts, and his relationship with Rosamond is in shreds because of it. Lydgate cannot stand Rosamond's repeated crying, and blaming him for her unhappiness. Now, he wishes he had married a woman of a like mind and spirit, so that their union might have survived this setback; instead, he is chained to Rosamond, when the union can no longer make either of them happy.

Analysis:

It seems that Bulstrode's downfall has already begun, though Caleb Garth is certainly too honorable to act as a catalyst. The juxtaposition of Caleb Garth and Bulstrode only serves to make Bulstrode look blacker, more manipulative; Caleb Garth looks all the more honorable in comparison. That Bulstrode tries to tell Caleb Garth that what Raffles might have said is untrue, and not to believe him over a neighbour, speaks even more poorly of Bulstrode's character. But, it is lucky for Caleb Garth that he refuses to get entangled with someone whose personal effects are so much in doubt.

That Raffles would dare come back to Middlemarch, and also spread the truth about Bulstrode, means that he is after more than just money. This event marks, and foreshadows, the end for Bulstrode. By this time, Raffles has become a symbol of disgrace and doom for him, rather than a person; thoughts about Raffles coming and his statements bringing Bulstrode down haunt him constantly. Raffles personifies all of Bulstrode's fears at this moment, and is sure to cause disgrace at any time. Caleb Garth becomes also a symbol, of providence; Bulstrode believes that Raffles was meant to run into Mr. Garth, and tell his story only to the one person who would not repeat it. Caleb will certainly do nothing to hasten Bulstrode's fall, but Raffles is still not neutralized as a potent threat.

Bulstrode's thoughts that he still might be saved, and Raffles' illness and his meeting with Caleb Garth arranged so that he might suffer no longer. This view is sure to prove an irony, the last hopeful wish of a fallen man. Also ironic is Lydgate's view that Bulstrode's friend Raffles is someone to whom he has chosen to show charity and kindness, to the neglect of "deserving" people like Lydgate. Bulstrode is not generous enough to show interest where there is no benefit to him; Lydgate assumes too kindly of Bulstrode, but also tries to blame his own troubles on him.

Lydgate finally repents of marrying Rosamond, as it is certain that there marriage will never be a happy one, unless he manages somehow to get rich. He finally sees that a man should marry someone whom he has things in common with, who he gets along with well and who is good company and conversation always. But, there is of course irony in this, as it is too late for Lydgate's wisdom to be of any use. His tone, when he speaks to Rosamond, becomes bitter and resentful; hers does the same. Everything around them seems unpleasant, as the thought of living without money upsets Rosamond more than anything, and Rosamond's blame and materialism in turn upsets Lydgate.

Chapter 70: Summary:

Bulstrode is with Raffles, tending to him according to Lydgate's orders, though wishing at the same time that Raffles would just die and leave him in peace. Bulstrode still thinks that fate is on his side, that Raffles will die and he will be free; he is not sorry for anything he has done, but is more intent on getting away with everything. Bulstrode decides that maybe another "good" deed will save him; he decides to give Lydgate the money he needs, thinking that this action will clear his conscience, and in case Raffles says something unpalatable, Lydgate will be obligated not to repeat it.

Raffles dies only a few days after coming to Bulstrode; Lydgate is there when he dies, and does not think to say that perhaps neglect led somehow to the man's death. Lydgate knows he is obligated to Bulstrode, and he is uneasy about this fact, because of Bulstrode's visitor and his demise. However, there is nothing else that he can do, since to renounce Bulstrode's help would mean ruin. Farebrother senses that Lydgate is still in a desperate condition, though his money woes are over. Lydgate admits as much, though he is now in a better position to continue his career and marriage.

Analysis:

The revelation that Bulstrode is not at all penitent just about says that he will not escape from punishment for what he has done. Bulstrode has tempted fate, through his pride, arrogance, and unwillingness to admit to himself or anyone else that wrong has been done. He has not learned any lessons yet, but he will have to before his story is done. Even now his conscience is getting heavy, which is a sign that perhaps redemption is possible. But, that he buys Lydgate's future silence with the thousand-pound loan means that Bulstrode still refuses to reform, even under threat of ruin. He still only acts with a show of benevolence when it is in his best interests, which shows that he has not really changed at all.

Bulstrode's behaviour upon Raffles' death also shows a great want for change. He never thinks to himself that his days of dishonesty are done, or that he will reform now that he has been spared. Indeed, Bulstrode will have to keep up the charade with his family, in trying to move them elsewhere, and in explaining falsely who the dead man is, and why he was there. Bulstrode seems determined as ever to profit from his good fortune, at the expense of others' misfortune; but surely, fate has surprises in store for him yet.

The main question that comes out of this Chapter, is whether Lydgate will manage to recover from his debt using the loan from Bulstrode, or whether Rosamond will continue to drive them into debt once more. Hopefully, Lydgate has had all the warning he needs about lacking money, and the desperation that comes with it. However, entangling himself with Bulstrode in such a compromising way can hardly come to good, and may damage Lydgate's practice and reputation even further.

Chapter 71: Summary:

It seems that Bulstrode has not effectively thwarted ruin; for Bambridge has heard how Bulstrode gained his fortune, and is ready to tell the lot of men at the Green Dragon. The story begins at this point to spread around Middlemarch, with mention of Will Ladislaw's family and how they were robbed by him too. When Bambridge mentions that the man's name was Raffles, someone present remembers that the funeral of Raffles was only the other day, that he died at Stone Court while Bulstrode was there. This looks very bad for Bulstrode; Caleb Garth confesses that he ceased all business with Bulstrode last week, which is taken as another proof of Bulstrode's wrong behaviour. Also, gossip about Lydgate suddenly being able to pay his debt, but without aid from Rosamond's family, becomes public knowledge. When it is found out that he was attending on Raffles while he died, and that the money came from Bulstrode, it appears that Lydgate took a bribe so that he wouldn't tell of any foul play that happened.

All of Middlemarch is buzzing with the gossip, and people wonder whether Bulstrode can be legally stripped of his money for gaining it through illegal and immoral means. People guess that Lydgate poisoned Raffles, with the money as a bribe; all kinds of things are flying around, and have been spread all through Middlemarch before Lydgate and Bulstrode are even aware of it. Bulstrode is accused at a medical meeting, and again tries to defend himself through his services to the town. But Middlemarch opinion is against him, and believes Lydgate to be an accomplice. However, Dorothea would not see Lydgate slandered if such things proved untrue, and is determined to get the truth about the whole thing.

Analysis:

Once again, the workings of Middlemarch are laid bare, and shown in greater detail and clearness than in previous Chapters. Eliot shows how a few words from one person can set an inquisition going against a member of the society; again, rumors and stories are credited as fact, and there are things that are true and untrue in the reports against Bulstrode. People's conjecture is also credited with having the force of truth, as people figure that Bulstrode must have bribed Lydgate, and then start to believe this as fervently as if it were proven fact. Without the aid of a judge and jury, Middlemarch has already condemned Bulstrode and Lydgate; and even if they can come up with some kind of defence, it seems that their names will be blackened forever in that region.

Lydgate's pride, at this point, has almost been too harshly

punished; he is certainly innocent of wrongdoing, and can be excused for not making the same inquiry of Bulstrode on such a difficult case. But will Lydgate be condemned, along with Bulstrode? The outcome is still somewhat unclear, and though it is possible that Lydgate may indeed be exonerated by Dorothea's kind help, it is likely that his practice will be reduced to nothing, and he will continue to struggle for a living.

Chapter 72: Summary:

Dorothea is set on proving Lydgate innocent, though this may prove difficult. Farebrother would certainly like to help, but he knows from the alteration and desperation in Lydgate's character of late, that is it completely likely that Lydgate did take the bribe, to save himself. Farebrother does not blame Lydgate, but at the same time knows how good people may be tempted, and fail. Sir James is definitely against Dorothea having anything to do with this issue; but Dorothea is still determined to do a good turn for Lydgate, especially after he helped her so much when her husband died. Dorothea is not the sort of person to allow a friend to be wronged, unless he is really guilty of what he is accused of.

Analysis:

Here, gender relations are at work, as Dorothea struggles to get support for her plan. Gender roles are the main consideration in the men's refusal to let Dorothea go to Lydgate's aid; as a woman, she is necessarily too weak minded and unwise to be entrusted with such a great undertaking, which might have undesirable consequences. It is unfair that Dorothea's noble plan is dismissed outright, because of her gender and the misconceptions of women that help to sabotage her. This is one of the defining themes, and trials of Dorothea's life; to be herself, and do what she wishes, despite the limitations and ideas that belie her intelligence and strength as a woman. Celia may have a more conventional view, that women must submit to men unless they know that the men are wrong, but it is necessary for Dorothea to find her own ways, or risk losing herself as she did when she was married to Casaubon.

Chapter 73: Summary:

Lydgate is now faced with the heavy task of exonerating himself, for he stands accused among everyone in Middlemarch. He wants to be able to stand up and say that he did not take a bribe from Bulstrode, and had no complicity in Raffles' death. However, his conscience troubles him, since he wonders if he would have acted differently in the situation had Bulstrode not given him the money. Lydgate determines not to run from the town's opinion, but to bear it with all possible strength; nothing he can do can clear his name now that public opinion is set against him, so he will have to weather it as best he can.

Analysis:

Lydgate shows that he is no longer a stranger to the workings of Middlemarch politics and society; but it is ironic and unjust that he be outcast for someone else's wrongs, and his wishes to do his duties. This situation might provide the final push to Lydgate, in his desire to be gone from the place; if his reputation is truly destroyed in the neighborhood, then his practice will become nonexistent.

Bulstrode's check has become a symbol of uneasiness for him; but he cannot decide whether it represents some failings on the part of his conscience and scruples, or the unfortunate entanglement of money in this situation. But, Lydgate's pride has not been checked by having to ask for aid from Bulstrode; indeed, it comes back in a rush to him. Lydgate's pride could still be his undoing, since it is his pride, more than any other consideration, which informs his decision. If Lydgate's pride steers him wrong once more, he and Rosamond may very well have to leave Middlemarch for good.

Chapter 74: Summary:

Now that Bulstrode and Lydgate have already been judged and condemned, it is the time for the wives of

Middlemarch to assess and judge how Mrs. Bulstrode and Rosamond might be to blame as well. Mrs. Bulstrode is acquitted of her husband's wrongdoing, because she is a good person, and all wrongs were done before they were even married. Rosamond is also pardoned for the most part, because she is also one of the Vincys, and has married an "interloper," as the townswomen say.

It takes Mrs. Bulstrode a while to find out what has happened with regard to her husband; she knows that he came home ill from the meeting, and seems much disturbed, but Lydgate will certainly not tell her why. Only through visiting her friends does she find out what has happened; her brother tells her everything, and she goes home, troubled at the knowledge. But though a light has been shed on her husband's character, she finds that there is no way for her to forsake him. She determines to try and live with him, and eventually to forgive him, though it will certainly be a long and painful time.

Analysis:

Without a trial or a judge, Bulstrode and Lydgate were found guilty, and shunned; now, the women of Middlemarch are convened to see if their wives deserve equal punishment. This is one of the quirks of small-town life, but it also reveals some of the less admirable tendencies of human nature; to judge others without mercy, be unwilling to forgive because of one's envy or other less honorable feelings, and to gossip viciously about others. At the same time, one person in a small town can inflict many wrongs, and do a great deal of damage; their measure is a mixture of necessary concern, and of vicious judgment too. Although Harriet Bulstrode really deserves none of the disgrace that she must be going through, the women are right in assuming that Rosamond needs a lesson. Lydgate has been too soft to correct her in matters of spending, materialism, and vanity; she desperately needs to be brought low, and reform her character. Vanity has been Rosamond's stumbling block for too long, and it has been too important a theme in her story and her actions; it is time she was through with it, and start to be more pleasant about having very little.

Mrs. Bulstrode proves all the positive appraisals about her character true; she resolves to be faithful to her husband and not desert him, but at the same time, is deeply grieved by what has happened. Mrs. Bulstrode is a very good, sensible woman, much more so than Rosamond could ever hope to be; she certainly does not deserve the lot she is in, nor did her husband deserve a wife like her. However, Mrs. Bulstrode shows her honor by choosing to keep to the vows she made at marriage; she is a much stronger woman than most, and deserves to be commended in how she handled this difficult situation.

Chapter 75: Summary:

It seems that Rosamond refuses to learn any lessons from her situation; to appease her vanity, she starts to think of Will Ladislaw, and imagines that he must love her instead of Dorothea, because she is so beautiful and charming. She continues to blame her husband for her unhappiness, not her rabid materialism; everything is someone else's fault, and she is still a creature who is perfectly innocent of blame. She gets a letter from Will, saying that he will be paying a visit sometime soon; Rosamond is cheered up by this, and decides to send out invitations for a dinner party. Of course, all invitations are denied, and Rosamond is still ignorant as to the reason why; she goes to visit her parents, and they tell her the terrible news. When she goes home, she tells her husband that she has heard about everything; she then reiterates that they must go to London, to lessen her suffering. He cannot stand to hear this, and storms out, without taking the time to correct her or explain anything.

Analysis:

It is a shame that Rosamond prefers to blame her husband for every fault she finds in marriage. To be more honest, Rosamond is just not suited to the necessities of marriage; even when she had all the material things she needed, still things were not to her liking. Rosamond lacks the ability to compromise with Lydgate on anything; either she gets her way and things are great, or she is denied, and she thinks him a terrible, hateful man. She thinks that it is his duty to make her happy, and always to be cheerful and pleasant himself; she gives no thought to how she might ease his worry, or make things better for him. She is unable to communicate, except to make demands, manipulate him into something, or to say something proper and charming to someone else; she is completely empty-headed, which means she can only serve as an ornament, and can do nothing that a real wife or woman could.

Rosamond's vanity has become like an addiction, almost like a drug; if her husband cannot satisfy her enough, or some charming young man, like Will or Captain Lydgate, cannot fill her needs, she will delude herself to the point where she believes that she is sated. Rosamond is a girl desperate for affection, attention, and approval; but what she really needs is correction, discipline, and impetus to change herself dramatically. What an irony, that the very quality that attracted Lydgate to Rosamond, and kept her bound to him during the courtship, is now proving to be their undoing.

With all that Lydgate and Rosamond have been through, it would have been hoped that they break through their communication barriers, and come to some understanding. Only Lydgate knows enough to know how to do this; but already, he regards his wife as a lost cause, and prefers that he suffer through her ignorance than take the easier step of talking to her about what is happening.

Lydgate and Rosamond's marriage seems oddly similar to the union of Casaubon and Dorothea. Lydgate's role is parallel to Dorothea's; both of them had the task of trying to soothe their spouse and make their spouse happy, though no amount of Herculean effort on their part ever seemed to suffice. Casaubon and Rosamond are parallel as spouses because they believe that it is their spouse's only job to please them. Both have very unreasonable expectations about what their spouse should do, and sacrifice, in order to satisfy their desires, which are sometimes very petty. Both of them believe in restrictive ideas of roles that each partner should play in marriage; but although they excuse themselves from their own marital duties, they believe that their partner should do twice as much in return.

Chapter 76: Summary:

Dorothea wrote a letter to Lydgate, bidding him to come and visit her. Against Mr. Brooke and Sir James' advice, she has decided to try and clear Lydgate, if she can, and also to continue and support the hospital as well. Lydgate begins to tell her the whole truth‹they are good friends, and often feel that they can confide in each other. He tells her everything about the situation with Bulstrode, the money, and his continuing reservations about having taken it. Dorothea and Lydgate also speak of his troubles in his marriage; Dorothea senses that there is much difficulty communicating in their union, and decides to see Rosamond, and try to reassure her about her husband's worth, if she can. Dorothea would like Lydgate to stay until the negative opinion of him in the town diminishes; she would also like to see the hospital continue, under his able leadership. Lydgate determines to leave, since he has little faith that he would be able to do good at the hospital. But, Dorothea is determined to have him stay and give him aid; she decides to give him a thousand pounds to work at the hospital, and to see Rosamond the next day.

Analysis:

Dorothea has truly matured and changed since her marriage to Casaubon a few years ago; her wish to help others has finally become a reality to her, as she now has the means, and the will, to accomplish whatever she wishes. She is more knowledgeable about how the world works, even about how Middlemarch works; it seems likely that if Lydgate stays and tends to the hospital, that he will be able to thrive sometime in the near future, as she says. Dorothea has a much bigger heart, and a much more epic sense of charity, than do so many other people in Middlemarch; that is why Sir James fears so much for her, because he thinks that she could be taken advantage of by the wrong person. Perhaps she could be, but Dorothea has sense enough to keep to people whom she has an intellectual and emotional connection with‹a bond that is not easily come by in a place like Middlemarch.

Dorothea and Lydgate are alike in more ways than just in their actions as spouses; they both have a sense that they could make big differences in the world, if they only have drive and care enough. Lydgate and Dorothea want to make things better for people in their community, and Lydgate, through medical discovery, wants to help scientific progress improve lives in a much larger arena. Their lives should be spent in trying to help as many people as they can, as they believe that they both have the capacity to bring great changes and health and happiness to a great number of people.

Chapter 77: Summary:

Rosamond has written a letter to Will, trying to make his visit come more quickly; she is still very unhappy with everything, and Lydgate has tried to avoid her, lest he upset her in some way. Dorothea has been thinking about Will a lot lately, as well; she still cannot help but think that he might be in love with her, though she also defends his honor fervently. Sir James and Mr. Brooke have tried to get her to see that Will is lowly, and the fact that his grandparents were Jewish pawnbrokers, though they were wealthy, means that his character is base. Dorothea, of course, will hear nothing of this; although she is not sure what Will's feelings toward her are, she is resolved to think the best of him.

However, when Dorothea gets to Rosamond's, she enters to find Rosamond crying, and Will clasping her hands. This scene upsets Dorothea, and seems to be proof that Will loves Rosamond, and not her. She rushes out, intent on attending to other errands, but still very upset and bothered by what has happened.

Analysis:

Dorothea is finally becoming herself, in the absence of any oppressive male presence, like Casaubon or Mr. Brooke. She is finally determined to live life on her own terms, and has forsaken all of society's rules about gender and women's limitations, two themes in the novel with which Dorothea struggled for some time. She no longer cares what people think of her unconventionality, or her wish never to be remarried; she knows that she has the ability to manage her own affairs, money, and property, though everyone else might think she needs a husband to do all of that for her.

Dorothea's kind character is shown to best effect in her care for Lydgate and Rosamond in their current situation. She looks past their flaws, to their good points when she appraises them; she gives both of them the benefit of the doubt in every possible way, and looks only to their misfortune. Perhaps she is overly kind and judicious in the way she regards them and resolves to help them. But at least she lacks the nasty, backstabbing tendencies and desire to believe the worst about people that so many other citizens of Middlemarch have.

Dorothea's strong, instinctive reaction upon seeing Will and Rosamond together is another confirmation of her very strong feelings for Will. If she merely regarded him as a friend, which she pretends to do, she would not feel the same shock and jealousy that came immediately to her when she saw them together. She would also not be filled as much with outraged energy that she could rush out and feel that she could do nearly anything. Hopefully, Will is able to sort out Dorothea's mistake, and correct her incorrect conclusions; but it seems that her good opinion of him is damaged, at least for the present.

Summary and Analysis of Chapters 78-Finale

Chapter 78: Summary:

Will and Rosamond are shocked at being found, and in a way that would look bad to Dorothea. Will realizes suddenly what Rosamond was trying to do; Rosamond wanted it to look like Will loved her, and kept him around in order to create this impression. He blows up at her, especially when she tries her methods that usually work on Lydgate. But her ways of quietly manipulating fail with Will; he gets very angry when she intimates that Will loves her, and says that the only woman he loves, or could think of loving, was Dorothea. Rosamond is very hurt, and her illusions and vanity are finally shattered. Will was a bit harsh toward her, but this was a lesson that she desperately needed, and hopefully it will do her good.

Analysis

Finally, Rosamond's vanity has backfired on her; for the first time, she has seen that not everyone she meets is instantly in love with her, and not all men find her irresistible. Her little fantasy of Will loving her over Dorothea has been shattered, and it is a very harsh, but very necessary blow to her. She needs to get over her vanity and become a real human being; but, chances are, she will only become more melancholy, and more blaming of her poor husband. How shallow Rosamond must be that one man saying that he loves someone other than her shatters her whole world, and makes her violently ill. But though her family and her husband will tolerate her and her delusions, the rest of the world will not, as she very reluctantly finds.

Will has never before expressed his love so forcefully or explicitly; this is a great step for him, meaning that he has gotten over his pride at last seeing her enough to admit openly that he loves her. Will wants to be with Dorothea more than ever, especially because she might be lost to him forever because of the little incident with Rosamond. But Will's drive, the force of his love, and Dorothea's love in return mean that in all likelihood they will end up together. Fate has a way of working among the people of Middlemarch, that hopefully will not leave a deserving couple like Will and Dorothea in want of love and happiness.

Chapter 79: Summary:

Lydgate puts Rosamond to bed, still not totally aware of what has caused her distress. Will comes over, but Rosamond has not mentioned Will's visit earlier in the day; Will makes no mention of it to Lydgate either. Lydgate tells Will a bit of what has been going on, and that his name has also been mixed up in the proceedings. Will is not surprised, and almost does not care, because he thinks that Dorothea has already given up on him. When Lydgate mentions Dorothea's name, he notices that Will has a very peculiar reaction; he suspects that there is something between the two, and in this, he is correct.

Analysis:

Even more interesting than what is said in this chapter, is what is left unsaid by the characters. Will leaves out his crucial information regarding Rosamond's "illness," and the major part he played in that; Rosamond does not tell her husband that Dorothea has been there, when this is information of the utmost importance. Will does not tell Lydgate that he too was offered money by Bulstrode, but was lucky enough to refuse it. Perhaps all these facts will come out, but perhaps not; if they do come out, they might do some minor damage or nothing at all, depending upon context and situation. Secrets have a peculiar way of acting, once they are out; it can never be predicted, especially in Middlemarch, what will come out, and what harm, if any, it will cause.

Chapter 80: Summary:

Dorothea goes over to the Farebrothers' house, which she does very often; her visits keep her from being lonely, and also keep her from criticisms that she needs a companion. But, when Will comes up, she suddenly feels that she must leave; that evening, she finally realizes that she loved Will, although she fears that this love has been lost. By the morning, she has put aside all the remorse and anger of the previous evening; she also begins to wear new clothes, symbolic of lesser mourning, since it has been a year since Casaubon died. She resolves to go and see Rosamond again, and to offer help as she meant to do the day before.

Analysis:

At last, both Will and Dorothea have declared their love openly; the only question that remains is whether they will be united. Unrequited love is a theme that comes up in the book on occasion, usually with reference to Farebrother and his love for Mary. At this point, though, both of them feel their love is unrequited, which makes their situation all the more desperate.

The irony of their situations is that neither realizes the extent of their love until they think they have lost it. Dorothea's finally realizes that her love has been a "very little seed" that has grown and grown in her, which it has taken until then to notice; the metaphor betrays how she has treasured it, and how slowly but steadily it has taken hold and grown. Will realizes that Dorothea might well be the only woman he could ever love, and curses himself for losing his chance. But, there are still barriers between Dorothea and Will. Dorothea is angry, and her good opinion of Will offended, by the thought that Will loves Rosamond too. Will is proud, and his reputation is not the best, which he fears might have driven her away.

It is a paradox inherent in Dorothea that she can feel so passionately one moment, and then be so collected the next; she feels great love for Will, which is replaced by great anger, which is replaced by a mature calmness, all within the course of hours. Dorothea is a great deal more mature than at the beginning of the novel, when she was mired in illusion and naivete, which have since been chiseled away. She is able to set aside her anger and hate for both Will and Rosamond, and consider how best she can help them and Lydgate; it takes a great deal of strength to do what Dorothea is doing, and again she is proving herself a noble, worthy person.

Chapter 81: Summary:

Dorothea finds Lydgate at home, and Lydgate thanks her for giving him the money with which to pay his debt to Bulstrode. Dorothea is only too happy to have been of service; she asks him in Rosamond is in, and finds Lydgate completely unaware of what went on the previous day. Rosamond is wary at the visit, but receives her anyway, and finds her quite different from the day before, though perhaps troubled. Dorothea reassures her that her husband is a good person, and is still welcomed in Middlemarch by people of character and influence, like herself, Sir James, Mr. Brooke, and Mr. Farebrother.

Dorothea then proceeds to speak about marriage, trying to address Rosamond and Lydgate's marriage in the process.

Dorothea hits on some of her own sadness though, and her anguish at the whole debacle with Will becomes apparent. Dorothea convinces Rosamond that Lydgate loves her very much, and that she needs to give the marriage a chance, because she still has his love; this cheers Rosamond up a bit, though her mind is still dazed from the previous day. Rosamond feels that she should clarify the situation with Will, so Rosamond tells her that Will was only there to explain that he loved someone other than Rosamond, and always would. Rosamond tells her this to try and exonerate herself somewhat, although Dorothea takes this statement as an expression of sympathy and goodness on Rosamond's part. Then, Lydgate enters, and the two part; neither can hold anything against the other anymore, and both their minds have been eased.

Analysis:

This Chapter is a turning point for Rosamond, and for Dorothea as well. Rosamond finally accepts the blow to her vanity that Will caused her, and does not let her offended vanity get in the way of telling Dorothea the truth, to ease her mind. Rosamond is not completely over the shock of the previous day, but at least she is able to let go of her pain long enough to show some emotion and talk with Dorothea, who she had focused her anger on after Will's slight.

It also seems that Rosamond might take Dorothea's advice on her marriage; she seems to have a moment of realization that her husband does care for her, and that maybe she needs to make her marriage more of a marriage. Hopefully, after this conversation, she will not treat him with such contempt and disregard; and also, she will hopefully not go back to her old, proud, vain ways, which caused her so much misery. But whether Rosamond will truly be able to get over her materialism is another issue completely. Hopefully, she will have learned that having Lydgate is more important than having nice things, but then again, lessons do not come very easily to poor Rosamond.

Here, Dorothea hits a peak of care for others, and her ability to transcend her own feelings in order to help others is admirable. But, at the same time, her ability to remember and value her own feelings is something new for her; she has broken the old habit of the Casaubon days to put other people first, which sometimes resulted in her own neglect and unhappiness. It seems that Dorothea is learning how to balance her interests in other people's welfare with her own, and how not to discount herself in light of other, pressing interests.

Chapter 82: Summary:

Will debates with himself whether he should leave Middlemarch altogether after the events of the previous day; in the end, he decides he cannot leave after making some amends to Rosamond after her shock. He is sorry that he got so angry at her, but at the same time, does not want to come straight out and apologize‹especially since this would mean that he would have to explain what happened to Lydgate, which is undesirable. Will does end up going, and is as affable as he can be to Rosamond, without betraying what went on before. Rosamond gives Will a note, saying that Dorothea has been told the truth about what happened; Will is somewhat relieved, but is worried about what might have transpired between Rosamond and Dorothea.

Analysis:

With everything that Will has been through, the fact that he still has affection for Dorothea at this point, and wants desperately to see her, is certainly a positive thing. At the least, they are bound to make amends; Will's desire to see her, and Dorothea's wish to set things right, strongly foreshadow a meeting between them, hopefully a cordial one. Rosamond still has not fully recovered, as Will sees from her note; it is written in an honest, but wounded and pouting, tone, but still sharpens Will's desire to see Dorothea. At least Rosamond has told Will, which represents another positive step on her part, but she still has some distance left to go in mending herself.

Chapter 83: Summary:

Dorothea is too agitated to set herself at any one task; she tries to memorize places on a map, before Miss Noble comes in, to greet her. Miss Noble tells her that Will is there, waiting outside, to greet her; Dorothea decides that she cannot turn him away, and has him sent into her. Dorothea is a little formal in her greeting to Will; he still cannot fathom whether she loves him or not. Will speaks to her carefully, hoping that she was not offended by the gossip attaching him to Bulstrode; Dorothea, however, knows that he has acted correctly in all things, and brightens up with affection. Will tries to say goodbye, but then is affected by passion; he says they cannot be together, yet it is a cruel thing. Dorothea decides that she cannot let him go again; she would rather give up the wealth that Casaubon has left her and go with Will, with the aid of her own fortune to support them.

Analysis:

The storm in this Chapter is highly symbolic; it represents all the barriers in the world to Will and Dorothea's relationship. Dorothea and Will's notice of the storm happens concurrently with the turn of their relationship to the future, and whether they can stay together. Many factors have tried to keep Will and Dorothea apart; Casaubon's spite when he was alive and as he showed in his will, Will's questionable reputation as an outsider and someone of lower class, the objection of all Dorothea's friends and relatives to the relationship, and Will's lack of money. The storm represents the immediacy of all these concerns in their decision whether or not to stay together.

Here, both Will's and Dorothea's passionate natures are inflamed by the possibility that they might be driven apart. They are similar in their show of concern for their possible union, but at the same time, both have finally learned to let passion overrule pride and any social concerns that might stand between them. This moment displays the course of change that Dorothea has been through in the novel; she began as one ruled by restraint, duty, and societal ideals, and she is at this moment only ruled by her own emotions and fervent wishes. Dorothea has truly become herself, and learned how to make decisions that will improve her life and make her happy.

Chapter 84: Summary:

Mr. Brooke, Sir James, Celia, and the Cadwalladers are all assembled at Sir James' home. Mr. Brooke has news to tell them of Dorothea and Will, and their impending marriage. Sir James is very angry, and objects strongly; he wants to try and protect Dorothea as he should have protected her from her marriage with Casaubon, though this time she does not need help. The others only consider Will's reputation and his money situation in evaluating the worth of the union; everyone still has a great deal of prejudice against Will, and much concern for Dorothea. Sir James sends Celia to go and talk her, but Dorothea is steadfast in her decision. Celia hopes for the best, though still, no one is very positive about the marriage.

Analysis:

In this chapter, Sir James, though he is a decent man, represents all the societal attitudes that have wronged Will Ladislaw, Will's mother, and Will's grandmother. He is a symbol of the strict ideals of marriage confirming status and class, and of the society who condemns women for marrying men whom they love, when those men have little property or renown. The irony is, that none of these women needed protection from their husbands, nor did they deserve to be disowned for making such a match. Sir James, however, is too consumed with the idea that Will is a lowlife, and that Dorothea has been taken in, to see the truth of the situation.

It seems that fate was at work in Dorothea's life, even in her marriage to Casaubon. She was destined to cross paths with Will, and end up with him; he is her one true love, and she is his. Also, from the moment that she found the portrait of Will's grandmother Julia, she has had a romantic and sympathetic disposition toward Julia's story and the consequences of her union. Dorothea already knew from the story what sacrifices that women in that situation had to make, and how they were treated. However, it seems that from the moment she learned of Julia, she was destined to relive her history. And Will too, whose father and grandfather were both worthy but poor and married women of higher rank and money, also seemed destined by family history to do the same. But perhaps the cycle of disentailment of heirs from these marriages, and of social consequences for the people in them, will end; and then the cycle of suffering and unjustness that started with Will's grandmother and has been his legacy will finally end.

Dorothea and Celia are juxtaposed in this Chapter, to clarify their characters. Previously, Celia seemed the far more sensible one of the two; however, Dorothea has learned and grown beyond what Celia could have imagined, and now seems to surpass her sister in sense and in worldly concerns. Dorothea has certainly turned out to be the more open-minded, free-spirited one of the two, and has shed her religious-like fervor and piety. Celia, in comparison, does not seem quite as great as she once did; but, Celia is at least herself and has found her own way as well, even if she is not as wise and as driven as her sister.

Chapter 85: Summary:

Bulstrode is getting ready to leave Middlemarch, since he cannot bear the scorn and shame of being there any longer. His wife has been constant, but at the same time, she has been worn down by grief and remorse in the past few months. She would like to do something nice for her family before she goes away; they decide to give the management of Stone Court to Fred, and a decent income, so that he may be able to save some money.

Analysis:

Bulstrode, though he has suffered, still has the idea that he is some sort of martyr, unfairly persecuted for his past sins. Bulstrode regrets that all of this is happening to him, but if he is not penitent by now, then he probably never will be. Hopefully, he has learned enough not to repeat his mistakes; it certainly seems that he has, especially with his wife's disappointment weighing so heavily on him. But still he has the money he gained through his indiscretions, and as long as he is living off this dirty money, the past will remain with him.

Chapter 86: Summary:

Caleb Garth tells Mary that the Bulstrodes want Fred to manage Stone court; Mary is very happy, though Mr. Garth is still not sure if Fred will make her a good husband. He questions his daughter, about her love for Fred, and whether she truly thinks she can spend her life with him; she does not want to see his daughter make a huge mistake in marriage, if he can help prevent it. But Mary knows what is right to do, and has a good deal of sense; she will marry Fred, and they will probably be happy. She tells Fred about the management of Stone Court, and he is very happy; they will have to be engaged for a while so he can save money, but yet they are content with their engagement.

Analysis:

Love has brought Fred Vincy full circle, from an irresponsible, hopeless youth, to a hard-working, determined young man. Though he still has some tendency toward laxity in him, he is still a good man, and much improved over his more youthful self. With Mary's help, he will become better still; Mary is a good match for Fred, and will certainly make up for his shortcomings with her intelligence and economy. Mary and Fred are the picture of another kind of ideal of marriage; it is one where the husband and wife are uniquely suited in character and affection, and will be able to weather any hard times through their kinship in spirit and in life.

Finale: Summary:

Mary and Fred did live happily ever after, with both of them prospering and becoming very happy in their marriage. Fred buys Stone Court, and they have three boys, two of whom resemble Fred, much to his mother's relief. Lydgate and Rosamond kept on going, but were not exceptionally happy. Lydgate was able to make a successful practice, but was not happy because he never did make any of his beloved scientific advances. Dorothea and Will were very happy together; Will goes into politics, and becomes a member of Parliament. They have a boy, who becomes the heir to Mr. Brooke's estate; the disastrous effects of disinheritance are for once avoided. Sir James allows Celia to see her sister, and Will and Dorothea make visits twice a year to Mr. Brooke's house. Dorothea is not able to make the big, sweeping impact she desired; however, she was able to spread happiness and have a wonderful family, and a very contented life.

Analysis:

There are no real surprises in this little epilogue to the novel; everyone's life continues on the whole course on which they were going at the end of the novel. Those people, who are well-suited, like Dorothea and Will and Mary and Fred, are happy together and make good lives with one another. Those who are not as happy, Rosamond and Lydgate in particular, muddle through, but are never able to change the dynamic of their relationship. Characters are not set in stone, but it seems that people in Middlemarch remain pretty much as they are. Love and honor do make some favorable changes in the way people act and live; but everyone seems to find their particular destiny, and everything happens according to the indications of fate.

Chaptet 10

Study Questions and Answers

Q. Write down a character sketch of George Eliot, The Victorian Writer ?

Or

Q. Write an essay on George Eliot ?

Victorian writer, a humane freethinker, whose insightful psychological novels paved way to modern character portrayals - contemporary of Dostoevsky (1821-1881), who at the same time in Russia developed similar narrative techniques. Eliot's liaison with the married writer and editor George Henry Lewes arise among the rigid Victorians much indignation, which calmed down with the progress of her literary fame.

"Marriage, which has been the bourne of so many narratives, is still a great beginning, as it was to Adam and Eve, who kept their honeymoon in Eden, but had their first little one among the thorns and thistles of the wilderness. It is still the beginning of the home epic - the gradual conquest or irremediable loss of that complete union which makes the advancing years as a climax, and age the harvest of sweet memories in common." (from Middlemarch, 1871-72)

Mary Ann Evans (George Eliot) was born in Chilvers Coton, Warwickshire. Her father was a carpenter who rose to be a land agent. When she was a few months old, the family moved to Griff, a 'cheerful red-brick, ivory-covered house', and there Eliot spent 21 years of his life among people that he later depicted in her novels. She was educated at home and in several schools, and developed a strong evangelical piety at Mrs. Wallington's School at Neneaton. However, later Eliot rejected her dogmatic faith. When her mother died in 1836, she took charge of the family household. In 1841 she moved with her father to Coventry, where she lived with him until his death in 1849. During this time she met Charles Bray, a free-thinking Coventry manufacturer. His wife, Caroline (Cara) was the sister of Charles Hennel, the author of a work entitled An Inquiry Concerning the Origin of Christianity (1838). The reading of this and other rationalistic works influenced deeply Eliot's thoughts. After her father's death, Eliot travelled around Europe. She settled in London and took up work as subeditor of Westminster Review.

In Coventry she met Charles Bray and later Charles Hennell, who introduced her to many new religious and political ideas. Under Eliot's control the Westminster Review enjoyed success. She became the centre of a literary circle, one of whose members was George Henry Lewes, who would be her companion until his death in 1878. Lewes's wife was mentally unbalanced and she had already had two children by another man. In 1854 Eliot went to Germany with Lewes. Their unconventional union caused some difficulties because Lewes was still married and he was unable to obtain divorce. Eliot did not inform her close friends Caroline and Sarah Hennell about her decision to live with Lewes - the both friends were shocked and angry because she had not trusted them.

Eliot's first collection of tales, Scenes of Clerical Life, appeared in 1858 under the pseudonym George Eliot - in those days writing was considered to be a male profession. It was followed by her first novel, Adam Bede, a tragic love story in which the model for the title character was Eliot's father. He was noted for his great physical strength, which enabled him to carry loads that three average men could barely handle. When impostors claimed authorship of Adam Bede, it was revealed that Marian Evans, the Westminster reviewer, was George Eliot. The book was a brilliant success. Her other major works include The Mill on the Floss (1860), a story of destructive family relations, and Silas Marner (1861). Silas Marner, a linen-weaver, has accumulated a goodly sum of gold. He was falsely judged guilty of theft 15 years before and left his community. Squire Cass' son Dunstan steals Marner's gold and disappears. Marner takes care of an orphaned little girl, Eppie and she becomes for him more precious than the lost property. Sixteen years later the skeleton of Dunstan and Marner's gold is found. Godfrey Cass, Dunstal's brother, admits that he is the father of Eppie. He married the girl's mother, opium-ridden Molly Farren secretly before hear death. Eppie and Silas Marner don't wish to separate when Godfrey tries to adopt the girl. In the end Eppie marries Aaron Winthorp, who accepts Silas Marner as part of the household.

Middlemarch (1871-72), her greatest novel, was probably inspired by her life at Coventry. The story follows the sexual and intellectual frustrations of Dorothea Brooke. Eliot weaves into her story other narrative lines, which offer a sad comment upon human aspirations. Among Eliot's translation works are D.F. Strauss's Das Leben Jesu kritisch bearbeitet (published anonymously in 1846), Ludwig Feuerbach's Das Wesen des Christentum, and Spinoza's Ethics (unpublished). Eliot's thoughts of religion were considered at that time advanced. When she visited Cambridge University in 1873 and discussed with F.W.H. Mayers of "the words of God, Immortality, and Duty", she pronounced "with terrible earnestness how inconceivable was the first, how unbelievable was the second, and yet how peremptory and absolute the third."

Middlemarch is a novel of English provincial life in the early nineteenth century, just before the Reform Bill of 1832. The book was called by the famous American writer Henry James a 'treasure-house of detail.' It fuses several stories and characters, creating a a network of parallels and contrasts. One of Eliot's main concerns is the way which the past moulds the present and the attempts of various characters to control the future. Harold Bloom has noted in The Western Canon (1994) the implicit but clear relation of the work to Dante's Comedy. Dorothea, an idealistic young woman, marries the pedantic Casaubon. After his death she marries Will Ladislaw, Casaubon's young cousin, a vaguely artistic outsider. Doctor Tertius Lydgate is trapped with the egoistic Rosamond Vincy, the town's beauty. Lydgate becomes involved in a scandal, and he dies at 50, his ambitions frustrated. Other characters are Bulstrode, a banker and a religious hypocrite, Mary Garth, the practical daughter of a land agent, and Fred Vincy, the son of the mayor of Middlemarch. For modern feminist readers Middlemarch has been a disappointment: Dorothea was not prepared to give up marriage. "'I know that I must expect trials, uncle. Marriage is a state of higher duties, I never thought of it as mere personal ease,' said poor Dorothea." However, Eliot's lament for Dorothea left no doubts about her views: "Some have felt that these blundering lives are due to the inconvenient indefiniteness with which the Supreme Power has fashioned the nature of women: if there were one level of feminine incompetence as strict as the ability to count three and no more, the social lot of women might be treated with scientific certitude. Meanwhile the indefiniteness remains, the the limits of variation are really much wider than any one would imagine from the sameness of women's coiffure and the favourite lovestories in prose and verse." - The book is required reading in university English courses.

In 1860-61 Eliot spent some time in Italy collecting material for her historical romance Romola. It was published serially first in the Cornhill Magazine and in book form in 1863. Henry James considered it the finest thing she wrote, "but its defects are almost on the scale of its beauties." In 1871 she mentioned to Alexander Main: "I have the conviction that excessive literary production is a social offence." When Harriet Beecher Stowe wrote admiringly of Silas Marner in 1869 Eliot began a correspondence with her. In a letter from 1876 she wrote about Daniel Deronda (1876): "As to the Jewish element in 'Deronda', I expected from first to last in writing it, that it would create much stronger resistance and even repulsion than it has actually met with. But precisely because I felt that the usual attitude of Christians towards Jews is - I hardly know whether to say more impious or more stupid when viewed in the light of their professed principles, I therefore felt urged to treat Jews with such sympathy and understanding as my nature and knowledge could attain to. Moreover, not only towards the Jews, but towards all oriental peoples with whom we English come in contact, a spirit of arrogance and contemptuous dictatorialness is observable which has become a national disgrace to us."

After Lewes's death Eliot married twenty years younger friend, John Cross, an American banker, on May 6, 1880. They made a trip to Italy and according to a story, he jumped in Venice from their hotel balcony into the Grand Canal. After honeymoon they returned to London, where she died of a kidney ailment on the same year on December 22. Cross never married again. In her will she expressed her wish to be buried in Westminster Abbey, but Dean Stanley of Westminster Abbey rejected the idea and Eliot was buried in Highgate Cemetery. Eliot's interest in the interior life of human beings, moral problems and strains, anticipated the narrative methods of modern literature. D.H. Lawrence once wrote: "It was really George Eliot who started it all. It was she started putting action inside." The young Henry James described her "magnificently, awe-inspiringly ugly," but also studied her work carefully, critically, and acknowledged her greatness as a writer: "What is remarkable, extraordinary - and the process remains inscrutable and mysterious - is that this quiet, anxious, sedentary, serious, invalidical English lady, without animal spirits, without adventures, without extravagance, assumption, or bravado, should have made us believe that nothing in the world was alien to her; should have produced such rich, deep, masterly pictures of the multifold life of man." (Henry James in The Atlantic monthly, May 1885)

Q. Discuss the relation of George Eliot with the Visual Arts ?

Q. Discuss the significance of Visual Arts in Middlemarch by George Eliot ?

Landscape and landscape painting afforded George Eliot great visual pleasure and spiritual refreshment. Her enjoyment and careful study of natural appearances found full expression in her novels, impelled by personal feeling and summoned by a tradition of landscape description that had become established in British and American fiction in the time of Mrs. Radcliffe, Scott, and Fenimore Cooper.1 Eliot's responsiveness to landscape views in fiction may be seen in her appreciation of Charles Kingsley's "scene-painting" in Alton Locke, Yeast, and Westward Ho! er own vision of landscape combined several important eighteenth- and nineteenth-century traditions. The cult of the picturesque and the English school of topographical painting, both of which had reached their prime in the eighteenth century, were second-nature to George Eliot in her perception and description of country scenes.

But she was also profoundly influenced by three nineteenth-century developments in landscape sensibility, each of which came to her in part through the work of Ruskin: the cult of detailed naturalism, which Ruskin advocated and the Pre-Raphaelites practiced; the nature poetry of Wordsworth, which Ruskin echoed in many parts of Modern Painters; and the moral critique of the cult of the picturesque, which finds its classic formulation in volume IV of Modern Painters To explore these five aspects of George Eliot's landscape vision is the purpose of the present Chapter.

Several of the traditions just mentioned work together harmoniously in the following passage of Middlemarch:

The ride to Stone Court, which Fred and Rosamond took the next morning, lay through a pretty bit of midland landscape almost all meadows and pastures, with hedgerows still allowed to grow in bushy beauty and to spread out coral fruit for the birds. Little details gave each field a particular physiognomy, dear to the eyes that have looked on them from childhood: the pool in the corner where the grasses were dank and trees leaned whisperingly; the great oak shadowing a bare place in midpasture; the high bank where the ash-trees grew; the sudden slope of the old marl-pit making a red background for the burdock; the huddled roofs and ricks of the homestead without a traceable way of approach; the grey gate and fences against the depths of the bordering wood; and the stray hovel, its old old thatch full of mossy hills and valleys with wondrous modulations of light and shadow such as we travel far to see in later life, and see larger, but not more beautiful. These are the things that make the gamut of joy in landscape to midland-bred souls — the things they toddled among, or perhaps learned by heart standing between their father's knees while he drove leisurely.

The narrator here is in part a Gilpinesque tourist, in search of the picturesque in all its roughness, variegation, chiaroscuro, and suggestive antiquity ("old, old thatch full of mossy hills and valleys with wondrous modulations of light and shadow such as we travel far to see in later life"). But there is also an element of Ruskinian naturalistic precision in the description of individual features in the landscape, the "little details" that give "each field a particular — physiognomy" such as "the great oak shadowing a bare place in mid-pasture." And finally there is a Wordsworthian emphasis upon the "joy" that such landscape brings in maturity to those who have grown up amidst it. All these tones are characteristic of the George Eliot landscape, which we may now examine in greater detail. "The power of description, both of scenery and of character... may be very puissant in the hands of a fine writer, gifted with a real sense of the picturesque," G. H. Lewes argued in "The Novels of Jane Austen".

The cult of the picturesque grew up in the late eighteenth century, making it fashionable to travel in search of landscape views that compose themselves pictorially.3 The models for such views derived in part from the neoclassical heroic landscapes of Claude Lorrain and the Poussins, in part from the wilder, more dramatic visions of Salvator Rosa, and in part from the leafy, aqueous, rock-strewn country scenes of Ruisdael, Hobbema, and other seventeenth-century Dutch painters. William Gilpin's initial definition of the picturesque in 1768 as "that peculiar kind of beauty which is agreeable in a picture" was refined by a complex debate in the 1790s and early 1800s to mean a kind of aesthetic effect which is neither awesomely sublime nor smoothly beautiful but a blend of those two extremes distinguished by roughness, variety, sudden contrast, chiaroscuro, signs of age or decay, and a power to stimulate in the viewer a piquant mixture of painful and pleasurable impressions and associations.

The coming of Romanticism modified but did not extinguish the cult of the picturesque. Christopher Hussey is more right than not when he asserts that "the picturesque became the nineteenth century's mode of vision" (It was certainly a natural mode for George Eliot, whose letters and journals are full of descriptions in the Gilpin tradition. Italy in 1860 showed her "Claude-like scenes of mountains, trees, and meadows, with picturesque accidents of building, such as single round towers, on the heights" Biarritz in 1867 seemed to G. H. Lewes, and doubtless to Eliot as well, "so picturesque that it may be called a succession of Prouts". Switzerland in 1860 was mediated through the novelist's prior experience of Alexandre Calame's landscape painting. Except for ruins, the valley of Bercka near Weimar in 1854 had all the necessary ingredients of the picturesque:

The hanging woods — the soft colouring and graceful outline of the uplands-the village with its roofs and spire of a reddish violet hue, muffled in luxuriant trees — the white Kurhaus glittering on a grassy slope — the avenue of poplars contrasting its pretty >primness with the wild bushy outline of the wood-covered hill, which rises abruptly from the smooth, green meadows — the clear winding stream, now sparkling in the sun, now hiding itself under soft grey willows — all this makes an enchanting picture.

Returning from Germany in 1855, the ardent tourist found a charming English landscape at Dover: "As I walked up the Castle hill this afternoon, the town, with its background of softly rounded hills shrouded in sleepy haze, its little lines of water looking golden in the sun, made a charming picture". Jersey in 1857 offered a feast for the wandering eye, and a stroll along the banks of the Trent near Newark in 1868 brought "some charming quiet pictures — Frith landscapes"

In 1879, less than two years before her death, Eliot sought to pass on her taste for the picturesque to young Blanche Southwood Lewes, who had just celebrated her seventh birthday with a visit to an exhibition and a boatride on the Thames: "I am sure you must have liked being on the river in the steamboat for the first time. The wide river, and the bridges, and the great buildings that can be seen a long way by the waterside, are all very beautiful, are they not? It would seem to you like another and grander sort of picture, after seeing the small pictures on the wall at the Exhibition". Eliot wanted Blanche's vision to be shaped and enriched, as hers was, by the experience of pictures.

Eliot's novels, from the start to the finish of her career, abound with picturesque descriptions in an eighteenth-century vein. She was especially fond of "pretty bits of midland landscape" like the one quoted above from Middlemarch. Here is another representative "bit," this time from Felix Holt.

The Rectory was on the other side of the river, close to the church of which it was the fitting companion: a fine old brick and-stone house, with a great bow-window opening from the library on to the deep-turfed lawn, one fat dog sleeping on the door-stone, another fat dog waddling on the gravel, the autumn leaves duly swept away, the lingering chrysanthemums cherished, tall trees stooping or soaring in the most picturesque variety, and a Virginian creeper turning a little rustic hut into a scarlet pavilion.

After reading a similar description of a parsonage and farm in "Mr. Gilfil's Love-Story," John Blackwood wrote to George Eliot: "The picture reminds me strongly of the genuine English rural landscapes with which we are all familiar on canvas or in nature". Blackwood's was precisely the sort of response Eliot wanted her language in such passages to elicit. The convention of the Gilpinesque tourist-guide may help to account for the anonymous observer who opens so many of George Eliot's stories, mediating between author, reader, and action.

The horseback traveller in Adam Bede, the armchair dreamer in The Mill on the Floss, the Florentine shade in Romola, and the stagecoach passenger in Felix Holt are visitors or revisitors on holiday, having no business in the scene except to appreciate it. They make a Gilpinesque discrimination of landscape and figures, and disappear as soon as they have drawn the reader into engagement with the prospect (though the traveller in Adam Bede does reappear later in the novel as the magistrate who helps Dinah gain admission to Hetty's prison cell). They are guides and tutors, demonstrating the quality of perception that the reader must learn to apply to the world within the novel.

Though it came so naturally to her, Eliot knew that the picturesque way of seeing has its dangers. For one thing, it can become facile and overgeneralized. She did not favor the Claudian technique, often imitated by Gilpin in his sketches of Wales and the Lake District, of reconstructing an actual landscape according to an ideal model; see Barbier, George Eliot's distaste for Claudian techniques may account for her inability to admire Karl Rottmann's Greek landscapes, which she saw at Munich in 1858. She preferred a sense of unique place and abundant local detail in landscape descriptions (see Barrell). From this preference stems her critique of Tom Tulliver's drawing lessons in The Mill on the Floss.

Tom found, to his disgust, that his new drawing-master gave him no dogs and donkeys to draw, but brooks and rustic bridges and ruins, all with a general softness of black-lead surface, indicating that nature, if anything, was rather satiny; and as Tom's feeling for the picturesque in landscape was at present quite latent, it is not surprising that Mr. Goodrich's productions seemed to him an uninteresting form of art... Tom learned to make an extremely fine point to his pencil, and to represent landscape with a "broad generality," which, doubtless from a narrow tendency in his mind to details, he thought extremely dull.

A broad generality in which no characteristic details can be discerned was not George Eliot's idea of a good landscape style. The picturesque must be tempered by the naturalistic. We shall see that in Adam Bede, as in Modern Painters, Claudian ideal landscape is something of a villain.

George Eliot's taste for the representation of actual places shows itself in her imitation of eighteenth-century topographical painting, especially in her descriptions of English country houses and their grounds. John Steegman has shown how the bird's-eye perspective and diagrammatic cartography of early country-house portraits gave way in the eighteenth century to a lower viewpoint, a placing of the house itself in the middle or far distance, and a bringing forward of human and/or animal groups into the intervening space (Steegman). Engraved views of noblemen's and gentlemen's country seats were especially popular between 1760 and 1840. J. P. Neale's six-volume set, published between 1818 and 1823, had a standard pictorial format that can be characterized in the words of John Dixon Hunt: "The typical English landscape garden as generally visualized would consist of undulating grass that leads somewhere down to an irregularly shaped piece of water over which a bridge arches, of trees grouped casually, with cattle or deer, about the slopes, and of houses and other buildings glimpsed in the middle or far distance".

When Phillipe Mercier, a transplanted imitator of Watteau, began around 1725 to make the figures in the foreground into portraits, he initiated a special and highly influential form of semitopographical English conversation piece which depicts "family groups in their proper setting, that is in their own park or garden, with a sight of the family home in the background."

Eliot's skill at country-house portraiture may be seen in her descriptions of Hall Farm and the Chase in Adam Bede, of Transome Court in Felix Holt, and of Offendene, Brackenshaw Park, the Abbey, Diplow, and Gadsmere in Daniel Deronda — see Adam Bede, Felix Holt, and Daniel Deronda. A favourite and recurring form of architecture in her novels is a plain red-brick structure built in the Queen Anne period, sometimes adjoining the ruins of a medieval abbey.

The gables, windows, and doors are ornamented with limestone, but the contrast between the limestone and the brick is diminished by the growth of a powdery, greenish-grey lichen. A flowery lawn cut by graveled, often tree-lined walks or driveways runs from the house to a plantation of trees which nearly surround the house or screen it on the north.

The plantation frequently contains Scotch firs, while one or two large firs or cedars or beeches may stand immediately adjacent to the house. If the estate is landscaped, the garden is in the picturesque style, with rolling lawns, man-made lakes, serpentine paths, clumps of trees, and perhaps an occasional glimpse of a white temple. Eliot's affection for "grounds, which are laid out with a taste worthy of a first-rate landscape gardener" was expressed in her early descriptions of the Belvedere gardens at Weimar. Eliot's most elaborate country-house portrait is of the neo-Gothic Cheverel Manor in "Mr. Gilfil's Love-Story." Here the topographical element is very strong; for, as Margharita Laski has said, "Cheverel Manor is photographically Arbury Hall," the Newdigate family seat in Warwickshire near which George Eliot grew up.

Her description is also a full-fledged conversation piece, beginning with close-up portraits of Caterina Sarti and Lady Cheverel, and then placing the sitters in their habitat: they sat down, making two bright patches of red and white and blue on the green background of the laurels and the lawn, which would look none the less pretty in a picture because one of the women's hearts was rather cold and the other rather sad.

And a charming picture Cheverel Manor would have made that evening, if some English Watteau had been there to paint it: the castellated house of grey-tinted stone, with the flickering sunbeams sending dashes of golden light across the many-shaped panes in the mullioned windows, and a great beech leaning athwart one of the flanking towers, and breaking, with its dark flattened boughs, the too formal symmetry of the front; the broad gravel-walk winding on the right, by a row of tall pines, alongside the pool-on the left branching out among swelling grassy mounds, surmounted by clumps of trees, where the red trunk of the Scotch fir glows in the descending sunlight against the bright green of limes and acacias; the great pool, where a pair of swans are swimming lazily with one leg tucked under a wing, and where the open water-lilies lie calmly accepting the kisses of the fluttering light-sparkles; the lawn, with its smooth emerald greenness, sloping down to the rougher and browner herbage of the park, from which it is invisibly fenced by a little stream that winds away from the pool, and disappears under the wooden bridge in the distant pleasure-ground; and on this lawn our two ladies, whose part in the landscape the painter, standing at a favourable point of view in the park, would represent with a few little dabs of red and white and blue.

Eliot's sensitivity to colour is evident here, and the reference to an "English Watteau" is entirely apt since, as we have noted, Watteau's fêtes galantes were the immediate predecessors of Mercier's pioneering English conversation pieces.l4 Eliot even includes the artist in her scene, as Mercier did in his seminal Viscount Tyrconnel with His Family in the Grounds of Belton House.

When the narrator moves inside Cheverel Manor to describe the dining-room and saloon, we seem to be observing two of Joseph Nash's views of The Mansions of England in the Olden Time (1839-49), staffed by figures in Georgian instead of Tudor or Restoration costume. What Neale had done for the exteriors of country houses, Nash did for their interiors, by publishing detailed engravings of their great halls, drawing-rooms, parlors, bay windows, galleries, bedchambers, staircases, porches, and chapels. Again, however, Eliot's description combines view-painting with portraiture, turning the picture into a conversation piece. She presents informal portraits of Sir Christopher Cheverel and Anthony Wybrow, surrounded by the architecture which is Sir Christopher's proudest domestic achievement.

George Eliot's penchant for topographical specificity in landscape also took a form that was more characteristic of the nineteenth century than of the eighteenth. Her passion for precise naturalistic detail was kindled by the teachings of Ruskin, the practice of the Pre-Raphaelite painters, and the scientific researches of G. H. Lewes. After reading the third volume of Modern Painters in February of 1856 and reviewing it in April, Eliot spent May and June at llfracombe on the north coast of Devon, where Lewes was conducting the fieldwork in marine biology that eventually led to the publication of his Sea-Side Studies (1858). Art and science were in perfect harmony during these happy months. The picturesque took on an ecological dimension:

From this end of the Capstone we have an admirable bit for a picture. In the background rises old Hillsborough jutting far into the sea-rugged and rocky as it fronts the waves, green and accessible landward; in front of this stands Lantern Hill, a picturesque mass of green and grey surmounted by an old bit of building that looks as if it were the habitation of some mollusk that had secreted its shell from the material of the rock; and quite in the foreground, contrasting finely in colour with the rest, are some lower perpendicular rocks, of dark brown tints patched here and there with vivid green. In hilly districts, where houses and clusters of houses look so tiny against the huge limbs of Mother Earth one cannot help thinking of man as a parasitic animal — an epizoon making his abode on the skin of the planetary organism.

It is difficult to know whether these words came originally from George Eliot or from Lewes, since they appear almost verbatim in Sea-Side Studies. But the ideas were in any case shared. Man, the figure in the landscape, becomes a mollusk or epizoon when viewed from a biological perspective. Ruskin's mixture of science and aesthetics was very much in Eliot's mind at llfracombe, as a letter sent from there to Barbara Leigh Smith suggests: "What books his last two are! I think he is the finest writer living". She must have been thinking in part of Ruskin's defence of the naturalistic landscapes of the Pre-Raphaelite painters:

I have talked of the Ilfracombe lanes without describing them, for to describe them one ought to know the names of all the lovely wild flowers that cluster on their banks. Almost every yard of these banks is a "Hunt" picture — a delicious crowding of mosses and delicate trefoil, and wild strawberries, and ferns great and small. But the crowning beauty of the lanes is the springs, that gush out in little recesses by the side of the road — recesses glossy with liverwort and feathery with fern... I never before longed so much to know names of things as during this visit to llfracombe. The desire is part of the tendency that is now constantly growing in me to escape from all vagueness and inaccuracy into the daylight of distinct, vivid ideas. The mere fact of naming an object tends to give definiteness to our conception of it — we have then a sign that at once calls up in our minds the distinctive qualities which mark out for us that particular object from all others.

The "Hunt" mentioned here could be either William

Henry ("Bird's Nest") Hunt, who had tutored Barbara Leigh Smith, or William Holman Hunt, whose landscape in The Hireling Shepherd Eliot had already praised for its "marvelous truthfulness". Both Hunts practiced a painstaking realism, and their treatment of vegetation made a lasting impression upon the novelist, who sought an equivalent precision in her own medium. She had been accustomed to think of "attention to vegetation as one of the most remarkable characteristics of the Pre-Raphaelite painters" by the essay on "Pre-Raphaelitism in Art and Literature" which she read and praised in the 1852 British Quarterly Review.

In his review of Modern Painters, volume IV, Lewes defined "the ideal of a pre-Raphaelite landscape" as "isolating one part of the landscape, and thus concentrating attention on it alone". This formulation was prompted by an experience he and George Eliot had in the Belvedere gardens at Weimar. Walking through the park, they came upon a set of "large glass globes of different colours" placed upon an artificial rock. "It is wonderful to see with what minute perfection the scenery around is painted in these globes," Eliot wrote. "Each is like a pre-Raffaelite picture, with every little detail of gravely walk, mossy bank, and delicately-leaved, interlacing boughs, presented in accurate miniature". The eighteenth-century connoisseur of the picturesque had composed his landscapes in a special mirror known as a Claude glass. But George Eliot's equivalent of the Claude glass isolated "every little detail" for special attention, heightening what Mario Praz in Mnemosyne has called the "microscopic structure" of represented reality.

Pre-Raphaelite attention to natural detail helped to shape George Eliot's technique of landscape description. The Huntian treatment of vegetation especially influenced her rendering of the hedgerows that she considered the most distinctive feature of the English midlands landscape. In the following passage from Felix Holt, the precise botanical naming imitates the Hunts' leaf-by-leaf drawing:

But everywhere the bushy hedgerows wasted the land with their straggling beauty, shrouded the grassy borders of the pastures with catkined hazels, and tossed their long blackberry branches on the corn-fields. Perhaps they were white with May, or starred with pale pink dog-roses; perhaps the urchins were already nutting amongst them, or gathering the plenteous crabs. It was worth the journey only to see those hedgerows, the liberal homes of unremarkable beauty — of the purple-blossomed ruby-berried nightshade, of the wild convolvulus climbing and spreading in tendrilled strength till it made a great curtain of pale-green hearts and white trumpets, of the many-tubed honeysuckle which, in its most delicate fragrance, hid a charm more subtle and penetrating than beauty. Even if it were winter the hedgerows showed their coral, the scarlet haws, the deep-crimsoned hips, with lingering brown leaves to make a resting-place for the jewels of the hoar-frost.

These hedgerows reappear in Adam Bede and Middlemarch, where George Eliot's prose again follows the principle laid down at Ilfracombe: to describe them one ought to know the names of all the lovely wild flowers that cluster on their banks." Passages like these inspired Ruskinian praises from at least one of George Eliot's contemporaries: "Marian Evans does really good landscape sketching, of an intensely truthful character"

Yet Eliot's strong local attachment to her native midlands scenery is due neither to the cult of the picturesque nor to the cult of outdoor naturalism. Rather it shows the Wordsworthian side of her landscape sensibility. "I am afraid you despise landscape painting," she wrote to an early correspondent, "but to me even the works of our own Stanfield and Roberts and Creswick bring a whole world of thought and bliss — 'a sense of something far more deeply interfused.' The ocean and the sky and the everlasting hills are spirit to me, and they will never be robbed of their sublimity" This is the voice of a young person who has been reading the early volumes of Modern Painters in conjunction with "Tintern Abbey" and mediating her Wordsworthian responses to landscape through the vision of the landscape painter. The enthusiasm was by no means temporary, for in her maturity George Eliot continued to pair Ruskin with Wordsworth and to draw inspiration from the association. "The two last volumes of Modern Painters," she wrote in 1858, "contain, I think, some of the finest writing of this age. He is strongly akin to the sublimest part of Wordsworth, whom, by the bye, we are reading now with fresh admiration for his beauties and tolerance for his faults".

Eliot read Wordsworth often from 1839 till the end of her life. As she indicated in "Impressions of Theophrastus Such," she felt a considerable affinity of temperament with the great poet: "And I often smile at my consciousness that certain conservative prepossessions have mingled themselves for me with the influences of our midland scenery, from the tops of the elms down to the buttercups and the little wayside vetches". This vocabulary of influences, mingling, and prepossessions reflects the change Wordsworth had wrought in the literary representation of landscape. Wordsworth "began in the picturesque," as J. R. Watson has noted.The early poem, "An Evening Walk," continues a tradition of loco-descriptive poetry that descends from John Denham and James Thomson. But as early as "Descriptive Sketches), Wordsworth began to grow restless with the picturesque apprehension of nature, and to evolve a new sense of landscape which placed greater emphasis upon the affective and experiential interchange between the observer and the scene.

The Wordsworthian observer is in fl the landscape and part of it, rather than separated from it by an aesthetic distance. He is more concerned to render the emotional impact of the outdoor setting, the sense of its total presence, than to distinguish and analyze its constituent parts. The landscape affects him in a diffuse but profound and permanent manner, creating in his memory an "obscure sense/Of possible sublimity" which is a source of both joy and moral strength in later years.28 This complex sense of an environment that functions in many ways as a deity was immensely congenial to George Eliot. "I never before met with so many of my own feelings, expressed just as I could like them," she declared shortly after reading Wordsworth in 1839 (Letters, I, 34). Having originated in a reaction against the picturesque tradition, the mature Wordsworthian mode is essentially nonpictorial. As Christopher Salvesen has noted Wordsworth is always much more aware of the presence of landscape, of its surrounding influence, than of any pictorial qualities it might have... the fundamental landscape of his best poetry is not at all detailed: the unifying force of nature is what creates it and holds it together, and this force is conveyed by Wordsworth's emotion rather than by his observation. He responds to a landscape rather than observes it: he feels it, almost, rather than sees.

The absence of pictorial qualities in Wordsworth's best poetry undermines most critical attempts to compare it with painting; see, for example, Kroeber and the critical review by E. D. H. Johnson. The distinction Salvesen is making could be illustrated by the well-known comparison between "I Wandered Lonely as a Cloud" and Dorothy Wordsworth's far more particularized journal description of the same field of daffodils (Nabholtz). The distinction may also be illustrated by two passages from George Eliot:

Janet's way thither lay for a little while along the highroad, and then led her into a deep-rutted lane, which wound through a flat tract of meadow and pasture, while in front lay smoky Paddiford, and away to the left the mother-town of Milby. There was no line of silvery willows marking the course of a stream — no group of Scotch firs with their trunks reddening in the level sunbeams — nothing to break the flowerless monotony of grass and hedgerow but an occasional oak or elm, and a few cows sprinkled here and there.

A very commonplace scene, indeed. But what scene was ever commonplace in the descending sunlight, when colour has awakened from its noonday sleep, and the long shadows awe us like a disclosed presence? Above all, what scene is commonplace to the eye that is filled with serene gladness, and brightens all things with its own joy? And Janet just now was very happy. And the mill with its booming — the great chestnut-tree under which they played at houses — their own little river, the Ripple, where the banks seemed like home, and Tom was always seeing the water-rats, while Maggie gathered the purple plumy tops of the reeds, which she forgot and dropped afterwards — above all, the great Floss, along which they wandered with a sense of travel, to see the rushing spring-tide, the awful Eagre, come up like a hungry monster, or to see the Great Ash which had once wailed and groaned like a man — these things would always be just the same to them.

The second of these passages is more truly Wordsworthian than the first, yet the first is more pictorial in the strict sense of the term. What makes it so is the addition of topographical and picturesque details to the basically nonpictorial Wordsworthian emphasis upon presences, awe, gladness, and joy. The second passage abounds with visual images, but they are not arranged pictorially. Their disposition is controlled rather by what Wordsworth might have called the inward eye of contemplation and memory, as opposed to the outward or bodily eye. It is not surprising, then, that Eliot's two most Wordsworthian novels — The Mill on the Floss and Silas Marner — are her two least pictorial. Although both are full of visually memorable scenes, the construction of those scenes is seldom indebted to the visual arts.

To be sure, the panoramic landscape which opens The Mill on the Floss is pictorial, as Reva Stump has pointed out. The passage appeals to other senses than sight in an effort to create the illusion of a total environment, but the dominant mode of the description is picturesque. The details constitute a virtual anthology of motifs from seventeenth-century Dutch landscape painting: a distant view of a town and river in a flat, wide, cultivated plain; a mill and cottage among trees by a stream; a covered wagon pulled by a team of horses across a bridge. It is tempting to connect this word-painting with

Constable's Suffolk landscapes, especially in view of the many affinities between Constable and Wordsworth. But the motifs are commonplace, and since George Eliot never mentions Constable in any of her published writings, there is no independent evidence that his work was important to her. (Eliot did know Constable's biographer, C. R. Leslie, and she could have seen the six important Constable pictures in the Sheepshanks bequest, which came to the South Kensington Museum in 1857. But Ruskin's low estimate of Constable's art would hardly have escaped her notice.) After its opening passage, the novel offers relatively little of a pictorial nature until Maggie emerges in Book 5 as a stately hamadryad among the Scotch firs in the Red Deeps.34 Pictures are used within the story to characterize the amusingly provincial taste of St. Ogg's, and to act as Hogarthian emblematic warnings of Maggie's fate, but the scenes and characters in the first four books of the novel are only rarely conceived as pictures.

Likewise in Silas Marner, as Norma Jean Davis has pointed out, "there is a general absence of pictorial patterns". The principal exceptions to this rule are two contrasting scenes in Godfrey Cass's parlor at the Red House; the introduction of Nancy Lammeter; and the description of the churchgoers which opens part 2 and shows the main characters after a lapse of sixteen years. But the climacffc discovery of Eppie by Silas turns upon Silas's nearsightedness and is therefore not visualized pictorially, while the famous scene at the Rainbow Inn, as we have seen, is not visually indebted to Dutch genre painting. Silas Marner, too, works mainly by the Wordsworthian inner eye of memory and feeling.

In Daniel Deronda the English landscape has a Wordsworthian potential to heal and integrate the human personality, but that potential is largely unrealized by the English characters. Gwendolen's family has led a rootless and nomadic modern life, and therefore lacks the sense of selfhood that comes from full integration with a relatively permanent environment. Although their new home at Offendene affords "a glimpse of the wider world in the lofty curves of the chalk downs, grand steadfast forms played over by the changing days" the inhabitants are unable to incorporate that stability. Mrs. Davilow passes untouched through a landscape which combines picturesque and Wordsworthian elements in the most characteristic George Eliot manner.

It was a fine mid-harvest time, not too warm for a noonday ride of five miles to be delightful: the poppies glowed on the borders of the fields, there was enough breeze to move gently like a social spirit among the ears of uncut corn, and to wing the shadow of a cloud across the soft grey downs; here the sheaves were standing, there the horses were straining their muscles under the last load from a wide space of stubble, but everywhere the green pastures made a broader setting for the corn-fields, and the cattle took their rest under wide branches. The road lay through a bit of country where the dairy-farms looked much as they did in the days of our forefathers-where peace and permanence seemed to find a home away from the busy change that sent the railway train flying in the distance.

But the spirit of peace and permanence did not penetrate poor Mrs. Davilow's mind..

Only at the very end of the novel, after suffering has burned away her alienation, does Gwendolen have "a more wakeful vision of Offendene" and its landscape, accepting them at last as her home. She is finally able to hear what George Eliot, in the "Impressions of Theophrastus Such," calls "the speech of the landscape".

Just as the portraiture in the Jewish part of Daniel Deronda contrasts with the portraiture in the English part, so the landscapes of the two plots differ. The Jewish landscape belongs to Mordecai, and is not Wordsworthian but Turnerian and visionary, Its distinguishing features are a brilliant yellow sun near the horizon, a luminous hazy atmosphere, water, and indistinct shapes of boats and men.

Thus, for a long while, he habitually thought of the Being answering to his need as one distantly approaching or turning his back towards him, darkly painted against a golden sky. The reason of the golden sky lay in one of Mordecai's habits. He was keenly alive to some poetic aspects of London; and a favourite resort of his, when strength and leisure allowed, was to some one of the bridges, especially about sunrise or sunset.... Leaning on the parapet of Blackfriars Bridge, and gazing meditatively, the breadth and calm of the river, with its long vista half hazy, half luminous, the grand dim masses or tall forms of buildings which were the signs of world-commerce, the oncoming of boats and barges from the still distance into sound and colour, entered into his mood and blent themselves indistinguishably with his thinking.... Thus it happened that the figure representative of Mordecai's longing was mentally seen darkened by the excess of light in the aerial background. When Daniel fulfills this vision, he is rowing downstream toward Blackfriars Bridge at the sunset hour of half-past four. He appears to Mordecai out of "a wide-spreading saffron clearness, which in the sky had a monumental calm, but on the river, with its changing objects, was reflected as a luminous movement".

Eliot clearly has the work of Turner in mind here, as Edward Dowden rightly sensed when he referred in 1877 to "the Turneresque splendour" of the bridge scenes. The novelist had acquired a firsthand knowledge of Turner's pictures in 1851. She had spoken of "a Turnerian haze of network" in "Janet's Repentance" and of "a faery landscape in Turner's latest style" in "Brother Jacob". She also mentioned Turner in connection with a London sunset in a letter of 1868 to Barbara BodichonTurner's visionary painting is well suited to the visionary temperament of Mordecai, in whom George Eliot boldly asserts the Romantic possibility of second sight and prophecy.

Turner, like Wordsworth, had gone beyond the picturesque mode; and so in a different way did Ruskin. In his discussion "Of the Turnerian Picturesque" in Modern Painters, Ruskin denied that the picturesque as traditionally defined is a valid aesthetic category, a tertium quid mediating between the sublime and the beautiful. Ruskin's preference was all for the sublime, and he argued that the qualities of roughness, variety, irregularity, and chiaroscuro are in fact qualities of the sublime which connoisseurs of the picturesque mistakenly transfer from mountains, trees, and other sublime natural growths to cottages, ruins, and other objects that are not inherently sublime.

He thus defined conventional picturesqueness as a parasitical sublimity, and since it was in his view an entirely superficial effect, he called it also the "surface-picturesque." The apprehension of the surface-picturesque involves a failure of the moral-aesthetic imagination, according to Ruskin, for the viewer not only fails to grasp the true nature of what he contemplates, but he also fails to sympathize with the human suffering which ruins and broken cottages so often imply. Ruskin declared that "the lower picturesque ideal is eminently a heartless one," and he characterized the lover of the lower picturesque as "kind-hearted, innocent, but not broad in thought; somewhat selfish, and incapable of acute sympathy with others". The only true form of the picturesque, Ruskin argued, is one in which the objects depicted express suffering, poverty, or decay in an unselfconscious manner. This mode of representation he called the noble, or Turnerian, picturesque, and attributed above all to Turner and Prout among contemporary painters.

A moral critique of the cult of the picturesque was not original with Ruskin. Gilpin was aware that banditti, though pictorially colorful, are morally reprehensible and socially undesirable. The moral question was also raised in the debates between Uvedale Price and Richard Payne Knight around 1800. By the mid-nineteenth century such reservations about the picturesque had become almost commonplace in England and America.43 But Ruskin's statement of the argument was classic for its eloquence, incisiveness, and passion; and it exercised a powerful influence upon contemporary readers such as George Eliot.

In the same volume of Modern Painters, in the famous chapter on "Mountain Gloom," Ruskin applies his critique compellingly. Here he is out to quash naive romantic notions of the beneficial effects of living close to nature. He undertakes to show that even the magnificent scenery of the Swiss Alps, created nature's nearest approximation to paradise, contains elements of suffering, poverty, and decay behind its picturesque surface. The landscape itself has a dark and ominous aspect, and its sublime influences do not protect its human inhabitants from squalor, misery, disease, ignorance, and Catholicism. Ruskin vividly describes the dismal condition of the Swiss peasantry and then contrasts their reality with false and sentimentally picturesque representations of peasant life in contemporary opera nightly we give our gold, to fashion forth simulacra of peasants in gay ribands and white bodices, singing sweet songs, and bowing gracefully to the picturesque crosses: and all the while the veritable peasants are kneeling, songlessly, to veritable crosses, in another temper than the kind and fair audiences dream of, and assuredly with another kind of answer than is got out of the opera catastrophe.

The chapter effectively advances the argument made throughout Modern Painters that the fallen world contains both good and evil, that the greatest art represents both the beauties and the imperfections of nature, and that any art which does not acknowledge the existence of evil is likely to be false and sentimental.

Ruskin's critique of the picturesque is an informing principle of George Eliot's great essay on Riehl's Natural History of German Life. Here the novelist-to-be transfers Ruskin's attack upon the opera to contemporary fiction and painting.

Opera peasants, whose unreality excites Mr. Ruskin's indignation, are surely too frank an idealization to be misleading; and since popular chorus is one of the most effective elements of the opera, we can hardly object to Iyric rustics in elegant laced bodices and picturesque motley, unless we are prepared to advocate a chorus of colliers in their pit costume, or a ballet of char-women and stocking-weavers. But our social novels profess to represent the people as they are, and the unreality of their representation is a grave evil.

When she turns to contemporary English painting, the unreality of the peasants she finds represented there prompts Eliot to grumble about "cockney sentimentality" and to draw unfavorable comparisons between Holman Hunt and Teniers or Murillo. English painters display "a total absence of acquaintance and sympathy with our peasantry," she argues. They "treat their subjects under the influence of traditions and prepossessions rather than of direct observation.... The painter is still under the influence of idyllic literature, which has always expressed the imagination of the cultivated, and town-bred, rather than the truth of rustic life". She proceeds to contrast, in thoroughly Ruskinian manner, a/sentimentalized view of hay makers seen from a safe aesthetic distance with a more realistic view from close up which does not shirk their coarseness and dependence upon drink. The artistic manifestoes of Ruskin and Eliot, both published in 1856, coincide historically with a general change in English rustic genre painting away from depictions of the countryside as a place of simple pleasures, pieties, and harmonies, toward depictions of "dreary landscapes" and scenes of rural poverty such as sickbeds, deathbeds, acts of charity, floods, evictions, redundancy, alcoholism, prostitution, workhouses, and emigration.

Social and moral concerns are reflected in the presentation of landscape throughout George Eliot's fiction. Felix Holt, for example, opens with a dioramic view of the midlands countryside circa 1832 as it passes before a hypothetical passenger on the outside box of a stagecoach. The reader is offered a rich description of such natural beauties as meadows, watercourses, ponds, lanes, willows, elders, yews, hedgerows, wildflowers, ricks, and cattle. But the landscape, as Arnold Kettle has pointed out, is sociological as well as pictorial; For an opposing view, see Conrad, Victorian Treasure-House,. It offers what Eliot, in the "Impressions of Theophrastus Such," calls "a piece of our social history in pictorial writing". The narrator of Felix Holt not only places a shepherd in the scene but pauses to characterize his mental horizons. She contrasts an impoverished, benighted cluster of laborers' cottages ("their little dingy windows telling, like thick-filmed eyes, of nothing but the darkness within") to a more prosperous, better-schooled village. Many of the visual details take on an emblematic moral significance, as they do so often in Ruskin's great set-piece descriptions.

Both Adam Bede and Middlemarch are deeply influenced by Ruskin's critique of the picturesque. The landscape of Adam Bede consistently reflects a Ruskinian awareness of the dark underside of an apparently Edenic setting. Loamshire at first seems the classic paysage riant, ideally fertile and perfectly suited to man's needs. But a close scrutiny of the opening prospect reveals some ominous tints. In the following passage the nameless Gilpinesque traveller begins and ends in the picturesque, but symbolic elements intervene.

On the side of the Green that led towards the church, the broken line of thatched cottages was continued nearly to the church yard gate; but on the opposite, northwestern side, there was nothing to obstruct the view of gently-swelling meadow, and wooded valley, and dark masses of distant hill. That rich undulating district of Loamshire to which Hayslope belonged, lies close to a grim outskirt of Stonyshire, overlooked by its barren hills as a pretty blooming sister may sometimes be linked in the arm of a rugged, tall, swarthy brother; and in two or three hours' ride the traveller might exchange a bleak treeless region, intersected by lines of cold grey stone, for one where his road wound under the shelter of woods, or up swelling hills, muffled with hedgerows and long meadow-grass and thick corn; and where at c very turn he came upon some fine old country-seat nestled in the valley or crowning the slope, some homestead with its long length of barn and its cluster of golden ricks, some grey steeple looking out from a pretty confusion of trees and thatch and dark-red tiles.

The distant glimpse of Stonyshire introduces a touch of mountain gloom into the agreeable vista (Creeger). Bleakness and barrenness, according to Gilpin, are distinctly nonpicturesque; here they function as emblematic reminders of an alternate and far less pleasant state of nature.

The traveller proceeds to analyze the landscape in the approved Claudian terms of foreground, middle distance, and background. The prospect accommodates this conventional zoning, first by falling away from the viewer, who occupies a middle elevation, and then by rising in the distance to its maximum elevation in the form of large hills. But the description emphasizes that the zoning is nature's rather than man's; and the foreground, with its "level sunlight lying like transparent gold among the gently curving stems of the feathered grass and the tall red sorrel, and the white umbels of the hemlocks lining the bushy hedgerows," is far more Pre-Raphaelite than Claudian.

Moreover, a strong consciousness of time invests the consideration of space. Although the moment is 18 June 1799, the description evokes the grand perennial cycle of nature, so that the reader seems to glimpse the same landscape under different seasonal aspects. The passage of time brings renewal to nature, but has a different meaning for mortal man. The "keen and hungry winds of the north" and the "sound of the scythe being whetted [which] makes us cast more lingering looks at the flower-sprinkled tresses of the meadow" remind man of his finite term, as they often do in traditional pastoral literature. The description suggests that man will be swallowed up from view, much as the "tall mansion" and its landscaped park are swallowed up from view by the woods and meadows

In his picture of Dinah Morris Preaching on Hayslope Green, E. H. Corbould neatly solves the problem posed by George Eliot's detailed and richly significant landscape description. He simply turns Dinah around, so that her backdrop is not the panoramic vista, as in the novel, but Hayslope village and a piece of the intervening green, an altogether more manageable subject.

The truly Ruskinian landscape always contains intimations of mortality as well as of immortality. The bay into which Romola's boat drifts is spectacularly beautiful and peaceful but contains a plague-stricken village. As Norma Jean Davis points out, "both Ruskin and Romola discover, in their exploration of Italian landscape, that behind the apparent picturesque beauty and green luxuriance are elements of death and decay". In Adam Bede Eliot twice introduces overt memento mori into apparently idyllic landscapes. Early in the novel Adam and Seth carry a coffin through a scene of "Eden-like peace and loveliness," creating, as the narrator says, "a strangely-mingled picture". A moment later they come upon their drowned father's body. This effect of moral chiaroscuro is repeated in the setting through which the pregnant Hetty sets off in search of Arthur. The early February landscape is astir with signs of spring and hope, but the narrator thinks of the wayside crucifix one might encounter in a Continental countryside on such a day:

an image of a great agony — the agony of the Cross. It has stood perhaps by the clustering apple — blossoms, or in the broad sunshine by the cornfield, or at a turning by the wood where a clear brook was gurgling below; and surely, if there came a traveller to this world who knew nothing of the story of man's life upon it, this image of agony would seem to him strangely out of place in the midst of this joyous nature. He would not know that hidden behind the apple-blossoms, or among the golden com, or under the shrouding boughs of the wood, there might be a human heart beating heavily with anguish; perhaps a young blooming girl, not knowing where to turn for refuge from swift-advancing shame; understanding no more of this life of ours than a foolish lost lamb wandering farther and farther in the nightfall on the lonely heath; yet tasting the bitterest of life's bitterness.

This appeal for sympathy is a virtual reprise of the third and fourth paragraphs of Ruskin's "Mountain Gloom." There, too, a naive traveller comes upon "a cross of rough-hewn pine, iron-bound to its parapet" amidst an inspiring landscape. This cross is an emblem of the misery of the peasants who inhabit the landscape and who die contemplating images of the suffering Christ. Eliot's comparison of the uncomprehending Hetty to a biblical lost lamb may have been prompted by Ruskin's comparison of the insensible Swiss peasants to the wild mountain goats which take no "passion of joy in all that fair work of God" surrounding them. The cross in the landscape is a reminder of unseen moral forces in nature. The moral intrudes upon the picturesque again in the climactic recognition scene of Adam Bede. Adam, passing through the Fir-tree Grove, stops to contemplate a beech-tree as Gilpin himself might have done in his Remarks on Forest Scenery. The sensitive carpenter registers aesthetic detail as well as potential board-feet:

Adam delighted in a fine tree of all things; as the fisherman's sight is keenest on the sea, so Adam's perceptions were more at home with trees than with other objects. He kept them in his memory, as a painter does, with all the flecks and knots in their bark, all the curves and angles of their boughs; and had often calculated the height and contents of a trunk to a nicety, as he stood looking at it. No wonder that, notwithstanding his desire to get on, he could not help pausing to look at a curious large beech which he had seen standing before him at a turning in the road, and convince himself that it was not two trees wedded together, but only one. For the rest of his life he remembered that moment when he was calmly examining the beech, as a man remembers his last glimpse of the home where his youth was passed, before the road turned, and he saw it no more. The beech stood at the last turning before the Grove ended in an archway of boughs that let in the eastern light; and as Adam stepped away from the tree to continue his walk, his eyes fell on two figures about twenty yards before him.

This is the moment of Adam's psychic fall from innocence to experience. His innocent perception of the picturesque variegation of tree-trunks and boughs gives way to a shattering recognition of Eve with her seducer. The recognition is still pictorial, since the "archway of boughs" makes a perfect frame; but the picture now admits the existence of treachery and evil in the idyllic scene. This episode may have been the model for the great recognition scene in Henry James's The Ambassadors, in which Lambert Strether, like Adam, sees two trusted friends in a compromised position amidst a landscape which only moments before had been a pleasant picture.

The Fir-tree Grove in Adam Bede is a delusory paradise for all who enter it. It is the regular trysting-place of Hetty and Arthur, and the scene of the seduction that has such tragic consequences. Michael Squires has rightly related the setting to the tradition of the locus amoenus in pastoral poetry, the erotic and magical pagan paradise which changes those who enter it the Red Deeps in The Mill on the Floss is a vestigial locus amoenus. Compare Ware Commons in chapter 12 of John Fowles's The French Lieutenant's Woman). But George Eliot treats the topos with a Protestant distrust that recalls Spenser's handling of the Bower of Blisse in The Faerie Queene. In pictorial terms, the grove is a Claudian mythological landscape, peopled with figures from Ovid. This ideal landscape is the symptomatic product of a mind that avoids reality to indulge in fantasies of self-gratification.

She thought nothing of the evening light that lay gently

in the grassy alleys between the fern, and made the beauty of their living green more visible than it had been in the overpowering flood of noon: she thought of nothing that was present. She only saw something that was possible: Mr. Arthur Donnithorne coming to meet her again along the Fir-tree Grove. That was the foreground of Hetty's picture; behind it lay a bright hazy something — days that were not to be as the other days of her life had been. It was as if she had been wooed by a river-god, who might any time take her to his wondrous halls below a watery heaven.

In other words, Hetty prefers a Heroic Landscape with Poseidon and Tyro to a more realistic picture along the lines of, say, Millais's Waiting. Claude's presumed avoidance of the nature immediately surrounding him makes him the chief villain in the historical drama of landscape painting presented by Ruskin in Modern Painters. By the same token, Claudian landscape is something of a villain in Adam Bede.

The aesthetic and the moral remain compatible in Adam Bede. Ruskin's critique of the surface-picturesque opens the way to a true landscape which intimates the possibility of salvation through moral struggle. The same is true in Middlemarch, but in the later novel the vision of true landscape is much more problematic. George Eliot explores more deeply than ever before the disturbing possibility that the aesthetic and the moral are incompatible, that art itself has no worthy human use. As Barbara Hardy has said: "The art/life antithesis is a very important subject in Middlemarch.... Many characters are defined and even tested by their response to art, and art itself is defined and even tested by its relevance and meaning for human beings of different kinds".

These issues are crystallized in Chapter 39, which narrates Mr. Brooke's visit to the farm of his tenant, Dagley. Here the lower picturesque is precisely what Ruskin called it: an eminently heartless ideal.

It is true that an observer, under that softening influence of the fine arts which makes other people's hardships picturesque, might have been delighted with this homestead called Freeman's End: the old house had dormer-windows in the dark-red roof, two of the chimneys were choked with ivy, the large porch was blocked up with bundles of sticks, and half the windows were closed with grey worm-eaten shutters about which the jasmine boughs grew in wild luxuriance; the mouldering garden wall with hollyhocks peeping over it was a perfect study of highly mingled subdued colour, and there was an aged goat (kept doubtless on interesting superstitious grounds) lying against the open back-kitchen door.

The mossy thatch of the cow-shed, the broken grey barn-doors, the pauper labourers in ragged breeches who had nearly finished unloading a wagon of corn into the barn ready for early thrashing [sic]; the scanty dairy of cows being tethered for milking and leaving one half of the shed in brown emptiness; the very pigs and white ducks seemed to wander about the uneven neglected yard as if in low spirits from feeding on a too meager quality of rinsings, — all these objects under the quiet light of a sky marbled with high clouds would have made a sort of picture which we have all paused over as a "charming bit," touching other sensibilities than those which are stirred by the depression of the agricultural interest, with the sad lack of farming capital, as seen constantly in the newspapers of that time. But these troublesome associations were just now strongly present to Mr. Brooke, and spoiled the scene for him.

At Freeman's End, picturesque unevenness betokens neglect and brown emptiness signifies want. As Eliot says in Daniel Deronda, again echoing Ruskin: "What horrors of damp huts, where human beings languish, may not become picturesque through aerial distance!" the narrator of Middlemarch will not indulge the nostalgia for "dear, old, brown, crumbling, picturesque inefficiency" which gives pleasure to the narrator of "Amos Barton". Even Mr. Brooke's connoisseurship gives way to a true perception of his tenant's misery.

The aestheticist view of life is questioned throughout Middlemarch. We have seen that Will Ladislaw accuses Naumann of looking at the world "entirely from the studio point of view". By the same token Dorothea's conscience is troubled by aesthetic apprehension as such. She is unable to bring the "severe classical nudities and smirking Renaissance-Correggiosities" in her uncle's art collection at Tipton Grange into "any sort of relevance with her life". Her trip to Rome helps her better to understand what Will calls the "old language" of classical and Renaissance art, but it does not bridge the gap between that art and her own sense of purpose. As Richard S. Lyons has pointed out in "The Method of Middlemarch, Dorothea renews her attack upon Mr. Brooke's collection after her return from Rome: "I used to come from the village with that dirt and coarse ugliness like a pain within me, and the simpering pictures in the drawing room seemed to me like a wicked attempt to find delight in what is false, while we don't mind how hard the truth is for the neighbours outside our walls". As the novel progresses, Ladislaw becomes less the aesthete, but Dorothea does not become more the connoiseuse.

Dorothea can find relevance in simple portraiture, which she values more for iconic than for aesthetic reasons. The miniature of Ladislaw's grandmother sustains her through some bad times because it reminds her of Will himself and of his great regard for her. Dorothea is also sustained by a hard-won vision of the English landscape, a vision that is partly pictorial but not sentimentally picturesque. She tends from the first to envision her own destiny as somehow involved with the midlands countryside. Even in the sculpture gallery of the Vatican Museum her first thoughts are of the English landscape: "She did not really see the streak of sunlight on the floor more than she saw the statues: she was inwardly seeing the light of years to come in her own home and over the English fields and elms and hedge-bordered highroads; and feeling that the way in which they might be filled with joyful devotedness was not so clear to her as it had been". Dorothea values nature and duty more highly than art, and her priorities reflect certain moments in George Eliot's own museum-going.

The landscape that matters most to Dorothea upon her return from Rome lies immediately outside the west window of her boudoir at Lowick. The window gives onto an avenue of lime-trees leading to an entrance-gate, beyond which may be seen a bit of road and a large expanse of open, flat field. Dorothea views this prospect under several different diurnal, seasonal, and emotional aspects, so that it affords a series of landscape images in which objective and subjective elements strive to achieve a stable balance. E. D. H. Johnson has pointed out in "The Truer Message" that the sequence of views from Dorothea's boudoir window provides an index to her growth toward self-knowledge.

The most important views occur in Chapters 28, 54, and 80; and they form a progression from despair through indifference to affirmation which corresponds roughly with the progression outlined by Carlyle in Sartor Resartus from the Everlasting Nay through the Centre of Indifference to the Everlasting Yea. In] Chapter 28 Dorothea is at an ebb, having suffered the disappointment of virtually all her marital hopes. The landscape outside her boudoir reflects her mood of cold constriction and drab imprisonment:

> she saw the long avenue of limes lifting their trunks from a white earth, and spreading white branches against the dun and motionless sky. The distant flat shrank in uniform whiteness and low hanging uniformity of cloud.... Her blooming full-pulsed youth stood there in a moral imprisonment which made itself one with the chill, colourless, narrowed landscape....

Dorothea's subjectivity dominates this landscape of despair. The description borders on the pathetic fallacy, a concept which George Eliot noted with interest in "Arts and Belles Lettres," her review of the third volume of Modern Painters. The novelist here displays what John Stuart Mill called "the power of creating scenery, in keeping with some state of human feeling; so fitted to it as to be the embodied symbol of it, and to summon up the state of feeling itself, with a force not to be surpassed by anything but reality". Mill was speaking of Tennyson's earliest poems, especially of "Mariana"; and indeed it is of "Mariana" and Millais's splendid painting of Tennyson's heroine that one is reminded most strongly by Chapter 28 of Middlemarch Dorothea's duty is no clearer to her in Chapter 54, but as a widow she suffers less acutely than she did as a wife. She has recuperated from the worst of her bereavement, and her condition is now comfortable but neutral and aimless. Again the landscape reflects her spiritual state:

> She had not yet applied herself to her work, but was seated with her hands folded on her lap, looking out along the avenue of limes to the distant fields. Every leaf was at rest in the sunshine, the familiar scene was changeless, and seemed to represent the prospect of her life, full of motiveless ease — motiveless, if her own energy could not seek out reasons for ardent action.

The prospect is no longer jaundiced by Dorothea's despair, but it is still dominated by her subjectivity. There is no fruitful interchange between objective and subjective, between nature and the perceiving mind.

The possibility of a more balanced relationship with the landscape is adumbrated in Chapter 37 and realized in Chapter 80. "She had been so used to struggle for and to find resolve in looking along the avenue towards the arch of western light," we are told in the earlier instance, "that the vision itself had gained a communicating power". Once the vision itself communicates, it can offer the joy and moral strength that work through time and memory to make up Wordsworthian maturity. Dorothea attains such maturity in chapter 80, after suffering through a night of dark despair brought on by Will Ladislaw's apparent rejection of her love. Her psychic resurrection is assisted by her recognition of an independent life in the landscape outside her boudoir window.

> She opened her curtains, and looked out towards the bit of road that lay in view, with fields beyond outside the entrance-gates. On the road there was a man with a bundle on his back and a woman carrying her baby; in the field she could see figures moving — perhaps the shepherd with his dog. Far off in the bending sky was the pearly light; and she felt the largeness of the world and the manifold wakings of men to labour and endurance. She was a part of that

involuntary, palpitating life, and could neither look out on it from her luxurious shelter as a mere spectator, nor hide her eyes in selfish complaining.

The landscape is no longer problematic; its objective reality affords Dorothea an alternative to self-pity, and makes possible a creative interaction between her mind and the world outside it. Though faith is gone, the world remains; and work still has meaning, as it does for Carlyle's Teufelsdrockh in the phase of the Everlasting Yea. The perception of otherness is not sickening, as in Sartre's La Nausée, but healing. The recuperation of Rex Gascoigne in Daniel Deronda begins with a similar act of attention to a landscape peopled by working figures immediately outside his own window.

The vista in Chapter 80 of Middlemarch holds its Wordsworthian and Carlylean elements within a highly pictorialized structure. The window provides a frame, and the prospect is divided into foreground, middle distance, and background. The lighting is specified and the figures in the scene are precisely located. Critics have sought analogues for the description in the paintings of Rubens and Millet, but the details given by Eliot are so minimal and generic as to defy identification with the work of any particular artist. They are at any rate not conventionally picturesque; they manifest no roughness, irregularity, vivid chiaroscuro, or ruin. Eliot is evoking not the surface-picturesque but the noble picturesque, which consists, according to Ruskin, in the unconscious expression of human suffering "nobly endured by unpretending strength of heart... the world's hard work being gone through all the while, and no pity asked for, nor contempt feared".

The best pictorial analogue for the window-scenes in Middlemarch is not to be found in landscape painting at all but in a popular motif of nineteenth-century Romantic genre painting: the figure looking out a window who presents his or her back to a viewer located inside the room. The motif is operative in European painting from the seventeenth century well into the twentieth; its classic nineteenth-century embodiment is in the work of Caspar David Friedrich, especially the Frau am Fenster of about 1822.[66] Millais's Mariana belongs to this tradition, as does Moritz von Schwind's Morgenstunde, a picture George Eliot might have seen at Munich in 1858. The real subject of such paintings, at least in the nineteenth century, is usually the spiritual interaction between the spectator and the prospect. Romantic Fensterbilder are an appropriate analogue to the window-scenes in Middlemarch because Dorothea's presence in those scenes is always visualized as carefully as the landscape itself, and because the quality of her apprehension is the true centre of the audience's interest.

In natural description, then, no less than in characterization and domestic scenes, George Eliot was deeply influenced by pictorial conventions. Her vision of nature was shaped by eighteenth-century traditions of the picturesque and topographical, and by nineteenth-century modes of landscape sensibility which came to her through Wordsworth, Ruskin, and the Pre-Raphaelites She was well aware that the beholder's share of perception may be conditioned by the experience of art. She lends this awareness to Daniel Deronda as he contemplates a Gothic capital at the Abbey:

'I wonder whether one oftener learns to love real objects through their representations, or the representations through the real objects,' he said, after pointing out a lovely capital made by the curled leaves of greens, showing their reticulated underside with the firm gradual swell of its central rib. 'When I was a little fellow these capitals taught me to observe, and delight in, the structure of leaves.'

These remarks are in the spirit of Ruskin, as Henry Auster has pointed out, but they must also reflect many of George Eliot's own encounters with the natural world. She knew that art can help one see and feel, and indeed she valued art chiefly because it can.

But what happened to Eliot's descriptive art when it became, in turn, subject to someone else's imagination — when, in short, an illustrator set about to render it into visual forms? Inevitably the pictures were modified from what the author had conceived. The next Chapter will examine Frederic

Leighton's illustrations of Romola, both for the light they throw upon the text and for the questions they raise concerning literary illustration in general.

Q. Write a passage on the Women in middlemarch by George Eliot ?

Women in Middlemarch

A major theme in George Eliot's novel, Middlemarch, is the role of women in the community. The female characters in the novel are, to some extent, oppressed by the social expectations that prevail in Middlemarch. Regardless of social standing, character or personality, women are expected to cater to and remain dependent on their husbands and to occupy themselves with trivial recreation rather than important household matters. Dorothea and Rosamond, though exceedingly dissimilar, are both subjected to the same social ideals of what women should be.

Dorothea and Rosamond are on different levels of the intricate social spectrum in Middlemarch. As a Brooke, Dorothea's connections "though not exactly aristocratic, were unquestionably ëgood'.

Rosamond is of a slightly lower status, especially given that her father has married an innkeeper's daughter, thus further lowering the family's social rank. Although Dorothea and Rosamond enjoy similar amenities such as servants, the detailed social continuum of Middlemarch separates them.

Dorothea and Rosamond's responses to their respective social classes differ much more widely than the actual social gap between them. Rosamond is particularly aware of her social standing; she "felt that she might have been happier if she had not been the daughter of a Middlemarch manufacturer. She disliked anything which reminded her that her mother's father had been an innkeeper" (). While Dorothea does not dissociate herself from her wealthy peers, she shows an affinity for the lower class by helping to improve the standard of living among them through new cottages. Dorothea's philanthropic view of the lower class contrasts with the distain Rosamond feels for them.

Accordingly, the two women's material views differ as well. Not only is Rosamond painfully aware of her social position vis-a-vis Dorothea's, she actively seeks to increase it by marrying Lydgate. When Lydgate's material wealth reaches its limit and Rosamond's dreams of social supremacy vanish, the marriage quickly deteriorates. Contrastingly, Dorothea relinquishes a great deal of money for her love of Will. Dorothea's lack of concern for material goods and Rosamond's preoccupation with them are a striking example of the disparity between them.

In spite of the vast differences between them, Middlemarch society applies the same tenets to both Dorothea and Rosamond. As females, both women are expected to follow certain social norms that hinder their personal objectives, material in Rosamond's case and intellectual in Dorothea's.

A key function of women in Middlemarch society is that of a wife. Lydgate marries Rosamond expecting someone who will compliment his busy lifestyle by making his home-life pleasant. He compares women to geese and men to ganders when reflecting on the psychological differences between them, namely: " the innate submissiveness of the goose as beautifully corresponding to the strength of the gander." (p.356) He presupposes Rosamond's obedient devotion. Caussabon, too, expects that Dorothea will aid him in his work. In his proposal to her, he writes: "But I have discerned in you an elevation of thought and a capability of devotedness - " (p.43). His letter is not a profession of love but an indication that he finds Dorothea worthy of assisting him. The men expect nothing but support from their wives.

Not only do the men demand complete dedication, they fail to comprehend the women's autonomous nature. To them, Dorothea and Rosamond entered into marriage not as equal partners, but as compliant, dependent supporters. Caussabon willingly recognizes that Dorothea will assist him with his work but refuses to entertain the idea that she has her own intellectual goals. Dorothea doubts her own intellect but retains her thirst for knowledge. " She would not have asked

Mr. Caussabon at once to teach her the languages, dreading of all things to be tiresome instead of helpful; but it was not entirely out of devotion to her future husband that she wished to know Latin and Greek." (p. 64) When Caussabon fails to fully include Dorothea in his studies, he undermines her intellectual ambitions and alienates her within the marriage.

Lydgate's views of women become apparent when, upon meeting Dorothea, he muses that a women with her intelligence and strong views would make a tiresome wife. He seeks a wife who will be complacent and not interrupt his budding career. As such a wife, Rosamond is supposed to occupy her time with trifling pursuits such as needlework and music. Lydgate presumes that Rosamond will help to reduce his debt from within the household by lowering expenditures, but refuses to listen to her ideas about appealing to the wealthy Sir Godwin. This forces Rosamond to go behind his back and ask for a loan herself. Not only does the request for help injure Lydgate's pride, but also, Rosamond's disobedience enrages him. He rebukes her, " - Have you sense enough to recognize now your incompetence to judge and act for meóto interfere with your ignorance in affairs which it belongs to me to decide on?" (p. 665) Lydgate cannot accept anything but Rosamond's ineptitude in managing financial affairs.

In addition to her husband's lack of confidence in her, Rosamond must deal with skepticism from other members of the community. When Sir Godwin receives her letter, he immediately assumes that Lydgate is behind it and admonishes him for dealing through his wife. It does not cross Godwin's mind that Rosamond herself generated the request. In Godwin's reply to Lydgate, he insists, "Don't set your wife to write to me when you have anything to ask - I never choose to write to a woman on matters of business." Lydgate's and Godwin's treatment of Rosamond in the matter of her request reveal general misogynistic tendencies of the society in Middlemarch.

Society puts pressure on Dorothea to conform to its model of the ideal woman as well. After the death of Caussabon, society deems it inappropriate for her to continue living at

Lowick alone, managing the parish. Even another woman, Mrs. Cadwallader, warns her, "You will certainly go mad in that house alone, my dear. You will see visions." (p.537) Society frowns upon the dependence of women, even Dorothea with her great inner strength.

Although Dorothea and Rosamond differ in almost every aspect, their husbands and society consider them simply as women and apply the same standards to each. By holding Dorothea and Rosamond to the same standards and ignoring the vast dissimilarity between them, society minimizes the unique nature of the two women and contributes to the oppression of females throughout the community.

Q. Write an essay on the 'Philosophical Power' and usage of 'Humor' by George Eliot.

Or

Q. What are the major highlights of George Eliot's style of writing?

AFTER all that has been written about George Eliot's place as an artist, it may be doubted if attention has been properly directed to her one unique quality. Whatever be her rank amongst the creators of romance (and perhaps the tendency now is to place it too high rather than too low), there can be no doubt that she stands entirely apart and above all writers of fiction, at any rate in England, by her philosophic power and general mental calibre. No other English novelist has ever stood in the foremost rank of the thinkers of his time. Or to put it the other way, no English thinker of the higher quality has ever used romance as an instrument of thought. Our greatest novelists could not be named beside her off the field of novel-writing. Though some of them have been men of wide reading, and even of special learning, they had none of them pretensions to the best philosophy and science of their age. Fielding and Goldsmith, Scott and Thackeray, with all their inexhaustible fertility of mind, were never in the higher philosophy compeers of Hume, Adam Smith, Burke, and Bentham. But George Eliot, before she wrote a tale at all, in mental equipment stood side by side with Mill, Spencer, Lewes, and Carlyle.

If she produced nothing in philosophy, moral or mental, quite equal to theirs, she was of their kith and kin, of the same intellectual quality. Her conception of Sociology was quite as profound as that of Mill, and in some ways keener in insight; if Lewes knew more of psychology or biology, she could teach him much in history and in morals. There are in "Silas Marner," "Adam Bede," and the "Spanish Gypsy," volcanic bursts of prophetic teaching which Teufelsdröckh never surpassed. That is to say, George Eliot, who at her death left no living novelist to be mentioned beside her, was all her life in intellectual fellowship with the first philosophic minds of her day. Turn it the other way.

None of our English thinkers of the first, second, or even third rank, have resorted to romance as a vehicle of thought. The only possible exceptions that occur to me are Swift, Dr. Johnson, and Miss Martineau; but "Gulliver," "Rasselas," and "Deerbrook" are romances only by courtesy for their authors. Abroad there have been examples of men of foremost intellectual force who have written novels. Of these one only—Goethe—has written a true novel in a vein worthy of himself. And it is to "Wilhelm Meister" that we may most aptly go for analogues to the George Eliot cycle of novels. Of course, as poet, as a secular force of European rank, Goethe himself stands apart.

But in his "Wilhelm Meister" we have those meditations upon life, human nature, and society, that supreme culture, and a certain Shakespearean way of looking down upon the world as from a vantage-ground afar, which again and again recur in George Eliot and give her the unique impression of tragic mystery amongst modern novelists.

Then again Voltaire, Rousseau, and Diderot wrote prose fictions which may by a stretch of language be called novels. But the wit of "Candide," the pathos of "The Religieuse," the passion of "Héloïse" do not make up a tale fit to be placed beside "Silas Marner," as a complete gem of art in the true field of romance. Voltaire, Rousseau, Diderot, Goethe, Victor Hugo, Carlyle may take rank above George Eliot in the sum of the intellectual impulse they gave to their time. But none of them, unless it be the author of the "Misérables," can be said to be her equal in the painting of real life and actual manners.

And here we may find at once the strength and the weakness of George Eliot. With a mental equipment of the first order, her principal instrument was art. And so she played a double part—as the most philosophic artist, or the most artistic philosopher in recent literature. It has been well said that there are flashes of hers which recall Pascal, Dante, Tacitus. There are certainly some which are worthy of Burke, Condorcet, or Vauvenargues. There are single passages which Bacon might have conceived, and others which Montaigne might have written. And again there are thoughts which Coleridge and De Maistre have never surpassed. One need not compare her in the sum with any of these famous thinkers. It is plain that in philosophy she has not produced work that can weight with theirs. But it is the sustained commerce with men like these, the continually recurring sense that we are in contact with a mind of their order, of the same intellectual family, which rouses in us so intense a delight in her novels that we are apt to indulge in hyperbolic language.

But the question comes in, and it must be answered, "Could she play the double part perfectly?" Did her philosophy, culture, moral earnestness, overweight her art? or was her art the complete and easy instrument for interpreting all that her brain and her soul contained? Few are now convinced that her art was always equal to so great a demand. For that reason it may be doubted whether it will ultimately take the very first rank. A few of the greatest sons of men have combined all that their age had attained with supreme creative ease. Milton, Shakespeare, Dante, and Virgil seem to use their vast intellectual power as if poetry were their mother tongue, their natural organ of thought. Alone of the moderns, Goethe wields his panoply of learning with perfect ease, bounding in his full suit of mail on to his charger like some paladin, and careering in it over the field as if it were a robe of tissue. But it is given only to the one or two of the greatest to interpret the profoundest thought, to embody the ripest knowledge, in the inimitable mystery of art.

And thus it comes about we so often feel the art of George Eliot to be short of perfect. The canvas of laborious culture is too often visible through the colouring of the picture. We find so much to think about that we crave a little rest for simple enjoyment. The chorus is very majestic; we are amazed by forked flashes of wisdom, sonorous gnomes, prophetic strains worthy of the immortal Trilogy; but the Chorus is often a little slow; and sometimes slightly senile, goody, prolix. We have come to a tragedy, we know; but we crave more business, incident, light and air....

Let us who love the art of George Eliot abstain, if only in obedience to her teaching, from all extravagance of eulogy. Certain that she belongs to the foremost intellectual forces of our time, and seeing that she is a novelist (for neither poems nor essays express her genius truly), some are apt to decide that she stands in the very front rank of the artists of the modern world. That is surely to claim a great deal too much. Cervantes, Fielding, Scott, of course, stand immeasurably apart and above, by virtue of their wealth of imagination, their range of insight into manners, and sympathy with character of every type. Goldsmith, Defoe, Richardson, I think too Sterne and Lesage, stand again in another class by virtue of their consummate art in producing, in some more limited field, images of pathos, humour, naïveté, or vitality, worthy in their own sphere of the mightiest master's hand.

The place of George Eliot will doubtless ultimately be found in the group where we set George Sand, Balzac, Jane Austen, Dickens, Thackeray, the Brontés. Judging her purely as artist, we can hardly hope that her ultimate popularity will quite equal theirs. That she is immeasurably superior to them all as thinker, teacher, inspirer of thought and purifier of soul will perhaps be little disputed. As facile creator of types, painter of varied character, veracious chronicler of manners, she has not their range, vivacity, irrepressible energy. In art very much must be given to mass of impression, vividness of enjoyment, fertility of creation. The inexhaustible charm of George Sand, the microscopic vivacity of Jane Austen, the pathetic oddities of Charles Dickens, the terrible Hogarthian pencil of Balzac and Thackeray were all deliberately foregone by a novelist who read so deeply, who looked on life so profoundly, and who meditated so conscientiously as George Eliot.—From a review of Cross's "Life of George Eliot," in the "Fortnightly Review" (March, 1885).

GEORGE ELIOT'S humour allies itself with her intellect on the one hand, and with her sympathies and moral perceptions on the other. The grotesque in human character is reclaimed from the province of the humorous by her affections, when that is possible, and is shown to be a pathetic form of beauty. The pale, brown-eyed weaver, gazing out from his cottage with blurred vision, or poring with miserly devotion over his golden hoard, touches us, but does not make us smile. The comedy of incident, the farcical, lies outside her province; once or twice, for reasons that appear hardly adequate, the comedy of incident was attempted, and the result was not successful.

The humour of George Eliot usually belongs to her entire conception of a character, and cannot be separated from it. Her humorous effects are secured by letting her mind drop sympathetically into a level of lower intelligence, or duller moral perception, and by the conscious presence at the same time of the higher self. The humorous impression exists only in the qualified organs of perception which remain at the higher, the normal point of view. What had been merely an undulation of matter, when it touches the prepared surface of the retina, breaks into light. By the fire of the "Rainbow Inn," the butcher and the farrier, the parish clerk and the deputy clerk puff their pipes with an air of severity, "starting at one another as if a bet were depending on the first man who winked," while the humbler beer drinkers "keep their eyelids down, and rub their hands across their mouths as if the draughts of beer were a funeral duty, attended with embarrassing sadness." The slow talk about the red Durham is conducted with a sense of grave responsibility on both sides. It is we who are looking on unobserved who experience a rippling over of our moral nature with manifold laughter; it is to our lips the smile rises—a smile which is expressive not of any acute access of risibility, but of a voluminous enjoyment, a mass of mingled feeling, partly tender, partly pathetic, partly humorous.

The dramatic appropriateness of the humorous utterances of George Eliot's characters renders them unpresentable by way of extract. Each is like the expression of a face which cannot be detached from the face itself. The unresentful complacency with which Dolly Winthrop speaks of the frailties of masculine human creatures is part of the general absence of severity and of high views with respect to others which belongs to her character, and receives illustration from her like complacent forbearance with the natural infirmities of the pups. "They will worry and gnaw—worry and gnaw they will, if it was one's Sunday cap as hung anywhere so they could drag it.

They know no difference, God help 'em; it's the pushing o' the teeth as sets them on, that's what it is." Contrast Dolly's indulgent allowances in men's favour, tempered by undeniable experiences of their scarcely excusable failings, with the keen and hostile perceptions of Denner, Mrs. Transome's waiting-woman, with mind as sharp as a needle, whose neat, clean-cut, small personality is jarred by the rude power, and coarse, incoherent manners of men. "It mayn't be good luck to be a woman," Denner said, "but one begins with it from a baby: one gets used to it. And I shouldn't like to be a man—to cough so loud, and stand straddling about on a wet day, and be so wasteful with meat and drink. They're a coarse lot, I think." We turn for a kindlier judgment to Dolly. "Eh, to be sure," said Dolly, gently (while instructing Silas in the mysteries of Eppie's wardrobe), "I've seen men as are wonderful handy wi' children. The men are awk'ard and contrairy mostly, God help 'em; but when the drink's out of 'em, they aren't unsensible, though they're bad for leeching and bandaging—so fiery and unpatient."—From "George Eliot" in "Studies in Literature"(1906).

Q. Discuss Fatal Marriages in George Eliot's "Middlemarch": Analysis of Vocational Marriage of Women. Discuss ?

Q. Write an Essay on the marriages in Middlemarch by George Eliot ?

Victorian novels are driven by the prospect of marriage, and George Eliot's masterpiece, Middlemarch, embodies through its various couples a nuptial kaleidoscope not matched since Chaucer's Wife of Bath. Conditions surrounding marriages in Victorian times for women were considerably different from what modern readers would surmise. Partly due to the deprivation of an equal opportunity to education, Victorian women were confronted with limited survival tactics. Richard Altick reminds readers in his Victorian People and Ideas that women could enter the female colleges of Cambridge and Oxford in 1869 and 1879 respectively but could not take degrees until 1920-21.

Middlemarch takes place in the years leading up to 1832, the year of the Reform Bill, and this bill was for the benefit of middle class men. Without an education women were subjected to vocations, actually jobs, not callings, that could hardly be called careers. The male defence of this narrowing of options was simply "the female brain was not equal to the demands of commerce or the professions, and women, simply by virtue of their sex, had no business mingling with men in a man's world". Competing with men and male-indoctrinated commerce without the added benefit of a formal education caused many Victorian women to seek the only alternative available, marriage as a vocation.

In Middlemarch Dorothea Brooke, the community's do-gooder, a virtual St. Theresa, longs to perfect amelioration for the entire town by architecturally improving housing. Her initial chance for this improvement comes in the person of Edward Casaubon though she could have been courted by Royalty in Sir James Chettam. In her attempts to fulfill her marriage career, Dorothea was more captivated by the vast library learning of Casaubon, and she exclaimed "what a lake compared with my little pool". Her sense of fulfillment in this boring but learned man was vested in her hope to become educated, to have her curiosity nurtured, and to be of constant usefulness to a man of sixty who really needed her nineteen year old eyes for reading. It is doubtful that modern readers would consider the above adequate reasons for marriage, but Dorothea "retained very childlike ideas about marriage". Part of Dorothea's naive formula for marriage stems from her bachelor uncle's Protestant upbringing.

Mr. Brooke, Dorothea's uncle, was well connected though not aristocratic and possessed property. He had acted as guardian for Dorothea and her younger sister Celia since the girls lost their parents at age twelve. The girls came to him with an inheritance of "seven hundred a-year each from their parents", but Dorothea's religious notions and her intensity given to causes might keep suitors at bay. Whether Uncle Brooke or the girls' parents were responsible for Dorothea's fanatical flares, Eliot did not make clear. The evidence readers do know about is vested in the uncle, a man who reigns in his "Puritan energy" and is somewhat stingy with his wealth and estate: "... he would act with benevolent intentions, and that he would spend as little money as possible in carrying them out".

The conservative uncle was criticized by many neighbors of Middlemarch for not introducing a new 'mother' to his nieces that might better prepare them for marriage. In the absence of the female perspective on the topic of marriage, Dorothea and Celia are still orphans to the selection process of good husbands. Whereas Mr. Brooke would consider religion "the dread of a Hereafter", Dorothea was in need of "the bridle" of motherhood, sadly lacking on Mr. Brooke's estate. Perhaps "bridle" should be bridal.

Had Dorothea had a mother's advice, she might have made some changes to Mr. Casaubon's Lowick Manor, her future home, to accomplish two things minimally: first, she would have made her feminine mark on her own environment which would have psychologically sent a message to her husband that life is to be shared; and secondly, by altering the drapes, for instance, to allow more light into her world and his, she could have made her world more conducive to her own preferences — those of enlightenment. Instead, Eliot chooses to have Miss Brooke deny even the advice of the narrator.

A woman dictates before marriage in order that she may have an appetite for submission afterwards. Dorothea's first opportunity on that "grey but dry November morning" even in the company of her uncle and sister to Lowick Manor failed to alter the "small-windowed and melancholy-looking" home she was to share with her dismal husband). Eliot forecasts the punishing tuition Dorothea is to experience for her education, for her vocation, and she does it eloquently with setting, mood, and character, but Dorothea, "on the contrary, found the house and grounds all that she could wish". DoDo's obsequiousness remains her helpmate to duty, and she treats her duty like an apotheosis to the exclusion of her own emotional well being.

What newsworthy worldly conditions existed at the time of Eliot's writing Middlemarch? After 1850 wage earners' income improved allowing them to purchase "penny dreadfuls" and "shilling shockers," a sort of dime novel, to tease a reading public. Serialized fiction, such as Middlemarch initially was, became a serious art form. The middle class became a reading class, and the written word was not the only area of change. Railroads connected smaller towns allowing a competitive commerce and more jobs.

The support industries of hotels and added health care advanced the population. Charles Darwin's Origin of Species, which changed the way the medical profession viewed genetics, and upset a many religious beliefs. It was an age of industrial revolution and reform that had a sweeping cadence that caught everyone in its rhythm, trumpeting the offer of new jobs and careers for everyone except women. The effect of political reform and laws favoring women that inevitably follow change would take place early in the next century. For women "marriage is the only conceivable career".

As the Victorian world was a complex, multifaceted fast-paced arena, powered by industrial innovations and sweeping reforms that added many threads to the fabric of society, so, too, were novels that attempted to weave the spin-offs from the reforming blanket of Victorian England and cover the feelings and philosophies of that time period. Eliot's concept of marriage in Middlemarch is showcased through many couples. Readers will form their own opinions about what makes a mutually beneficial marriage, but Eliot peels away the layers of trust in Dorothea and Edward as Mr. and Mrs. Casaubon. If trust is the cornerstone of a sound relationship, then its eroding would certainly collapse a marriage. Erosion occurs with the Casaubons.

Edward's jealousy and insensitivity, along with his selfish compulsive drive to finish and publish his gargantuan treaty, "Key to All Mythologies," prevents him from loving Dorothea romantically, a need that she has. Her choice in Casaubon is met with askance by modern readers even from the moment of Casaubon's letter of engagement and, consequently, Dorothea's three-time written response. Though Mr. Casaubon writes flatteringly only of Dorothea's cerebral qualities and her "devotedness", the engagement letter reads like an employment contract for a secretary. Disappointment and unhappiness surrounds Dorothea's career. And precisely this is what Eliot is indicating when she portrays marriage vocation for girls like Dorothea and Celia.

England was full of such girls in Victorian days; their choices already narrowed for living a fulfilled life by virtue of their sex, what were the alternatives? They could serve as maids, work in a textile factory, or teach school provided they had a modest education. Old maids could remain in their father's home but would endure unfavorable treatment by parents or guardians, mocked for being childless, thus, becoming the topic of the town's gossip. Their best choice was to marry well, but there they are at the mercy of the novelist.

Unlike Edward's failure to inform Dorothea of his work, which was his life, the Garths of Middlemarch are touchingly communicative and share everything with each other. When Fred Vincy was on the verge of losing Mary Garth due to his clerical vocation, he proposed to Caleb Garth employment within the Garth business, which Caleb thought was a practical option. Caleb's habit was to "take no important step without consulting Susan," his wife and mother to Mary.

The Garths communicate everything to each other and enjoy the most blissful marriage in Middlemarch. Susan even knows when to "make herself subordinate" to Caleb, which the narrator declares is only one percent of the time Fred apparently reminds Caleb of himself when he was courting Susan, for Caleb fell short of the matrimonial measure as well, and Mrs. Garth knows her daughter could be engaged to a man "worth twenty Fred Vincys" (. Caleb affirms his daughter through loving her mother dearly and is rewarded with Susan's reciprocal feelings:

She rose and kissed him, saying, "God bless you, Caleb! Our children have a good father."

On another occasion with Fred still the focus of Caleb's heart, Caleb proposed to Mr. Bulstrode, Middlemarch's prosperous banker with a dubious past, that Fred serve as tenant at Bulstrode's Stone Court and to enjoy the option of buying stock when he could afford it. Caleb would still be responsible for its management. As always Caleb let his dear wife in on the plans immediately taking her into his confidence and giving credence to her suggestions. Caleb can wave his hand, and the sign is not misinterpreted by his wife. Susan knows "a sign of his not intending to speak further on the subject". Susan, unlike Dorothea, made wiser choices in her matrimonial career or at least made the necessary changes to become a happy marriage partner. The Garth marriage of communication is enjoyed by readers especially by contrast to others less communicable.

As Mary Garth would never engage herself "to one who has no manly independence," Rosamond Vincy did marry Mr. Lydgate, an innovative surgeon, a man of "good birth", most important to Rosamond, and a man who unfortunately Eliot gives poor political skills and a failing practice at least initially. Mr. Lydgate is an outsider to Middlemarch, which causes the town's doctors to distrust his modern notions of medicine. As a newcomer, Mr. Lydgate is building his practice and does not consider marriage from romantic interests but from practical ones; perhaps marrying would increase his clientele, and he shallowly wants a wife for ornamentation.

Rosy's motivations for marriage and her future vocation as wife also deserve close scrutiny. Her prescription for marital vocation did not include "the inward life of a hero, or his serious business in the world," but rather she just wanted to climb the social status ladder and find a seat among the aristocracy. This element of Victorian snobbery was critical to middle-class women seeking to advance to the next level. Rosamond's first hint of being found attractive by Lydgate causes her to groom herself as an upper-middle-class lady, playing the piano, sketching, considering her wardrobe, reading novels and poetry, and "having an audience in her own consciousness".

Despite the fact that she could afford and did attend the best preparatory school for young ladies (, she would soon waste her education when taking Lydgate as her husband — wasted in the sense that what came after her wedding has little to do with the skills she learned at Mrs Lemon's. What has Rosy absorbed through her upbringing and education that prepare her for the hardships of marriage distress inevitably to be experienced by all couples at one time or another? And, furthermore, what has Mr. Lydgate developed in his character traits that will spare the storm of threatening divorce? They will both rethink their vocations before Eliot introduces the St. Theresa rescue.

Lydgate felt sure that if ever he married, his wife would have that feminine radiance, that distinctive womanhood which must be classed with flowers and music, that sort of beauty which by its very nature Virtuous, being molded was only for pure and delicate joys.

Eliot's words certainly bear fruit near the conclusion of her novel when Mr. Lydgate and Rosy by proxy suffer social shame, unjustly, but shame nonetheless. Of all the things to befall "poor" Rosamond with her superficial importance on what others believe or perceive about her station in life, financial shame and a husband's darkened reputation certainly depicts poetic justice.

If it were a known fact that daughters advance their lives by the marriage vocation, why did not Mr. and Mrs. Vincy school Rosamond in the art of selecting a suitable husband? Eliot knows the human factor that enters the marriage equation can not be interpreted by anyone other than the bride. Rosy is given to readers with a shallow outlook on life indicative of the importance she places on appearances.

Even her premature baby born dead by the tragic disobedient horse ride has unused "embroidered robes and caps" signifying membership and ownership of the Lydgate Crest, something Rosamond esteemed worthy, not her husband. Furthermore, it was Rosy who believed the visit by "Captain Lydgate, the baronet's third son," would be pleasantly interpreted by the public with amplified implication as to her station in life. In the Dickens novel, Our Mutual Friend, Rosy could have been the daughter of the Veneerings. The marriage of openness and consultation enjoyed by the Garths was a road seldom traveled by Rosamond. Her "aloof and independent" nature that the doctor found attractive from the beginning was now a source of aggravation and sorrow in the Lydgate marriage. She was not practical, and he was in debt.

The sacrifice of selling furniture and jewelry to live responsibly was not part of Rosamond's marriage formula. Her first response to the news of living within one's means was to suggest getting the money from "papa" so as to continue to live impractically. Her next suggestion centered on their leaving Middlemarch which Rosy calculated would require less money, but more importantly would rid her of imagined gossip and shame, and perhaps she could still live as a queen among the imagined aristocratic Lydgates of London. When her suggestions were negated and trumped by her wiser and more practical husband, "the thought in her mind was that if she had known how Lydgate would behave, she would never have married him". After Rosy leaves her husband's negotiation table without resolution or partnered comfort, readers anticipate a Victorian divorce, perhaps a first in Victorian literature.

The real laws did not favor women in divorce court. Fortunately for this pair, Eliot had a more benign treatment in mind. In fact she constantly has a compassionate "feeling expressing itself in knowledge" with all of her couples. Eliot's depth of understanding of human frailty is paramount to her characterization in all of her novels. The fatal marriages that occur in Middlemarch are at times temporary due to one of its members dying. It is not the efficaciousness of the death tactic that demonstrates Eliot's genius but rather her sensitive suffering treatment during the couples' trying times that captures the attention and sympathy of readers. There are many egregious marriages today just as in Victorian times, but the marital fallout during Victorian times left women without any options other than to suffer. Their job was marriage. Consequently, in the absence of divorce "yoked lonliness" ruled their lives for worse, having once enjoyed the better).

As Eliot used Eppie, the "golden-haired child" that Silas adopted in Eliot's novel, Silas Marner, to win this miser back to society, so did the author use Dorothea to "warm" the cold Middlemarch marriages facing fatalistic demise. Confessions by Tertius Lydgate to Dorothea that he had no knowledge of Raffles' secrets and that his medical treatment of Raffles was within practical and reasonable limits was communicated to Rosamond by Dorothea. Readers know through the narrator that Bulstrode was responsible for the aborted recovery and consequential death of Raffles, but Dorothea's intimate conversation with Rosamond and the latter's character development are some of literature's most touching moments:

But you will forgive him. It was because he feels so much more about your happiness than anything else — he feels his life bound into one with yours, and it hurts him more than anything, that his misfortunes must hurt you.

It is Dorothea through her own pain of unrequited love for Ladislaw, fearing his affection for Rosamond, and Lydgate's confessions that lead her to rectify the damaging misconceptions choking Rosamond's marriage. Dorothea convinces Mr. Brooke, Mr. Farebrother, and Sir James Chettam, the town's strata of nobility and whose opinions Rosy holds dear, of Lydgate's innocence. Had the town's opinion not been reversed, it is doubtful that Rosy would have been obliging to her husband even knowing herself that he was innocent. Yet, she does break down in this scene and confesses to Dorothea that the Ladislaw/Rosamond togetherness the previous day was "not as you thought").

'He was telling me how he loved another woman, that I might know he could never love me,' said Rosamond... He has never had any love for me.. He said yesterday that no other woman existed for him beside you.

The soul purging that takes place in this scene not only remedies Middlemarch rumors but also brings to the surface Rosamond's previously latent strength of character, the kind that provides the basis for rebuilding a marriage. Dorothea tells her: "Marriage is so unlike everything else. There is something even awful in the nearness it brings". Dorothea's remarks to Rosamond enable her to repair her marriage and enjoy "solid mutual happiness" (. Dorothea's truthful benevolence helps Will Ladislaw as well.

The relationship between Dorothea and Will Ladislaw has been regarded by many of Eliot's readers "as one of the artistic weaknesses of Middlemarch". The grounds for this criticism lie in the beklief that "Ladislaw is too idealized or too lightweight to be worthy of Dorothea". After all, he is a romantic character despite — or perhaps because of — his dilettante nature.

He has been educated at Heidelberg, one of the centers of German Romanticism. Mr. Brooke compares him to Shelley twice, and Mrs. Cadwallader, a wise but town gossiper, described him as "a sort of Byronic hero" in Chapter 38. Eliot uses 'pride', 'defiance', and 'rebellion' to describe Ladislaw — all of which words have a Byronic connotation. Dorothea's prescription for a marriage partner would certainly take these attributes into consideration, especially after she experienced essentially the opposite as Mrs. Casaubon. In addition, Ladislaw is an outsider to Middlemarch though is connected to Mr. Casaubon as his cousin. He is as ardent as Dorothea in his feelings which is significant for her. They feel passionately about life and share the power that 'passionates' emanate. A qualifying question asked by Dorothea to Ladislaw in her quest for vocation and his response indicates the romanticism Eliot develops:

Q. What is your religion? I mean not what you know about religion, but the belief that helps you most?

To love what is good and beautiful when I see it. But I am a rebel: I don't feel bound, as you do, to submit to what I don't like.

Eventually, Dorothea molds this romantic 'Byron' into doing much more good for Middlemarch society than he ever could with his rootless existence. The shaping of men's character by women is a favourite theme in many of Eliot's novels. Silas Marner's love for Eppie and her refusal to live with her biological father, Godfrey, is but one example where feminine love brings about change in the men of Eliot's novels. Silas, like Ladislaw, is brought back to a social nucleus where "an ardent public good" can be harvested. Dorothea's garden for this harvest, like Eppie's actual garden, is her soft criticism of Will which brings forth his change for the better. Only Dorothea knows that Will could be strong by her idealistic conception of him, and he draws strength by measuring up to this concept.

Will has a need "to earn her respect," and this need "brings out tendencies in himself that might otherwise have been overwhelmed by his attraction to egotistic Romantic attitudes". Dorothea is the lamp for most of Middlemarchers, holding up an ideal for others, which is the cornerstone of her womanhood. Being helpful to her friends and loved ones is far more important than her Casaubon inheritance which she ultimately sacrifices in her marriage to Ladislaw. Her vocation of marriage which yielded a son by Ladislaw seems to some readers a mild concession when considering Dorothea's full potential. However, this son does inherit Mr. Brooke's estate upon his death, and Dorothea's second marriage proved infinitely happier than her first. Since Sir James "never ceased to regard Dorothea's second marriage as a mistake," then most Middlemarchers thought the same way.

Society's judgment whether a couple's marriage will succeed when their engagement is known sometimes hinges on that couple's collective income. Sometimes it hinges on valid parentage. Other times it might be the age difference that casts dispersion upon the couple's uniting. Dorothea's ability to select a good husband and fulfill her vocation seems suspect when her only income in the absence of Casaubon dollars is derived from her parents, 700 pounds yearly, still a considerable sum but not enough to own a coach and carriage.

As an editor of The Pioneer, Ladislaw has no real income. And Will's parentage makes him despised by society. After Rosamond's disclosure to Dorothea that Will loved her and not Rosamond, nothing now prevented honest communication between Will and Dorothea. Eliot's "Sunset and Sunrise" chapter finds Dorothea and Ladislaw alone in the Lowick library illuminated by lightening when Dorothea declares: "I don't mind about poverty — I hate my wealth". Without an estate or family approved bloodline, Dorothea and Will sealed their engagement. She has found a new vocation, one where she will be loved, and Middlemarch opinions can be damned, especially those from nobility like Sir James, her new brother-in-law via Celia.

Certain sacrifices occur when Victorian women choose a husband for their career. Celia reveals Dorothea's sacrifices when she says:

— you never can go and live in that way. And then there are all your plans! You never can have thought of that. James would have taken any trouble for you, and you might have gone on your life doing what you liked.... to think of marrying Mr. Ladislaw, who has got no estate or anything.

Celia's concern for her sister stems partly from the fear of never seeing Dorothea if she movesw to London. Dorothea, who does not feel the sting of those sacrifices at first, continues to educate her worried sister about how fond she is of Ladislaw, telling her, "you would have to feel with me, else you would never know". Eliot emphasizes the importance of feelings as a way of knowing. Knowledge comes to Dorothea through her feelings, and she causes all those around her to come to grips with theirs. Eliot concludes that Dorothea's marriage to Ladislaw is not totally triumphant as there was always "something better she might have done". It seems a sacrifice to some readers that Dorothea, a woman of extraordinary breath and character, should "be absorbed" into a man's vocation and "be known in certain circles as a wife and mother". How does one applaud the millions of women who do just that?

What would modern day readers say of Mrs. Bulstrode's loyalty to her husband? Modern critics might note that the advanced age of Mrs. Bulstrode prevented her from a successful second marriage if she chose as the younger Dorothea did. Mr.Bulstode has not passed away like Mr. Casaubon leaving few options for Mrs. Bulstrode. She, unlike her husband, was not "an object of dislike", and the townspeople considered her "a handsome comfortable woman" though some exclaimed "Ah, poor woman". Before she married, Mrs. Bulstrode was Harriet Vincy. Eliot does not consider the courtship of the Bulstrodes, but readers are reminded of duty in marriage, loyalty in marriage, and a woman's heart in Mrs. Bulstrode's commitment to her husband. She does not act upon Mrs. Hackbutt's advice: "she ought to separate from him". As Mr. Bulstrode has replaced Mr. Casaubon late in the novel as an evil character, Mrs. Bulstrode persists in trying to save what she considers a redeemable husband:

> But this imperfectly-taught woman, whose phrases and habits were an odd patchwork, had a loyal spirit within her. The man whose prosperity she had shared through nearly half a life, and who had unvaryingly cherished her — now that punishment had befallen him it was not possible to her in any sense to forsake him.

Mr. Bulstrode kept his past hidden from Harriet Vincy twenty years earlier when she was receiving marriage proposals. His robbing his stepchildren's inheritance for his own selfish gain was forgiven by a loyal wife, a wife who thought better of her vocation. Eliot indicates that delayed communication in marriages can be unhealthy. Mrs. Bulstrode balances Mr. Bulstrode and "society's conflicting values regarding religion, medicine, money, status, and marriage").

When readers finish Middlemarch and its marriage narratives, they find as Dorothea did that feelings serve as both a blessing and a curse. Through them Dorothea matured and served as a catalyst for many of Middlemarch's couples including her own. Fatalistic threats to happy marriages are common place in all marriages, whether Victorian or otherwise, but the heroines of Eliot's novels prove that women more than men safeguard success in marriages. After all, marriage is a vocation, a precious business to women. Eliot sums up women vocational responsibilities of marriage in the voice of Mary when she says: "husbands are an inferior class of men, who require keeping in order". Perhaps the fact that Mary gives birth to only boy-children is Eliot's irony. Dorothea's child by Ladislaw is likewise a boy. Imaginative readers like to think that these boys will grow up to become gentlemen who will treat their wives with sensitivity, and they will respect the wifely taps of correction as husbands and as employers who stand a chance for improvement.

Q. Characters in Middlemarch are delineated in a complex way". Discuss ?

The mature reader's ability to understand the extensive range of emotions felt by characters in fiction stems from the reader's own life experiences, as George Eliot was well aware when writing Middlemarch. According to Virginia Wolfe, Eliot's novel is "one of the few English novels for grown-up people." Middlemarch has characters disillusioned by the self-deception and deception of others that they see around them. Middlemarch is about the process of understanding the experiences and perceptions of others, and of suffering through self-deception and disillusionment, social positioning, class consciousness, and the ambition for self-improvement with its concomitants: education and money.

Several scholars praise Eliot's novel because of the realistic characters that allow her readers sympathetic identification and participation. Huge Witemeyer says, for example, "The variety of meanings it [Middlemarch] can encompass, from the moral and psychological to the historical and sociological, makes Eliot's literary portraiture richer than that of any earlier novelist in English". Although characters within her novel may engage in deceit or suffer disillusionment, Eliot's focusing on their human condition allows readers to connect with each character's situation. This attachment, this connection between the reader and the character, enables Eliot to present a convincingly real world and enables her novel to convey the essential truths about human nature. For example, the women in Eliot's novel, though fictional, are faced with the same life decisions and responsibilities as the women in Victorian society.

Upper-middle and upper-class Victorian women, for example, were expected to "marry money," stay home to raise the family, and be responsible for the management of domestic affairs. As a result, women, who lacked the opportunity for the kind of education men had, were praised chiefly for their ability to act properly towards their husbands. Dorothea Brooke is an intelligent and independent young woman, who differs from the conventional woman of the Victorian Age. While other Victorian ladies worried about fashion and marriage, Dorothea concerns herself with issues of philosophy, spirituality, and service. Eliot points out Dorothea's genuine beauty in describing her physical appearance:

> Miss Brooke had the kind of beauty which seems to be thrown into relief by poor dress. Her hand and wrist were so finely formed that she could wear sleeves not less bare of style than those in which the Blessed Virgin appeared to Italian painters; and her profile as well as her stature and bearing seemed to gain the more dignity from her plain garments, which by the side of provincial fashion gave her the impressiveness of a fine quotation from the Bible, — or from one of our elder poets, — in a paragraph of to-day's newspaper.

Eliot, who emphasizes the plainness of Dorothea's clothing, alludes to paintings of the Virgin Mary to describe her, thereby accentuating Dorothea's dignity and purity. Because Dorothea does not concern herself with fashion, most people in Middelemarch perceive her to be odd, and "sane people did what their neighbors did, so that if any lunatics were at large, one might know and avoid them". Eliot mocks the social norm by praising the purity of the young and "inexperienced" Miss Brooke.

I think Dorothea is almost too perfect, but she evolves from her immaculate persona after she goes astray and marries Edward Casaubon. Dorothea's feelings for him are influenced by his supposed wisdom and her hopes that it will allow her to "become educated, to have her curiosity nurtured, and to be of constant usefulness to a man of sixty who really needed her nineteen year old eyes for reading". Bernard J. Paris sees Dorothea as a mimetic character whose desire for intensity, greatness, an epic life are not manifestations of spiritual grandeur but of a compulsive search for glory. Her craving for "illimitable satisfaction" is an expression of insatiable compensatory needs, and her "self-despair" results from hopelessness about actualizing her idealized image of herself as a person of world-historical importance. She misperceives Casaubon because "her need for glory leads her to idealize him" (31-32). Dorothea realizes "the fault of her own spiritual poverty", and is "sobbing bitterly" when she is left alone by Mr. Casaubon, who goes towork alone at the Vatican on their honeymoon.

In Middlemarch education and money "greatly determine" the characters' lives and opportunities, and Eliot takes as her central topic the unfit preparation of women for life. This theme is as crucial for understanding Rosamond Vincy as it is for understanding Dorothea. Rosamond comes from a family familiar with the comfortable lifestyle of middle-class society. Her egocentric character does not adapt to the sacrifices or adjustments in one's style of living necessary when money is scarce. In contrast to Dorothea's, Rosy's marital vocation does not include "the inward life of a hero, or his serious business in the world"; rather, she just wants to climb the social ladder and find a seat among the aristocracy (Thompson 3). Eliot reveals Rosamond's egotistical nature when she describes how theyoung girl wishes her father would invite Lydgate to a dinner party:

She was tired of the faces and figures she had always been use to — the various irregular profiles and gaits and turns of phrase distinguishing those Middlemarch young men whom she had always known as boys. She had been at school [Mrs.

Lemon's establishment] with other girls of higher position, whose brothers, she felt sure, it would have been possible for her to be more interested in, than in these inevitable Middlemarch companions.

Rosamond wants to meet Lydgate, "the new aspiring doctor," because she is utterly disappointed with the eligible bachelors in her immediate community. Eliot utilizes Rosamond's character to reveal her attitude towards provincial middle-class society by describing Rosamond's social circle as "inevitable Middlemarch companions." Rosamond knows what she wants out of life: to become a member of the aristocracy, but her marriage to Lydgate is not what she expects. Her upbringing and education do not prepare her for the hardships all married couples experience. Eliot uses her — as a foil to Dorothea — as an example of the misfortunes of shallow women. Or, she may be highlighting the importance of seeing reality instead of appearance.

Lydgate exemplifies the desires of an epic life, as Dorothea does, but unlike her he finds his vocation in the study of medicine, who works hard for success in his medical practice. Eliot's introduction of Lydgate, however, hints at his coming failure:

> For surely all must admit that a man may be puffed and belauded, envied, ridiculed, counted upon as a tool and fallen in love with, or at least selected as a future husband, and yet remain virtually unknown—known merely as a cluster of signs for his neighbours' false suppositions. There was a general impression, however, that Lydgate was not altogether a common country doctor, and in Middlemarch at that time such an impression was significant of great things being expected from him.

Lydgate has the drive and ambition to make a difference in the world by advancing studies in the medical field. He is aware of the risk that such an unknown field of study poses because the common people would have no proof that newly discovered cures would work. On the other hand, Lydgate's belief that there is a vast field for discovery and improvement in medicine makes him persevere. Lydgate's plan for his future is "to do good work for Middlemarch, and great work for the world". But he remains "virtually unknown" in his because of his passion for women. He becomes enamored of Laure when he sees her on stage while he is a student in Paris, but he is in love with her "as a man is in love with a woman whom he never expects to speak to". He does speak to her, though, but only after she murders on stage her husband who plays the part of her lover. Lydgate is convinced of her innocence until she confesses to him that she "meant to do it" because her husband had wearied her by being "too fond". Lydgate realizes that his passion will lead to his own destruction, so he returns to his studies, convinced that he will not make such a mistake again (Paris. Inevitably Lydgate's passion resurfaces when he meets Rosamond, and his emotional neediness leads to an impulsive proposal.

Lydgate's descent into debt makes Rosamond very unhappy, and his busy career makes her and other characters believe she is neglected. After dinner Mrs. Vincy sympathetically tells the other ladies around them: "It is dreadfully dull for her when there is no company"). Rosamond is used to having company in a "cheerful house" which is "very different from a husband out at odd hours, and never knowing when he will come home". Her unhappiness is encouraged by those around her. Perhaps Lydgate's willingness to sacrifice his own interests to ensure her happiness could have been appreciated by another wife. Instead, he sacrifices himself without any real hope of reciprocated affection. Although Lydgate accepts his own doom, he still has the ambition to make something in the world better, and that is his marriage. These are only a few examples of the wide range of characters in Middlemarch with whom readers can either identify with or understand. While representing an entire community, George Eliot invites her readers to become a part of Middlemarch, allowing them to enter into her characters' lives because she gives readers access to the characters' thoughts throughout the novel.

Chaptet 11

Critical Essays on Middlemarch

Dorothea Brooke's 'Awakening Consciousness' and Pre-Raphaelite Aesthetic in "Middlemarch"

A knowledge of the visual arts has long been considered essential to a full understanding of Middlemarch, and in this paper I hope to demonstrate that this understanding is considerably deepened when we take into account the major role played in the novel by George Eliot's treatment of Pre-Raphaelitism, and in particular her response to one Pre-Raphaelite painting: William Holman Hunt's Awakening Conscience (1853-4).

Hitherto, analysis of that role of Pre-Raphaelitism in Middlemarch has been almost exclusively devoted to the ideas expressed by the Nazarene artist Adolf Naumann and his pupil, Will Ladislaw, in the Rome section of the book (chapters 19-22). For this reason I shall begin my examination of the Pre-Raphaelite aesthetic in Middlemarch in Rome, with a brief consideration of Eliot's presentation of German Pre-Raphaelitism. While Will Ladislaw has traditionally been regarded as a figure who mediates, however satisfactorily, between Romantic and Victorian aestheticism, my concern is with an area of his artistic development which is often overlooked: his rejection of German Pre-Raphaelitism for its later, English, counterpart.

This shift in Will's sensibilities interestingly reflects the change which occurred in George Eliot's own taste in Pre-Raphaelite art in the 1860s. Eliot's increasing interest in English Pre-Raphaelitism reached its height early in the 1870s when

Middlemarch was being written, and is apparent in her presentation of three of its characters: Will Ladislaw, Rosamond Vincy, and Dorothea Brooke.

Finally, I shall consider in detail the implications of the sequence of allusions Eliot makes in Middlemarch to Hunt's Awakening Conscience. Ilese allusions clearly reveal Eliot's considerable indebtedness to John Ruskin for her understanding of Pre-Raphaelite aesthetics. Nevertheless, they also demonstrate her unique ability to weave a rich Pre-Raphaelite strand into the complex web of her novel, by making the development of a Pre-Raphaelite sensibility an integral part of Dorothea Brooke's growth in spiritual awareness — what Eliot calls her 'awakening consciousness.'

Chapter 19 of Middlemarch takes 'Mrs Casaubon, bom Dorothea Brooke', on 'her wedding journey to Rome', and begins with a paragraph of narrative which, even by the standards of the rest of the novel, is unusually ostentatious. Repeatedly in Middlemarch the narrator draws attention to the forty year difference between the period when the story is set 1829-32 — and the period in which it was written and published — 1870-2. In chapter 19 the first paragraph serves to contextualise the immensity of the culture shock Dorothea feels on her first visit to Rome, by explaining that 'in those days the world in general was more ignorant of good and evil by forty years than it is at present.' Moving, significantly, from broad moral to art-historical concepts of 'good and evil', the narrator describes the state of terrible ignorance in which the British tourist traveled to Europe in the 1820s, knowing nothing of 'Christian art', in particular. Exemplifying the ignorance of this period is 'the most brilliant English critic of the day', William Hazlitt, 'who mistook the flower flushed tomb of the ascended Virgin' in Raphael's Coronation of the Virgin 'for an ornamental vase', thus failing to recognise the floral resurrection symbolism of the painting.

Served by such inept English art criticism as this it is not surprising that travellers such as Mrs Casaubon were completely overwhelmed by Roman culture. However, as chapter 19 is also designed to demonstrate, not all of the inhabitants of the world of the novel are as ignorant as Hazlitt or Dorothea.

Blessed with the knowledge of German scholarship deemed so vital in Middlemarch, the Nazarene painter Adolf Naumann and his protégé, Will Ladislaw, see a vision of Dorothea statuesquely but spontaneously posed before the 'reclining Ariadne' in the Vatican Museum, which sends them into an aesthetic ecstasy. Although the narrator is decidedly amused by the ensuing debate between Naumann and Will, in which they offer conflicting Nazarene and Lessingite interpretations of Dorothea and Ariadne, nevertheless their enthusiastic and informed response to Dorothea invests her with a new value hitherto unperceived in Middlemarch. Alerted to the need for a heightened aesthetic awareness by chapter 19, the Victorian reader of Middlemarch would have appreciated the full significance of the moment when Dorothea comes into conjunction with a work of art and is found to be superior to it, or have frisked being tarred with the same brush as Hazlitt.

Modern readers have been enabled to appreciate fully the significance of the Rome chapters of Middlemarch because of the work of one critic in particular, Hugh Witemeyer. In George Eliot and the Visual Arts [full text] Witemeyer shows that although she was sympathetic towards some of the ideas of the German Pre-Raphalites, and modelled the figure of Naumann on the Nazarenes Fuhrich and Overbeck, nevertheless Eliot was ultimately dissatisfied with the Nazarenes' Christian Revivalist aesthetic.

In Middlemarch Eliot's criticisms of German Pre-Raphaelitism are articulated by Naumann's apprentice, Will. For although Will portentously tells Dorothea that Naumann is 'one of the chief renovators of Christian art, one of those who had not only revived but expanded that grand conception of supreme events as mysteries at which the successive ages are spectators', he soon reassures her that: 'I am not as ecclesiastical as Naumann, and I sometimes twit him with his excess of meaning'.).

Here Will appears to imply the desirability of finding an

aesthetic which offers a happy medium between the 'excess of meaning' contained in the Nazarenes' monumental Christian allegories, and Hazlitt's complete failure to find any meaning at all in Raphael's Coronation of the Virgin. In this as in many other respects Will is ahead of his time — in this case because he is saying in 1830 what George Eliot was thinking in the 1870s. In his Introduction to the Penguin edition of Middlemarch W. J. Harvey describes Will as being 'as close in some respects to the Pre-Raphaelites as to the later Romantics'). The vagueness of this identification fairly reflects the vagueness of Will's characterisation as an aesthete. Variously perceived in the novel as being Shelleyan and Byronic, Will is a failed De Quincey who may yet become a Chatterton: in short, he is a composite Romantic poet who aspires to be a Pre-Raphaelite painter.

Historically speaking, the Pre-Raphaelite painter whom Will most resembles is Ford Madox Brown. Although Brown was never invited to join the Pre-Raphaelite Brotherhood when it was formed in September 1848, he was a close associate of theirs and their only link with the Nazarenes, having met Overbeck in Rome and been influenced by him in his work of the 1840s. Having met Overbeck herself in 1860, during the 1860s Eliot also met most of the English Pre-Raphaelites. In 1868 she and Lewes were introduced to the Bume-Joneses, and through them the Leweses soon met William Morris and D.G. Rossetti, thereby completing 'the original circle of the Pre-Raphaelites,' since they 'had already met Holman Hunt in 1864 and Thomas Woolner in 1866').

In June 1870, a year after the gestation of Middlemarch had begun, the Leweses were holidaying in Cromer on the Norfolk coast and 'reading aloud' from Trollope and Balzac, and 'Rossetti's Poems and Morris's Earthly Paradise'). Eliot's increasing social contact with the English Pre-Raphaelites and growing awareness of their literature in this period helps account for her inclusion of a thumbnail history of Pre-Raphaelitism in Middlemarch, but I wish to suggest that the role of Pre-Raphaelitism in the novel goes considerably deeper than this.

Commentators have been struck by the similarities between scenes in Middlemarch and specific Pre-Raphaelite paintings, such as Dorothea's boudoir-window view in chapter 28 which reminds Witemeyer) of Millais's Mariana (1850-51). While Dorothea appears appropriately in this scene as a withdrawn Pre-Raphaelite figure, the robust Mary Garth is explicitly portrayed with Rembrandtesque honesty when compared with the local beauty Rosamond Vincy in chapter.

Rosamond's preoccupation with her 'hair of infantine fairness" in front of her toilette mirror clearly echoes the sinister narcissism of Rossetti's golden-haired Lilith in his sonnet 'Body's Beauty' and the iconography of its companion painting Lady Lilith (1868), which shows Lilith lovingly combing her blond hair before a mirror.

It is possible that the Leweses saw the painting Lady Lilith, or sketches for it, at Rossetti's studio in Chelsea when they visited in January 1870. It was begun in 1864 and finished in 1868, but not sold until Rossetti's death. When Eliot acknowledged receipt of the copy of Rossetti's Poems in May 1870 which she and Lewes subsequently read at Cromer, Eliot told Rossetti that 'the Sonnets towards "The House of Life" attract me peculiarly').

It is not therefore surprising to find that while Rossetti's Lilith weaves a 'bright web' with her hair and is surrounded by her flowers, 'the rose and poppy', in Middlemarch the sylph-like Rosamond exerts her channs on Lydgate by appearing to him 'as if the petals of some gigantic flower had just opened and disclosed her', and by habitually touching her web of 'wondrous hair-plaits'.

One particularly seductive strand in the 'mutual web' woven between Rosamond and Lydgate is Rosamond's musicianship. Indeed, when all the detailr of their 'young love-making' have been presented in chapter 36, the narrator reveals that 'all this went on in the comer of the drawing-room where the piano stood'. The piano presides over the courtship of Rosamund and Lydgate and makes its next appearance seven chapters later, strategically placed at, the beginning of Book Five, when Dorothea Casaubon visits Dr

Lydgate to consult him about her husband's condition, but finds he is 'not at home': 'Is Mrs Lydgate at home? said Dorothea, who had never, that she knew of, seen Rosamond, but now remembered the fact of the marriage. Yes, Mrs Lydgate was at home. 'I will go in and speak to her, if she will allow me. Will you ask her if she can see me — see Mrs Casaubon, for a few minutes?'

When the servants had gone to deliver that message, Dorothea could hear sounds of music through an open window — a few notes from a man's voice and then a piano bursting into roulades. But the roulades broke off suddenly, and then the servant came back saying that Mrs Lydgate would be happy to see Mrs Casaubon... Dorothea out her hand with her usual simple kindness, and looked admiringly at Lydgate's lovely bride — aware that there was a gentleman standing at a distance, but seeing him merely as a coated figure at a wide angle. The gentleman was too much occupied with the presence of the one woman to reflect on the contrast between the two —a contrast that would certainly have been striking to a calm observer.

The social significance of this meeting is registered by the self-conscious formality of Dorothea, whose repeated use of the word 'Mrs' draws attention to the newly-married status of herself and Rosamond, whom she has never met, and prepares the reader for a decorous meeting between two Middlemarch wives. However, the sound of music through an open window, which is suddenly interrupted, combines with Dorothea's sense of awkwardness to create an indefinable impression of unease. This impression is heightened by the formal tone of the narrator who refers to Mrs Lydgate's companion—whom the short-sighted Dorothea cannot identify—first as 'a gentleman' and then as 'the gentleman'. The awkwardness of this repetition draws attention to the narrator's sudden loss of omniscience: she does not know who is in the room with Mrs Lydgate — or she is deliberately not saying.

The ambiguous status of Eliot's anonymous 'gentleman' acquires added point when we realise that she is clearly alluding to the scenario in Holman Hunt's painting, The Awakening Conscience. In this picture a gentleman absent-mindedly fingers the keyboard of a piano while gazing blankly at his mistress. As John Ruskin pointed out in a letter published in the Times on May 25 1854: 'the poor girl has been sitting with her seducer, some chance words of the song 'Oft in the the stilly night,'have struck upon the numbed places of her heart'; her conscience is awakened, and she is saved. As the words of her seducer's song strike a chord with the fallen woman, her salvation is also brought about by her sudden vision of the sunlight streaming through the open French windows, which the spectator can see in the mirror at the back of the room, and falling in a shaft of light in the right foreground of the painting.

While these open windows provide the literal source of illumination for Hunt's fallen woman, when it was first exhibited at the Royal Academy in 1854 The Awakening Conscience was shown as the companion piece to Hunt's best known pictorial source of illumination The Light of the World (1851-53). Discussing this painting in a letter to the Times (May 5 1854) which preceded his exegesis of The Awakening Conscience, Ruskin claimed that 'the lantern, carried in Christ's left hand' is the 'light of conscience. Its fire is red and fierce; it falls on the closed door... thus marking that the entire awakening of the conscience is not merely to committed, but to hereditary guilt'. In The Awakening Conscience the girl's guilt is committed' rather than 'hereditary', but because her doors are opened and not closed, the light which falls on her lurid red carpet triggers 'the entire awakening of the conscience.'

Both Hunt and Ruskin had a considerable impact on the development of George Eliot's aesthetic. Witmeyer believes that Hunt was Eliot's 'favourite Pre-Raphaelite painter', although he notes the same ambivalence towards Hunt's work which characterised her response to ihe Nazarenes. For while she considered Hunt 'one of the greatest painters of the pre-eminently realistic school', Eliot still regarded his portrayal of The Hireling Shepherd as a failure in terms of its realistic portrayal of 'peasants', even though the landscape exhibited 'marvellous truthfulness' ("Natural History of German Life' 268). Eliot's idea of realism was, like Hunt's, profoundly influenced by the writings of Ruskin, and when she writes to Caroline Bray about The Light of the World it is significant that Eliot specifies she has seen it through Ruskin's eyes:

Tell Sara [Hennell] I did notice Hunt's picture, he being an immense admiration of mine, and that I did read Ruskin's letter. I understand all the beauties Ruskin points out, and it is impossible to look at the picture without feeling the power there is in it — but it is too medieval and pietistic to be rejoiced in as a product of the present age.

It is possible that while Eliot reacted to the 'pietistic' medievalism of The Light of the World much as Will did to Naumann's Christian allegories, she was attracted to the modern-life realism of its material counterpart, and companion at the Royal Academy in 1854, The Awakening Conscience. For the religious implications of this painting are sufficiently secularised and humanised to have been acceptable to Eliot's Positivist beliefs.

Thus, when Dorothea Casaubon finds out that Will Ladislaw is the 'gentleman'who has been accompanying Mrs Lydgate in her husband's absence, her short-sightedness and the narrator's calculated ignorance combine effectively to transform Will into the anonymous male of Holman Hunt's painting. Realising the compromising nature of the situation he is in, Will tries to extricate himself from it by offering to fetch Lydgate. This offer is refused by a dazed Dorothea who hastily departs to see Lydgate herself, leaving Will to utter the priceless lines: ' 'It is always fatal to have music or poetry interrupted. May I come another day and just finish the rendering of 'Lungi dal caro bene'?"

While Ladislaw contemplates being far from his beloved, Dorothea broods: Her decision to go, and her preoccupation in leaving the room had come from her sudden sense that there would be a sort of deception in her allowing any further intercourse between herself and Will which she was unable to mention to her husband, and already her effand in seeking

Lydgate was a matter of concealment. That was all that had been explicitly in her mind; but she had also been urged by a certain discomfort. Now that she was alone in her drive, she heard the notes of the man's voice and the accompanying piano, which she had not much noted at the time, returning on her inward sense; and she found herself thinking with some wonder that Will Ladislaw was passing his time with Mrs Lydgate in her husband's absence.

In Hunt's painting the awakening conscience belongs to a fallen woman. In Middlemarch the only woman in danger of falling is Rosamond Lydgate, yet she remains unrepentant while the conscience of the woman who only fleetingly senses Rosamond's corruption is stricken. Nevertheless, Dorothea feels guilty about her own behaviour because the sounds heard through Lydgate's open window objectify it for her: Mrs Lydgate's compromised situation with Will provides an analogue for Mrs Casaubon's. Furthermore, the fact that this moment of illumination is not pictorial but musical not only ties in neatly with Eliot's depiction of Rosamond as the Middlemarch siren in chapter 31, but also recalls Ruskin's explanation of the iconography of The Awakening Conscience, which passes over the girl's vision of sunlight to argue that her salvation is brought about by what she suddenly hears. Presumably some 'chance words of the song' 'Lungi dal caro bene' strike upon the numbed places of Dorothea's heart.

However, the full significance of this scene only becomes apparent to Dorothea and to the reader when it is repeated in chapter 77. This repetition occurs some time after Dorothea has been widowed and discovered the codicil to Casaubon's will which states that if she should marry Ladislaw she will lose her inheritance. Under a cloud because the Middlemarchers now perceive him to be a bounty hunter, Will Ladislaw prepares to take his leave of Dorothea for an embarrassing second time, having already bid farewell to Middlemarch two months ago. Meanwhile Mrs Cadwallader is moved to express her contempt for Will in these terms in front of Dorothea:

Mr Orlando Ladislaw is making a sad dark-blue scandal

by warbling continually with your Mr Lydgate's wife... It seems nobody ever goes into the house without finding this young gentleman lying on the rug or warbling at the piano.

With these words ringing in her ears Dorothea returns to Lowick Manor in tears, still trying to believe the best of Will:

but while all the while the remembrance to which there had always clung a vague uneasiness would thrust itself on her attention - the remembrance of that day she had found Wili Ladislaw with Mrs Lydgate, and had heard his voice accompanied by the piano.

By now it is abundantly clear that Dorothea's encounter with Will and Rosamond in chapter 43 is intended to be central to the novel's development, and not just a vivid but isolated scene. Further proof of the scene's importance is provided when Dorothea finds Will awaiting her at Lowick. Self-dramati singly he tells Dorothea that because of what Casaubon's will implies against his 'character" he may never return to Middlemarch. Ladislaw then adds: 'What I care for more than I can ever care for anything else is absolutely forbidden to me'; a cryptic compliment to Dorothea which Will assumes she understands. 'But', the narrator tells us, 'Dorothea's mind was rapidly going over the past with quite another vision than his... images crowded upon her which left the sickening certainty that Will was referring to Mrs Lydgate.'

Remarkably, Dorothea's faith in Ladislaw's love revives, until chapter 77, when he returns to Middlemarch. In chapter 76 Dorothea's sense of sympathy for and 'human fellowship' with the ruined Lydgate is kindled as she reviews 'all the past scenes which had brought' him 'into her memories.' Inevitably one of these scenes is Dorothea's discovery of Will with Rosamund, and the narrator now reveals that

The pain had been allayed for Dorothea, but it had left in her an awakening conjecture as to what Lydgate's marriage might be to him, a susceptibility to the slightest hint about Mrs Lydgate. These thoughts were like a drama to her, and made her eyes bright, and gave an attitude of suspense to her whole frame, though she was only looking out from the brown library onto the turf and the bright green buds which stood against the dark evergreens. Suddenly, but quite unmistakably, Dorothea's 'awakening conjecture" about the state of Lydgate's marriage causes her to adopt the pose of the girl in The Awakening Conscience, who stands bright-eyed and gazes onto an Edenic garden with promises her redemption. Again, Hazlitt's mistaken non-reading of the floral resurrection symbolism in The Coronation of the Virgin which was held up for our contempt in chapter 19 now reminds us that Eliot's ideal reader will not miss the significance of 'the bright green buds' in either Hunt's painting or her corresponding tableau.

Furthermore, if we turn from the symbolism of Hunt's painting to Ruskin's analysis of it, we also discover the source of Dorothea's sudden sense of the 'drama' of Lydgate's marriage. For besides indicating to the Times' readers that 'the fair garden flowers, seen in the reflected sunshine of the mirror... have their language, Ruskin also invokes the time-honoured Aristotelian principles of tragedy to argue that The Awakening Conscience 'is based on a truer principle of the pathetic than any of the common artistical expedients of the schools. 'Ruskin concluded his Times letter by expressing the hope that Hunt's painting would' subdue the severities of judgment into the sanctity of compassion. 'The sentiments expressed here by Ruskin are fundamentally the same as those expressed by Eliot in her observation that:

If Art does not enlarge man's sympathies, it does nothing morally... and the only effect I ardently long to produce by my writings, is that those who read them should be better able to imagine and to feel the pains and joys of those who differ from themselves in everything but the broad fact of being struggling erring human creatures.:

With her sympathies enlarged by her new dramatic sense of others' suffering, Dorothea expresses the 'sanctity' of her 'compassion' for Lydgate in characteristically practical, philanthropic fashion.

She lends him £1000 to relieve him of the debt to Bulstrode which has ruined his reputation, and also agrees to speak to Rosamond 'about her husband' in the hope of saving the Lydgates' marriage. In a state of cheerful optimism Dorothea approaches the Lydgates' drawing room for the second time, where - to her astonishment — she finds that history is repeating itself:

Dorothea had less of outward vision than usual this morning. being filled with images of things as they had been and were going to be. She found herself on the other side of the door without seeing anything remarkable, but immediately she heard a voice speaking in low tones which startled her as with a sense of dreaming in daylight, and advancing unconsciously a step or two beyond the projecting slab of a bookcase, she saw, in the terrible illumination of a certainty which filled up all outlines, something which made her pause motionless, without self-possession enough to speak.

Speaking with his back towards her on a sofa which stood against the wall on a line with the door by which she had entered she saw Will Ladislaw...

This scene is almost unbearable to read because, despite the absence of the tell-tale piano music, the ominously sudden recurrence of [60/61] Dorothea's chronic myopia and the low voices behind the door, are painfully familiar. However, the sense of dijd vu inevitably and deliberately attached to this scene by Eliot, is mitigated by the way in which she modifies her characters' responses to it.

In chapter 43 Will is strongly but only momentarily embarrassed by the interruption of his flirtation with Rosamond, while she herself was enjoying the discovery 'that women, even after marriage, might make conquests and enslave men'. Now, by contrast, both are 'motionless' - frozen like the girl in Hunt's painting - in a moment of 'terrible illumination'. For Will has finally realised that 'No other woman exists by the side of' Dorothea, and he tells Rosamond so. Thus disillusioned, the narrator reveals that 'Rosamond... was almost losing the sense of her identity, and seemed to be waking into some new terrible existence'.

More remarkable, however, than either of these unprecedented reactions by Rosamond and Will, is Dorothea's delayed response to her second encounter with them, and her traumatic realisation of how much she needs Will: and now, with a full consciousness which had never awakened before, she stretched out her arms towards him and cried with bitter cries that their nearness was a parting vision: she discovered her passion to herself in the unshrinking utterance of despair.

By the time this moment of revelation occurs, the phrase 'awakened consciousness' and its variants, has acquired a powerful resonance. For the central story of Middlemarch is the story of Dorothea Brooke's 'awakening consciousness' — George Eliot's dechristianised equivalent of Holman Hunt's Awakening Conscience. This awakening begins in Rome when Mrs Casaubon's statuesque reaction to the horrors of her married life is witnessed by a German Pre-Raphaelite and his pupil. But it is not until Dorothea acquires the vision of an English Pre-Raphaelite painter, and his critic, Ruskin, that she is able to overcome her bouts of recurrent myopia.

When Dorothea awakes from her night of despair at the, end of the novel she has 'the clearest consciousness that she' is 'looking into the eyes of sorrow'. In his analysis of The Awakening Conscience, Ruskin says that 'even to the mere spectator a strange interest exalts the accessories of a scene in which he bears witness to human sorrow'. Now realising that in her encounter with Will and Rosamond she had really only been a 'mere spectator' Dorothea began now to live through that yesterday morning again, forcing herself to dwell on every detail and its possible meaning. Was she alone in that scene? Was it her event only? She forced herself to think of it as bound up with another woman's life..

Having successfully applied these Ruskinian principles to the scene she witnessed in the Lydgates' drawing-room, Dorothea sees another vision, as for the last time Eliot evokes Hunt's Awakening Conscience and invokes Ruskin:

there was a light piercing into the room. She opened her curtains, and looked out towards the bit of road that lay in view, with fields beyond, outside the entrance-gates. On the road there was a man with a bundle on his back and a woman carrying her baby... She was part of that involuntary, palpitating life, and could neither look on it from her luxurious shelter as a mere spectator, nor hide her eyes in selfish complaining. No longer counter among the ranks of Ruskin's mere spectators, Dorothea sets out 'as quietly and unnoticeably as possible' on 'her second attempt to see and save Rosamond'. Dorothea's reward for this act is to receive the benefit of Rosamond's one unselfish act in the novel: the liberation of Will Ladislaw to marry her.

Middlemarch, by George Eliot

A review by Arthur George Sedgwick

The verdict which public opinion has pronounced, or, rather, is from time to time pronouncing, on the writings of George Eliot is certainly a very complicated one. That she is an acute delineator of character, a subtle humorist, a master of English, a universal observer and a comprehensive student, a profound moralist,—all this is part of her established reputation. That she is, besides this, a poet of great force and originality would, if we took as the test the most widely published criticism, be also established.

That she has also succeeded,—in an age in which the public has been satiated with novels, and critics have begun even to doubt whether novel-writing were not a thing of the past,—if not in founding a new school of novel-writing, at least in proving that this literary form could be adapted, in skilful hands, to purposes which her predecessors had never dreamed of. Thackeray, Dickens, Bulwer, Disraeli,—between them and George Eliot there is no relationship; and yet George Eliot, in the hold which she maintains upon the public interest, is certainly their successor.

But is this all? Does not everyone who reads generalizations like these involuntarily say to himself, this is nothing? To say of an author like George Eliot that she is distinguishable by this or that abstract quality is very much like trying to revive the effect produced upon our imaginations by a broad and majestic river by describing the general direction of a body of flowing water, the height of the banks between which it flows, the measurements of its soundings taken by the latest hydrographical survey. When we think of all the immense variety of her books, from the Scenes of

Clerical Life to Middlemarch, of the range of feeling and thought that they cover, and the wonderful manner in which the work has been done, one is tempted to give up the task of studying this student, of observing this author who has devoted her life to observation, or of analyzing this professor of analysis.

Several critics have agreed, and it is almost becoming the fashion to say, that the leading trait in all of George Eliot's works is the constant presence of the idea of Fate or Destiny, of the helplessness of man in his pitiful attempt to struggle with the eternal forces of nature; and no one will dispute that both The Mill on the Floss and Middlemarch have given undue reason for this opinion. But the idea of fate is very different in different minds, and it seems to us by no means clear that the fate of George Eliot is of a sort of which has hitherto been known to literature. The conception of destiny with which we are most familiar is that of the Grecian tragedies and myths,—an individual fate, or at most a family fate, which attends, during a long succession of years, a particular man or family. They are born into the world together; they move through life together; perhaps even, they struggle for the mastery: at last the fate is accomplished, whether for good or evil.

In the Arabian Nights we find a conception of somewhat the same kind in the story of the young prince who is fated to die on coming of age, and whom his father, the king, sends out of the kingdom to an island, where he is to live in a subterranean palace until the fatal moment is past; but to the same island comes by accident a traveller who discovers the prince's retreat, and lives with him on terms of great intimacy and affection, consoling him for his solitude. At last the prince's birthday—the last of his imprisonment—arrives, and the king's vessel is descried above the horizon coming to take his son home in safety. The moment, however, has come; the prince, reclining on a sofa, asks his friend for a knife from a shelf above; there is a misstep, and the king arrives to find the fate fulfilled.

Perhaps the destiny which appears in Scott's novel—in the Bride of Lammermoor, for instance, or Guy Mannering—

is of the same essential kind as that of the Greeks, but the coloring is totally different; while the Mohammedan, with his "will of God be done," has given to the idea a religious character, again of a quite opposite kind. The idea takes a thousand different forms, which a scientific treatment of the subject would no doubt show in their real order and historical sequence.

The fate of George Eliot is not one of them. Hers is a more modern and truer conception. The destiny which surrounds her characters, which leads to their several allotted ends the lives of Tito, Maggie Tulliver, Tom, Hetty, Romola, Lydgate, the Vincys, or the poor drunkard whose last agonies are described with such minuteness in Middlemarch, is the compounded destiny of natural laws, character, and accident which we call life. It leaves nothing out of view; neither the material nor the moral forces; neither the immutable fixity of physical succession, nor the will. Man is, in these novels, neither a creature who controls us and who controls nor who is controlled by nature; he is himself part of nature.

We would not, however, overlook the fact,—which is of the first importance,—that George Eliot's fate is a moral fate, or, to put what we mean in other words, that the moral lessons enforced by life are the most important lessons for her. It is not the strangeness and awfulness of life, it is not the joy of life, it is not the misery of life, nor the absurdity of life, that is first with her: all these she understands and feels; but what she most keenly understands and most keenly feels are the lessons which all this strangeness, awfulness, joy, misery, and absurdity bring for those who will read them aright, as well as the obligation that she herself is under to help others to read them aright.

This is not merely saying over again that she is a moralist. There have been many moralists in literature, particularly English literature, who would have been quite at a loss to understand the meaning of this morality; moralists to whom the bare idea of fate or destiny was anathema, and who could not have even imagined the connection between it and duty.

That fate should, in English hands, assume a moral colour

is natural enough; but if we compare the novels of George Eliot with those of a Continental writer whose novels have a distinctly fatalistic turn, we shall begin to doubt perhaps whether this view of life is the growth of any one soil. Turgenieff's character, or at least some of his characters, are the playthings of fate quite as much as any of his English contemporary. And Turgenieff, too, is impressed with the moral side of his subject. His Liza, if it were not for the pervading sadness of the book, might be distributed as a tract among refined people. Yet, after all, the sadness is more fundamental than the morality, and perhaps it would be fairer to say that there is a general way of looking at life, peculiar to modern men, which Turgenieff happened to take in Liza, although he certainly did not very distinctly grasp it, as George Eliot always does.

And what is this modern view of life, which is different from all others,—so sad, and so moral, so ironical, and so didactic, yet so undogmatically didactic? M. Taine, in his English Literature, after speaking of Byron's unhappy career, and that of the poets whom he calls "romantic," answers this question in a way that, whatever may be thought of the criticism in other respects, is complete: "So lived and so ended this unhappy great man; the malady of the age had no more distinguished prey; around him, like a hecatomb, lie the rest, wounded also by the greatness of their faculties, and their immoderate desires,—some extinguished in stupor or drunkenness, others worn out by pleasure or work; these driven to madness or suicide; those beaten down by impotence, or lying on a sick-bed; all agitated by their acute or aching nerves; the strongest carrying their bleeding wound to old age, the happiest having suffered as much as the rest, and preserving their scars, though healed.

The concert of their lamentations has filled their age, and we have stood around them, hearing in our hearts, the low echo of their cries. We were sad like them, and, like them, inclined to revolt. The institution of democracy excited our ambitions without satisfying them; the proclamation of philosophy kindled our curiosity without contenting it. In this wide-open career the plebeian suffered for his mediocrity, and the sceptic for his doubt.

The plebeian, like the sceptic, attacked by a precocious melancholy, and withered by a premature experience, delivered his sympathies and his conduct to the poets, who declared happiness impossible, truth unattainable, society ill-arranged, man abortive or marred. From this unison of voices an idea sprang,—the centre of the literature, the arts, the religion of the age,—that there is, namely, a monstrous disproportion between the different parts of our social structure, and that human destiny is vitiated by this disagreement. "What advice have they given us for its remedy? They were great: were they wise? 'Let deep and strong sensations rain upon you; if your machine breaks, so much the worse!....Cultivate your garden, busy yourself in a little circle; reenter the flock, be a beast of burden..... Turn believer again, take holy water, abandon your mind to dogmas, and your conduct to hand-books.... Make your way; aspire to power, honors, wealth.' Such are the various replies of artists and citizens, Christians and men of the world. Are they replies? And what do they propose but to satiate one's self, to become beasts, to turn out of the way, to forget? There is another and a deeper answer, which Goethe was the first to give, which we begin to conceive, in which issue all the labour and experience of the age, and which may perhaps be the subject matter of future literature. 'Try to understand yourself and things in general.' A strange reply, seeming barely new, whose scope we shall only hereafter discover.

For a long time yet, men will feel their sympathies thrill at the sound of the sobs of their great poets. For a long time they will rage against a destiny which opens to their aspirations the career of limitless space, to shatter them, within two steps of the goal, against a wretched post which they had not seen. For a long time they will bear, like fetters, the necessities which they must embrace as laws. Our generation, like the preceding, has been tainted by a malady of the age, and will never more than half be quit of it. We shall arrive at truth, not at calm. All we can heal at present is our intellect;

we have no hold upon our sentiments. But we have a right to conceive for others the hopes which we no longer entertain for ourselves, and to prepare for our descendants the happiness which we shall never enjoy."

But we have not yet reached the fortunate isles. The future may have in store for those who are to come after us a thousand blessings of which we can only dream; for the present we live in a period of intellectual and moral tumult of revolt against the old, mixed with dread of the new, indeed, not half understanding the new, but half loving the old. Science has opened the portals of knowledge, and we are not scientific; science has revealed a new harmony of the feelings, and yet in our dull ears the old, incongruous, sentimental melodies go on ringing. Science offers us the key to the moral law which governs the world, yet we cannot bring ourselves to turn it. Is it any wonder that, amid this doubt, hesitation, and, it may be, despair, we find a wonderful zest in humour, in analysis, in irony, in the purely critical study of the world? Such a life as ours is too complicated, too revolutionary, too full of sudden surprises and absurdities, too sad, too merry, too horribly real, too shamefully false, to admit of that repose which furnishes the only sure foundation for happy art. Our business is not creation but criticism.

When we have said that George Eliot is almost an inspired critic, have we not said what is really the most important thing about her? No doubt at such an opinion thousands of her admirers would hold up their hands in horror. "Inspired critic!" they would exclaim; "how can an author of singular dramatic power, and of equally singular power of human delineation, be called a critic?" This, however, is the question. If George Eliot has real dramatic power, and has imagined real characters, there is no doubt that it is folly to say that she is primarily a critic. But we think she has not.

What she has done has been to describe, with such wonderful minuteness and ironical force, the thoughts and feelings which, under given circumstances, a certain kind of person might have, that we are forced to admit the possibility of the picture, or, to speak more accurately, the reality of the report. Besides this, she has a wonderful power of reproducing scenes of every sort, with which she is familiar, or, rather, with which her audience is familiar,—a faculty which seems to us, at least, not a pictorial or imaginative one, but rather that faculty of description which comes of the observation and general power of statement.

That this is true may be occasionally seen when George Eliot attempts remote studies, like that, for instance, of the mediaeval Italian barber shop in Romola,—a shop in which we feel too acutely sensible of the daylight of the English intellect of the nineteenth century, as well as the keenness of George Eliot's humour, to make ourselves quite at home. Even in the English scenes, as has been well said by a recent critic, we are from time to time oppressed by a sense that the village worthies who make reflections on life and on each other are, after all, only masks through which George Eliot is ventriloquizing.

To turn to the more noted and distinct characters,—are they characters?—no one, we suppose, except a woman would claim the actual existence for Adam Bede, or Felix Holt, or Will Ladislaw; but there are, besides such failures as these, remarkable successes in Maggie Tulliver, in Arthur Donnithorne, in Hetty, in Tom Tulliver, in Philip, in Tito, in Romola, in Lydgate, in Rosamond Vincy, Dorothea, and a very long list besides.

But if an artist were to be asked to illustrate these books, would he not find considerable difficulty in drawing these characters, so that they would be recognized? Would he not find, for instance, a strange family likeness between Romola and Dorothea? Would not Rosamond Vincy with a few slight touches (an alteration of coloring or outline), change into Hetty? Would not any one of a dozen Englishmen do for Lydgate? And can the other characters we have mentioned by fastened upon, and their likeness really kept? Perhaps Maggie, Arthur, Philip, and Tito make more against our theory than the rest; but though their psychological situations are always interesting, they seem always to be doing the work of representation of man or woman,—not that they are types, but that their movements seem a trifle too much in the control of the wonderful exhibitor who is half concealed behind the show. Romola was once illustrated; but the illustrations were rather of the situations than of the people. Thackeray's characters and Dickens's caricatures live and move of their own accord. Compare Becky Sharp with Rosamond Vincy,—both women in whom selfishness is the moving principle, and whose married life is the principal subject of treatment. If we were to meet Becky we should know her at once; Rosamond we should be perfectly certain to mistake for some one else. The honest farcical countenances of the members of the Pickwick Club are as familiar to us as those of own acquaintances; but Mr. Brooke, who is really almost as farcical, would not have the slightest difficulty in proving an alibi at any time.

To be sure, it may be said that Thackeray has been educated as an artist, and that he illustrated his own books. But he was an artist because it was his disposition to see certain things picturesquely or pictorially, and this is not George Eliot's disposition. Thackeray used to say, in reply to people who complained of Esmond's "marriage with his mother-in-law," that he had done nothing to arrange the match; he could not prevent his characters doing what they chose. Nobody can conceive of George Eliot's being able to make such a reply as this; yet both Thackeray and George Eliot are moralists. Thackeray was a moralist of the old school, however, his vanitas vanitatum was but the echo, after all, of the vanitas vanitatum handed down to us by tradition,—a charming echo, but still an echo. George Eliot is a moralist because her epoch is a moralizing epoch: it is her profession, her life.

The author of these volumes is a critic. Her maxim—"Know thyself and things in general"—she has taken profoundly to heart, and as a result we have a body of what might be called sympathetic erudition such as no one else ever dreamed of. History, science, art, literature, language, she is mistress of. Upon all these fields she draws. Human life, however, is her interest; in this all her studies centre. Her observation is always beginning, never ending. Certainly if writers are divided as Goethe somewhere suggests into those who are born to say some one thing, to produce some single literary flower and die, and those whose life is one constant development, like that of Nature herself, in which education and production go on side by side to the end, George Eliot would be included in the latter class. Goethe himself belonged to it, and, as M. Taine says, Goethe was the first of modern men to appreciate the changed relations between man and nature which the new renaissance was to introduce.

It would be a mere waste of time to go into a minute criticism of Middlemarch. The plots are too numerous, the characters too multitudinous, and the whole too complicated. Out of the history of Dorothea's marriage and domestic life, Lydgate's marriage and domestic life, Bulstrode's crimes and hypocrisy, the love-affair of Mary and Fred, and the adventures of Ladislaw, a library of novels might be made; while on the humour, the observation, reflection, and suggestion contained in the book a regiment of writers of social articles might support themselves for a lifetime. It is an interesting question, whether this Study of Provincial Life is success or a failure; whether it is a work which, judged by its own standard, reaches or falls short of that standard.

This question, however, we must leave to others to answer, partly because it seems now a little too soon to make up our minds, and partly because we find great difficulty in knowing what the standard is. It is A Study of Provincial Life, but this is about as indicative of the character of the books as Romans nationaux are in the case of Erckmann-Chatrian. It is, says one critic, the study of the effects of the narrow English provincial life of forty years ago on the characters of the story which interests the author, and therefore should interest the reader.

If this is so, we say that, somehow or other, the effects of this narrow provincial life on the characters is the last thing in the world we should have supposed the central point of interest. In Cranford, this is undoubtedly the main thing, and we think we may with great safety ask any one who has ever lived in a village—a real village, we mean, not a "quarter section" of town lots—to say in which book the relation in question is brought out most distinctly. In Cranford, do we not feel in every line the remoteness of the world, the whimsical pettiness of the interests, the eccentricity of the characters, the village life, with the thrill of reality which real art always produces? Of course, Middlemarch is not Cranford: Middlemarch is a county, Cranford is a village; but,after all, a county is a place, and there is, for some reason or other, no locality whatever for Middlemarch. Someone else says that it is Dorotheas' life which is the main thing; the struggle of an ardent, impassioned, and noble nature with surrounding obstacles; with a pedantic sham of a husband, with her own duty to this husband, with her love for Ladislaw, with her sense of duty to her family, and, in short,with provincial life.

But though there is certainly some reason for this opinion, there is just as much for the opinion that Lydgate is the central figure. Probably a good deal of difficulty of the same kind would be found in some of her other books, in Adam Bede, for instance, and The Mill on the Floss. Is Adam the principal figure in the first? If he is, it is in the same way that the figure-head of a ship is. What is the esoteric meaning of The Mill on the Floss? Certainly, compared with one or two of the former novels, Middlemarch is not a success. There is no such Satanic omniscience shown as we had in the analysis of Arthur Donnithorne's unhappy conscience. There is nothing here like Tito or the pathetic yet beautiful description of the gradual alterations in the relations between Maggie and Tom Tulliver. Yet Middlemarch is certainly infinitely more interesting than Felix Holt.

And yet,—and yet these rambling suggestions seem only worth making that we may take them all back in the end. In the attempt to play the critic of such works as these, one cannot help feeling that to properly analyze and explain George Eliot, another George Eliot is needed, and that all suggestion can do is to indicate the impossibility of grasping, in even the most comprehensive terms, the variety of her powers. An author whose novels it has really been a liberal education to read, one is more tempted to admire silently than to criticise at all.

"George Eliot" by Virginia Woolf

George Eliot was the pseudonym of novelist, translator, and religious writer Mary Ann Evans (1819-1880). This article by Virginia Woolf was first published in The Times Literary Supplement, 20th November, 1919.

To read George Eliot attentively is to become aware how little one knows about her. It is also to become aware of the credulity, not very creditable to one's insight, with which, half consciously and partly maliciously, one had accepted the late Victorian version of a deluded woman who held phantom sway over subjects even more deluded than herself. At what moment and by what means her spell was broken it is difficult to ascertain.

Some people attribute it to the publication of her Life. Perhaps George Meredith, with his phrase about the 'mercurial little showman' and the 'errant woman' on the dais, gave point and poison to the arrows of thousands incapable of aiming them so accurately, but delighted to let fly. She became one of the butts for youth to laugh at, the convenient symbol of a group of serious people who were all guilty of the same idolatry and could be dismissed with the same scorn. Lord Acton had said that she was greater than Dante; Herbert Spencer exempted he novels, as if they were not novels, when he banned all fiction from the London library. She was the pride and paragon of all her sex.

Moreover, her private record was not more alluring than her public. Asked to describe an afternoon at the Priory, the story-teller always intimated that the memory of those serious Sunday afternoons had come to tickle his sense of humour. He had been so much alarmed by the grave lady in her low chair; her had been so anxious to say the intelligent thing. Certainly, the talk had been very serious, as a note in the fine clear hand of the novelist bore witness. It was dated on the Monday morning, and she accused herself of having spoken with due forethought of Marivaux when she meant another; but not doubt, she said, her listener had already supplied the correction. Still, the memory of talking about Marivaux to George Eliot on a Sunday afternoon was not a romantic memory. It had faded with the passage of years. It had not become picturesque.

Indeed, one cannot escape the conviction that the long, heavy face with its expression of serious and sullen and almost equine power has stamped itself depressingly upon the minds of people who remember George Eliot, so that it looks out upon them from her pages. Mr Gosse has lately described her as he saw her driving through London in a Victoria: a large, thick-set sybil, dreamy and immobile, whose massive features, somewhat grim when seen in profile, were incongruously bordered by a hat, always in the height of Paris fashion, which in those days commonly included an immense ostrich feather.

Lady Ritchie, with equal skill, has left a more intimate indoor portrait: She sat by the fire in a beautiful black satin gown, with a green shaded lamp on the table beside her, where I saw German books lying and pamphlets and ivory paper-cutters. She was very quiet and noble, with two steady little eyes and a sweet voice. As I looked I felt her to be a friend, not exactly a personal friend, but a good and benevolent impulse.

A scrap of her talk is preserved. 'We ought to respect our influence,' she said. 'We know by our own experience how very much others affect our lives, and we must remember that we in turn must have the same effect on others.' Jealously treasured, committed to memory, one can imagine recalling the scene, repeating the words, thirty years later, and suddenly, for the first time, bursting into laughter.

In all these records one feels that the recorder, even when he was in the actual presence, kept his distance and kept his head, and never read the novels in later years with the light of a vivid, or puzzling, or beautiful personality dazzling his eyes. In fiction, where so much of personality is revealed, the absence of charm is a great lack; and her critics, who have been, of course, mostly of the opposite sex, have resented, half consciously perhaps, her deficiency in a quality which is held to be supremely desirable in women. George Eliot was not charming; she was not strongly feminine; she had none of those eccentricities and inequalities of temper which give to so many artists the endearing simplicity of children. One feels that to most people, as to Lady Ritchie, she was 'not exactly a personal friend, but a good and benevolent impulse'. But if we consider these portraits more closely, we find that they are all the portraits of an elderly celebrated woman, dressed in black satin, driving in her victoria, a woman who has been through her struggle and issued from it with a profound desire to be of use to others, but with no wish for intimacy, save with the little circle who had known her in the days of her youth. We know very little about the days of her youth; but we do know that the culture, the philosophy, the fame, and the influence were all built upon a very humble foundation - she was the granddaughter of a carpenter.

The first volume of her life is a singularly depressing record. In it we see her rising herself with groans and struggles from the intolerable boredom of petty provincial society (her father had risen in the world and become more middle class, but less picturesque) to be the assistant editor of a highly intellectual London review, and the esteemed companion of Herbert Spencer. The stages are painful as she reveals them in the sad soliloquy in which Mr Cross condemned her to tell the story of her life. Marked in early youth as one 'sure to get something up very soon in the way of a clothing club', she proceeded to raise funds for restoring a church by making a chart of ecclesiastical history; and that was followed by a loss of faith which so disturbed her father that he refused to live with her.

Next came the struggle with the translation of Strauss, which, dismal and 'soul-stupefying' in itself, can scarcely have been made less so by the usual feminine tasks of ordering a household and nursing a dying father, and the distressing conviction, to one so dependent upon affection, that by becoming a bluestocking she was forfeiting her brother's respect. 'I used to go about like an owl', she said, 'to the great disgust of my brother'. 'Poor thing', wrote a friend who saw her toiling through Strauss with a statue of the risen Christ in front of her, 'I do pity her sometimes, with her pale sickly face and dreadful headaches, and anxiety, too, about her father.'

Yet, though we cannot read the story without a strong desire that the stages of her pilgrimage might have been made, if not more easy, at least more beautiful, there is a dogged determination in her advance upon the citadel of culture which raises it above our pity. Her development was very slow and very awkward, but it had the irresistible impetus behind it of a deep-seated and noble ambition. Every obstacle at length was thrust from her path. She knew everyone. She read everything. Her astonishing intellectual vitality had triumphed. Youth was over, but youth had been full of suffering. Then, at the age of thirty-five, at the height of her powers, and in the fulness of her freedom, she made the which was of such profound moment to her and still matters even to us, and went to Weimar, alone with George Henry Lewes.

The books which followed so soon after her union testify in the fullest manner to the great liberation which had come to her with personal happiness. In themselves they provide us with a plentiful feast. Yet at the threshold of her literary career one may find in some of the circumstances of her life influences that turned her mind to the past, to the country village, to the quiet and beauty and simplicity of childish memories and away from herself and the present. We understand how it was that her first book was Scenes of Clerical Life and not Middlemarch.

Her union with Lewes had surrounded her with affection, but in view of the circumstances and of the conventions it has also isolated her. 'I wish it to be understood', she wrote in 1857, 'that I should never invite anyone to come and see me who did not ask for the invitation.' She had been 'cut off from what is called the world', she said later, but she did not regret it. By becoming thus marked, first by circumstances and later, inevitably, by her fame, she lost the power to move on equal terms unnoted among her kind; and the loss for a novelist was serious. Still, basking in the light and sunshine of Scenes of Clerical Life, feeling the large mature mind spreading itself with a luxurious sense of freedom in the world of her 'remotest past', to speak of loss seems inappropriate. Everything to such a mind was gain. All experience filtered down through layer-after layer of perception and reflection, enriching and nourishing. The utmost we can say, in qualifying her attitude towards fiction by what we know of her life, is that she had taken to heart certain lessons learnt early, if learnt at all, among which, perhaps, the most branded upon her was the melancholy virtue of tolerance; her sympathies are with the everyday iot, and play most happily in dwelling upon the homespun of ordinary joys and sorrows.

She has none of that romantic intensity which is connected with a sense of one's own individuality, unsated and unsubdued, cutting its shape sharply upon the background of the world. What were the loves and sorrows of a snuffy old clergyman, dreaming over his whisky, to the fiery egotism of Jane Eyre? The beauty of those first books, Scenes of Clerical Life, Adam Bede, The Mill on the Floss, is very great. It is impossible to estimate the merit of the Poysers, the Dodsons, the Gilfils, the Bartons, and the rest with all their surroundings and dependencies, because they have put on flesh and blood and we move among them, now bored, now sympathetic, but always with that unquestioning acceptance of all that they say and do, which we accord to the great originals only. The flood of memory and humour which she pours so spontaneously into one figure, one scene after another, until the whole fabric of ancient rural England is revived, has so much in common with a natural process that it leaves us with little consciousness that there is anything to criticize.

We accept; we feel the delicious warmth and release of spirit which the great creative writers alone procure for us. As one comes back to the books after years of absence they pour out, even against our expectation, the same store of energy and heat, so that we want more than anything to idle in the warmth as in the sun beating down from the red orchard wall. If there is an element of unthinking abandonment in thus submitting to the humours of Midland farmers and their wives, that, too, is right in the circumstances. We scarcely wish to analyse what we feel to be so large and deeply human. And when we consider how distant in time the world of Shepperton and Hayslope is, and how remote the minds of farmer and agricultural labourers from those of most of George Eliot's readers, we can only attribute the ease and pleasure with which we ramble from house to smithy, from cottage parlour to rectory garden, to the fact that George Eliot makes us share their lives, not in a spirit of condescension or of curiosity, but in a spirit of sympathy. She is no satirist. The movement of her mind was too slow and cumbersome to lend itself to comedy. But she gathers in her large grasp a great bunch of the main elements of human nature and groups them loosely together with a tolerant and wholesome understanding which, as one finds upon rereading, has not only kept her figures fresh and free, but has given them an unexpected hold upon our laughter and tears.

There is the famous Mrs Poyser. It would have been easy to work her idiosyncrasies to death, and, as it is, perhaps, George Eliot gets her laugh in the same place a little too often. But memory, after the book is shut, brings out, as sometimes in real life, the details and subtleties which some more salient characteristic has prevented us from noticing at the time. We recollect that her health was not good. There were occasions upon which she said nothing at all. She was patience itself with sick child. She doted upon Totty. Thus one can muse and speculate about the greater number of George Eliot's characters and find, even in the least important, a roominess and margin where those qualities lurk which she has no call to bring from their obscurity.

But in the midst of all this tolerance and sympathy there are, even in the early books, moments of greater stress. Her humour has shown itself broad enough to cover a wide range of fools and failures, mothers and children, dogs and flourishing midland fields, farmers, sagacious or fuddled over their ale, horse-dealers, inn-keepers, curates, and carpenters. Over them all broods a certain romance, the only romance that George Eliot allowed herself- the romance of the past.

The books are astonishingly readable and have no trace of pomposity or pretence. But to the reader who holds a large stretch of her early work in view it will become obvious that the mist of recollection gradually withdraws. It is not that her power diminishes, for, to our thinking, it is at its highest in the mature Middlemarch, the magnificent book which with all its imperfections is one of the few English novels written for grown-up people. But the world of fields and farms no longer contents her. In real life she had sought her fortunes elsewhere; and though to look back into the past was calming and consoling, there are, even in the early works, traces of that troubled spirit, that exacting and questioning and baffled presence who was George Eliot herself.

In Adam Bede there is a hint of her in Dinah. She shows herself far more openly and completely in Maggie in The Mill on the Floss. She is Janet in Janet's Repentance, and Romola, and Dorothea seeking wisdom and finding one scarcely knows what in marriage with Ladislaw. Those who fall foul of George Eliot do so, we incline to think, on account of her heroines; and with good reason; for there is no doubt that they bring out the worst of her, lead her into difficult places, make her self-conscious, didactic, and occasionally vulgar. Yet if you could delete the whole sisterhood you would leave a much smaller and a much inferior world, albeit a world of greater artistic perfection and far superior jollity and comfort.

In accounting for her failure, in so far as it was a failure, one recollects that she never wrote a story until she was thirty-seven, and that by the time she was thirty-seven she had come to think of herself with a mixture of pain and something like resentment. For long she preferred not to think of herself at all. Then, when the first flush of creative energy was exhausted and self-confidence had come to her, she wrote more and more from the personal standpoint, but she did so without the unhesitating abandonment of the young. Her self-consciousness is always marked when her heroines say what she herself would have said. She disguised them in every possible way. She granted them beauty and wealth into the bargain; she invented, more improbably, a taste for brandy. But the disconcerting and stimulating fact remained that she was compelled by the very power of her genius to step forth in person upon the quiet bucolic scene.

The noble and beautiful girl who insisted upon being born

into the Mill on the Floss is the most obvious example of the ruin which a heroine can strew about her. Humour controls her and keeps her lovable so long as she is small and can be satisfied by eloping with the gipsies or hammering nails into her doll; but she develops; and before George Eliot knows what has happened she has a full-grown woman on her hands demanding what neither gipsies, nor dolls, nor St Ogg's itself is capable of giving her. First Philip Wakem is produced, and later Stephen Guest.

The weakness of the one and the coarseness of the other have often been pointed out; but both, in their weakness and coarseness, illustrate not so much George Eliot's inability to draw the portrait of a man, as the uncertainty, the infirmity, and the fumbling which shook her hand when she had to conceive a fit mate for a heroine. She is in the first place driven beyond the home world she knew and loved, and forced to set foot in middle-class drawing-rooms where young men sing all the summer morning and young women sit embroidering smoking-caps for bazaars. She feels herself out of her element, as her clumsy satire of what she calls 'good society' proves.

Good society has its claret and its velvet carpets, its dinner engagements six weeks deep, its opera, and its faery ball rooms... gets its science done by Faraday and its religion by the superior clergy who are to be met in the best houses; how should it have need of belief and emphasis?

There is no trace of humour or insight there, but only the vindictiveness of a grudge which we feel to be personal it its origin. But terrible as the complexity of our social system is in its demands upon the sympathy and discernment of a novelist straying across the boundaries, Maggie Tulliver did worse than drag George Eliot from her natural surroundings. She insisted upon the introduction of the great emotional scene. She must love; she must despair; she must be drowned clasping her brother in her arms. The more one examines the great emotional scenes the more nervously one anticipates the brewing and gathering and thickening of the cloud which will burst upon our heads at the moment of crisis in a shower of disillusionment and verbosity. It is partly that her hold upon dialogue, when it is not dialect, is slack; and partly that she seems to shrink with an elderly dread of fatigue from the effort of emotional concentration. She allows her heroines to talk too much. She has little verbal felicity. She lacks the unerring taste which chooses one sentence and compresses the heart of the scene within that. 'Whom are you doing to dance with?' asked Mr Knightley, at the Weston's ball. 'With you, if you will ask me,' said Emma; and she has said enough. Mrs Casaubon would have talked for an hour and we should have looked out of the window.

Yet, dismiss the heroines without sympathy, confine George Eliot to the agricultural world of her 'remotest past', and you not only diminish her greatness but lose her true flavour. That greatness is here we can have no doubt. The width of the prospect, the large strong outlines of the principal features, the ruddy light of her early books, the searching power and reflective richness of the later tempt us to linger and expatiate beyond our limits. But is it upon the heroines that we would cast a final glance. 'I have always been finding out my religion since I was a little girl,' says Dorothea Casaubon. 'I used to pray so much - now I hardly ever pray. I try not to have desires merely for myself...' She is speaking for them all.

That is their problem. They cannot live without religion, and they start out on the search for one when they are little girls. Each has the deep feminine passion for goodness, which makes the place where she stands in aspiration and agony the heart of the book - still and cloistered like a place of worship, but that she no longer knows to whom to pray. In learning they seek their goal; in the ordinary tasks of womanhood; in the wider service of their kind. They do not find what they seek, and we cannot wonder.

The ancient consciousness of woman, charged with suffering and sensibility, and for so many ages dumb, seems in them to have brimmed and overflowed and uttered a demand for something - they scarcely know what - for something that is perhaps incompatible with the facts of human existence. George Eliot had far too strong an intelligence to tamper with those facts, and too broad a humour to mitigate the truth because it was a stern one. Save for the supreme courage of their endeavour, the struggle ends, for her heroines, in tragedy, or in a compromise that is even more melancholy. But their story is the incomplete version of the story that is George Eliot herself.

For her, too, the burden and the complexity of womanhood were not enough; she must reach beyond the sanctuary and pluck for herself the strange bright fruits of art and knowledge. Clasping them as few women have ever clasped them, she would not renounce her own inheritance - the difference of view, the difference of standard - nor accept an inappropriate reward.

Thus we behold her, a memorable figure, inordinately praised and shrinking from her fame, despondent, reserved, shuddering back into the arms of love as if there alone were satisfaction and, it might be, justification, at the same time reaching out with 'a fastidious yet hungry ambition' for all that life could offer the free and inquiring mind and confronting her feminine aspirations with the real world of men. Triumphant was the issue for her, whatever it may have been for her creations, and as we recollect all that she dared and achieved, how with every obstacle against her - sex and health and convention - she sought more knowledge and more freedom till the body, weighted with its double burden, sank worn out, we must lay upon her grave whatever we have it in our power to bestow of laurel and rose.

Bibliography

Daniel Deronda. Ed. Graham Handley. Oxford: Clarendon Press, 1980. [standard scholarly text] PR4658

Essays of George Eliot. Ed. Thomas Pinney. London: Routledge and Kegan Paul, 1963.

Felix Holt, the Radical. Ed. Fred C. Thomson. Oxford: Clarendon Press, 1980. [standard scholarly text]

Middlemarch. Ed. David Carroll. Oxford: Clarendon Press, 1986. [standard scholarly text]

The Mill on the Floss. Ed. Gordon S. Haight. Oxford: Clarendon Press, 1980. [standard scholarly text]

The George Eliot Letters. Ed. Gordon S. Haight. 7 vols. New Haven and London: Yale University Press, 1954-55.

Works. Cabinet Edition. Edinburgh and London: William Blackwood and Sons. 1877-80.

Beer, Gillian. George Eliot. Bloomington: Indiana University Press, 1986.

Beer, Gillian. "Music and the Visual Arts in the Novels of George Eliot," The George Eliot Fellowship Review, 5 (1974), 17-20.

Bloom, Harold. (ed.). Modern Critical Interpretations: George Eliot's Middlemarch. New York: Chelsea House, 1987.

Carpenter, Mary C. "George Eliot and the Landscape of Time. Chard, M. Joan. "Sacred and Secular: George Eliot's Concept of Pilgrimage." George Eliot Fellowship Review 20 (1989): 14-17.

Cross, John Walter. George Eliot's Life as Related in Her Letters and Journals. Cabinet Edition. 3 vols. Edinburgh and London: William Blackwood and Sons, 1885.

Deegan, Thomas. "George Eliot's Novels of The Historical Imagination." Clio 1 (1972): 21-33.

Ermarth, Elizabeth. "George Eliot's Conception of Sympathy." Nineteenth-Century Fiction 40, 1 (June 1985): 23-42.

"George Eliot." Dictionary of Literary Biography, ed. Ira B. Nadel and William E. Fredeman. Detroit: Gale Research, 1987. Volume 21.

George Eliot: The Critical Heritage, ed. David Carroll London: Routledge and Kegan Paul, 1971.

Haight, Gordon S. George Eliot: A Biography New York and Oxford: Oxford University Press, 1968.

Handley, Graham. "George Eliot and Marriage." George Eliot Fellowship Review 20 (1989): 10-11.

Perlis, Alan. A Return to the Primal Self: Identity in the Fiction of George Eliot. New York: Peter Lang, 1989.

Smalley, Barbara. George Eliot and Flaubert: Pioneers of the Modern Novel. Athens: Ohio University Press, 1974.

Stump, Reva. Movement and Vision in George Eliot's Novels. Seattle: University of Washington Press, 1959.

Uglow, Jennifer. George Eliot. New York: Virago/Pantheon Press, 1987.

Witemeyer, Hugh. George Eliot and the Visual Arts. New Haven: Yale University Press, 1974. [full text]

Individual Works: The Mill on the Floss

Modern Critical Interpretations: George Eliot's The Mill on the Floss. Ed. Harold Bloom. New York: Chelsea House, 1988.

Draper, R. P. (ed.). George Eliot's The Mill on the Floss and Silas Marner: A Casebook. London: Macmillan, 1977.

Hardy, Barbara. "Implication and Incompleteness: George Eliot's Middlemarch." The Victorian Novel, ed. Ian Watt. New York: Oxford University Press, 1971. Pp. 289-310.

Harvey, W. J. "The Intellectual Background of the Novel: Casaubon and Lydgate." The Victorian Novel, ed. Ian Watt. New York: Oxford University Press, 1971.

Knoepflmacher, U. C. "Middlemarch: Affirmation through Compromise." Laughter and Despair: Readings in Ten Novels of the Victorian Era. Berkeley: U of California Press, 1971.

Middlemarch: Critical Approaches to the Novel. ed. arbara Hardy. London: The Athlone Press, 1967. Individual Works: Silas Marner

Alley, Henry. "Silas Marner and the Balance of Male and Female." Victorians Institute Journal 16 (1988): 65-73.

Bonaparte, Felicia. "Carrying the Word of the Lord to the Gentiles: Silas Marner and the Translation of Scripture into a Secular Text." Religion and Literature 23, 2 (Summer, 1991): 39-60.

Cohen, Susan. "'A History and a Metamorphosis' : Continuity and Discontinuity in Silas Marner." Texas Studies in Language and Literature 25, 3 (Fall, 1983): 410-26.

Fisch, Harold. "Biblical Realism in Silas Marner." Identity and Ethos, ed. Mark H. Gelber. New York: Peter Lang, 1986. Pp. 343-360.

Hawes, Donald. "Chance in Silas Marner." Journal of the English Association 31, 141 (Autumn, 1982): 213-218.

Knapp, Shoshana, "George Eliot and W. S. Gilbert: Silas Marner into Dan'l Druce." NCF 40 (1985): 438-459.

John, Joseph. "Aspects of George Eliot's Characterization." Unisa English Studies 26, 1 (April 1988): 8-13.

Levine, George. "George Eliot Studies: 1980-84." Dickens Studies Annual 16 (1987): 377-407.

Marks, Louis. "Silas Marner: Filming the Novel." George Eliot Fellowship Review 18 (1987): 18-23.

Preston, John. "Silas Marner: The Community of the Novel." George Eliot Fellowship Review 11 (1980): 109-130.

Rechelson, Meri-Jane. "The Weaver of Raveloe: Metaphor as Narrative Persuasion in Silas Marner." Studies in the Novel 15, 1 (Spring, 1993): 35-43.

Roberts, Janene. "Literature on PBS: Three 'Masterpiece Theatre' Productions of Nineteenth-Century British Novels." Text and Performance Quarterly 9, 4 (Oct., 1989): 311-21.

Shuttleworth, Sally. "Fairy Tale or Science? Physiological Psychology in Silas Marner." Languages of Nature: Critical Essays on Science and Literature, ed. L. J. Jordanova. New Brunswick: Rutgers University Press, 1986. Pp. 244-288.

Swindon, Patrick. Silas Marner: Memory and Salvation. Twayne's Masterwork Studies. New York: Twayne, 1992.

Wiesenfarth, Joseph. "Demythologizing Silas Marner." ELH 37 (1970): 226-244.